17.50

POW D

Haiti and the Great Powers, 1902–1915

Haiti and the Great Powers, 1902–1915

Brenda Gayle Plummer

Louisiana State University Press
Baton Rouge and London

Copyright © 1988 by Louisiana State University Press
All rights reserved
Manufactured in the United States of America

10 9 8 7 6 5 4 3 2 1

Designer: Laura Roubique Gleason
Typeface: Aldus
Typesetter: The Composing Room of Michigan, Inc.
Printer: Thomson-Shore, Inc.
Binder: John H. Dekker & Sons, Inc.

Library of Congress Cataloging-in-Publication Data

Plummer, Brenda Gayle.
Haiti and the great powers, 1902–1915 / Brenda Gayle Plummer.
   p. cm.
  Includes index.
  ISBN 0-8071-1409-X (alk. paper)
  1. Haiti—Politics and government—1844–1934. 2. Elite (Social
sciences)—Haiti—Attitudes—History—20th century. 3. Businessmen—
Haiti—Attitudes—History—20th century. 4. Haiti—Economic
conditions. 5. Mercantile system—Haiti—History—20th century.
6. Haiti—Foreign relations. 7. Haiti—Social conditions.
I. Title.
F1926.P68   1988   87-33873
972.94'04—dc19   CIP

Parts of this study were originally published, in slightly different form, as
"The Metropolitan Connection: Foreign and Semiforeign Elites in Haiti,
1900–1915," in *Latin American Research Review*, XIX (1984), 119–42.

For Charles and Elizabeth Plummer

Contents

Illustrations

Preface

IN THE early 1900s, the great powers viewed Haitian political instability with increasing distaste. Regarding the seemingly endless succession of palace revolutions through a lens clouded by racial and cultural prejudices, they thought of mounting operations to "clean house" in the Black Republic and put its affairs in order. Haiti's critics found ample support among the social scientists of the period. Historians in particular played an important role in rationalizing and justifying efforts at intervention and destabilization.

Haitians were not slow to respond to scholars' assaults. Attempts to address them were made early in the century by such statesmen as Anténor Firmin and J. N. Léger. In 1940 the American historian Rayford W. Logan revised the desultory and pejorative interpretation of Haitian-American relations then standard in academic circles in the United States. Although Logan and subsequent investigators skillfully exposed the bleak effects of racism and imperialist domination on Haiti, they worked within a conceptual framework that gave American state papers a prominence that obscured much of the underlying richness of the history and forced it into categories that reflected the priorities of the United States.

The historiography of Haitian relations with the great powers continues to rely substantially on the massive collection of U.S. state papers in the National Archives and Library of Congress, but it is infinitely less hostile than formerly to other sources of information. In the past, the vast Haitian literature, in printed and manuscript form, public and private, was only spottily consulted by diplomatic historians, who also neglected the extensive archive of European state papers and personal manuscript collections. There were two main reasons for this, and one principal result.

First, until recently, the history of foreign relations was narrowly construed as investigation of the formal relations among states. To strict constructionists, the full range of social, intellectual, and economic exchange among peoples had no place in their field but rather belonged to social and cultural history. Second, though the events of the last few decades have given greater legitimacy to the experience of the relatively powerless (and consequently have altered social history), such testimony has not always been trusted. Just as Afro-Americans were at one time automatically assumed to be inferior witnesses to their own history, so were accounts written by Haitians of their national experience seen as lacking authority. The consequences of the narrow parameters adopted for the history of foreign relations and of historians' distrust of a substantial part of the evidence led to a historiography that so confounded itself with the policy objectives of the strong and so readily clothed itself with their cultural and ideological assumptions that it primarily served rather than clarified the behavior of the great powers.

This study aims to avoid these problems through a focus that treats the behavior of states as originating in the matrices of the civil societies from which the states were created—centers where the roots of domestic and foreign policy are inextricably entwined. It also seeks to balance the enormous historiographic weight imposed by the sheer volume of American documentation with a variety of data sources, both domestic and foreign.

Examination of Haiti's relations with the great powers begins in 1902 and continues until the Marine invasion of Haiti in 1915, which abruptly terminated Haitian sovereignty. The dependent Haitian economy remained overwhelmingly mercantile, and mercantilism continued to be the most important link binding Haiti to the world imperialist system. Mercantilism possessed a social character that expressed itself in the elaboration of cosmopolitan values and ways of life among the traders, Haitian and foreign, who lived in the port cities. Cosmopolitanism is an orientation toward society that minimizes ethnic boundaries to seek the broadest class allegiances across national lines. The allegiances cosmopolites seek, however, are limited by the class-specific character of the cosmopolitan phenomenon. While cosmopolites take national affiliations lightly, they do not subscribe to the collectivism associated with internationalism in either its liberal or its proletarian form. Their apolitical stance is rooted in the individualism that lies at the base of the cosmopolitan attitude. In popular speech, such common synonyms for cosmopolitan as "urbane," "sophisticated," and "blasé" (the last word retaining its

French connotation of "jaded") reveal a worldliness without the invigorating qualities of idealism.

The growth of cosmopolitanism in so nationalistic a country as Haiti is due in large measure to the development of maritime trade. The migration of the Haitian merchant class to the cities in the nineteenth century, its exposure to European culture as part of the process of legitimating its own claims to superior knowledge and authority, and the ties of kinship and friendship that evolved from sociocultural and professional transactions with foreigners created a strong cosmopolitan identity within the bourgeoisie. Foreigners resident in Haiti had congruent experiences. Many had weak allegiances to home countries that they rarely, if ever, visited. Some were of uncertain nationality, their families having lived and traded on numerous islands for generations before the widespread use of travel documents. They had friends and relatives in various parts of the Caribbean and often, if they were from long-established mercantile families, were better known in the region by name than by putative citizenship. Nationality did play a role, however, in consolidating important business contacts, and in spite of the detachment with which many sophisticated Haitians and foreign residents alike regarded patriotism, they frequently became identified with the interests of a particular major power.

In Haiti, specifically, cosmopolitanism and mercantilism were linked in several ways. First, traders enjoyed a strategic position in an economically dependent society, including a social prominence entirely disproportionate to their numbers. Second, the commercially oriented urban stratum identified itself and was identified at home and abroad with its business connections in the metropoles; members of this urban stratum served politically and socially as representatives of particular metropolitan interests. Third, multilateralism as a key factor in Haitian foreign relations encouraged these broker communities to perceive themselves as independent of Haitian national interests. Multilateral diplomacy appealed to Haitians because the elimination of the secrecy associated with one-to-one relations between states maximized the possibility that the major powers would not agree on any one issue, and thereby reduced the leverage that any one power could exert on Haiti. Multilateralism made diplomacy a public process and widened the latitude a weak state could enjoy. One of the principal tasks of Haitian policy makers was to diffuse the impact of the political and economic demands that foreigners made on the state by ensuring that no one nation achieved preeminence in Haiti. Haitian statesmen wanted to widely distribute their country's heavy dependence on external resources among the great powers, but were not always successful in achieving this goal. This traditional concern meshed well with the counterrole played by cosmopolites.

In contrast to, and in spite of, this pattern, Haitian civil society retained a strongly nationalist character. Oppositions characteristic of the 1902–1915 period did not involve matters of class and race only, but also turned on the tension that existed between cosmopolites and those who continued to define a unique Haitian identity, rooted in the possession and defense of a patrimony, with concomitant attachments to honor, republicanism, and a Creole culture. The interplay between cosmopolitanism and nationalism, and their joint contribution to political instability, was a factor in the United States' invasion in 1915. The American mission could not restore or reform Haitian institutions eroded by years of foreign intrigue, internal warfare, corruption, and penury but would attempt to terminate multilateralism in Haitian diplomacy and political culture. Its failure to do so, though generally unnoticed, was nevertheless significant.

The Introduction presents the context in which Haiti's relations with the great powers is explored. In the first chapter, historical background about Haiti and the development of its society is provided. This chapter treats the peasantry; the issues of race, class, and color; and the question of military superstructure and landed proprietorship.

Chapter II discusses trade and diplomacy in the context of an expanding mercantile capitalism. It analyzes the leading commercial issues of the period and how they were addressed by Haitian and foreign principals. The impact of trade on culture and class is also considered.

The institutional and ideological origins of Haiti's peculiar place in the world community are examined in Chapter III. The creation of a repressive state as a reaction against reform and as a response to encroaching imperialism is described in Chapter IV. The manner in which social peace was achieved and the metropoles' role in effecting it are studied.

The much-vaunted arrival of finance capitalism in Haiti by 1910 is the subject of Chapter V. The origins, operations, and politics of this finance capitalism are viewed against a backdrop of increasing multilateral corporate penetration and diplomatic machinations.

Chapter VI is concerned with the characteristics and policies of the governments of 1911–1914, and the increasing American concern with Haitian affairs. Wilsonian foreign policy, extremely hostile to the politics of revolutionary insurgency, dictated the United States' response to events in the Black Republic. It examines the governments that rose to power on the shoulders of peasant mercenaries, the effects of rural unrest in the North, the urban coalition of professional politicians, the impact of war in Europe, and the increasing efforts of the great powers to destabilize Haitian regimes.

The consensus of the great powers on Haiti is taken up in Chapter VII, and the discussion includes the issues of strategic security, commercial rights, demands for control of the state, and the ultimate collapse of the government. The Epilogue looks back on the 1902–1915 period from the vantage point of the American occupation era and concludes with observations on the historical development of those troubled years before the Great War.

Acknowledgments

T HIS PROJECT was completed with the assistance of people in four countries. I would like to thank those who graciously accorded me interviews: Mercer Cook, Dr. and Mrs. William R. Furniss, Mr. and Mrs. Robert D. Heinl, Mme. Celestin Jacquet, the late Gérard Jolibois, the late Rayford W. Logan, Dana Munro, and René Piquion. The thoughtful courtesies of Fred Conway, Mme. Gérard Jolibois, and William B. Jones greatly facilitated my investigations. I have also profited from the invaluable counsel of Walter LaFeber, my advisor at Cornell, and the moral support and research assistance provided by Donald R. Culverson. To my benefit, Cedric Robinson reviewed many versions of parts of this work with his customary acuity.

I drew heavily on the professional expertise of the personnel at numerous archival repositories and received invaluable help from the staffs of the Archives of the Episcopal Church, Austin, Texas; the Bibliothèque de Saint-Louis de Gonzague, Port-au-Prince, Haiti; the Moorland-Spingarn Collection of Howard University, Washington, D.C.; the Library of Congress; the National Archives; the archives of the Ministry of Foreign Affairs, Paris; the National Archives of the Republic of Haiti; the Public Record Office, London; the Schomburg Research Center of the New York Public Library; the United States Marine Corps Museum; and Yale University Library.

Throughout the various stages of research and writing, grant support was supplied by the Center for Afro-American Studies, University of California, Los Angeles; the Center for Black Studies, University of California, Santa Barbara; the Dorothy Danforth Compton Foundation; the

University of Minnesota College of Liberal Arts; and the University of Minnesota Graduate School.

I also thank Franklin Knight, David Geggus, Richard Long, and Thomas Schoonover for their thoughtful review of this study, and Beverly Peavler for her skillful editing of the manuscript.

Abbreviations

AN	Archives Nationales de la République d'Haïti
CD	U.S. Department of State, Consular Dispatches
DF	U.S. Department of State, Decimal File
FO 35	Great Britain, Foreign Office, *British and Foreign State Papers, Hayti and San Domingo, General Correspondence*
FO 371	Great Britain, Foreign Office, *British and Foreign State Papers, Hayti and San Domingo, Hayti*
FR	U.S. Department of State, *Papers Relating to the Foreign Relations of the United States*
LC	Library of Congress
NA	National Archives
NF	U.S. Department of State, Numerical File
NR	U.S. Navy, Naval Records Collection, Areas C and 8, Record Group 45
NYPL	New York Public Library
QDO	Archives of the Ministry of Foreign Relations, Quai d'Orsay, France, Correspondance politique et commerciale, nouvelle série, Haïti
SI	U.S. Senate, Inquiry into the Occupation and Administration of Haiti and Santo Domingo, *Hearings Before a Select Committee on Haiti and Santo Domingo*, 2 vols., 67th Cong., 1st and 2nd Sess.

Haiti and the Great Powers, 1902–1915

Introduction

Changana, changana.
What's mine is mine.

—Haitian proverb

THE TRAVEL literature of the early twentieth century is replete with works on the Caribbean. The old books depicted palmy, indolent islands, where time seemed suspended in the dust and heat of quaint colonial streets. Even riots and civil wars, as described by the occasional journalist or commercial traveler, peculiarly lacked a sense of urgency. Caribbean politics moved as in a dream or in a hazy costume drama. The independent republics spent their energy and resources, it appeared, engaged in short, violent revolutions, and the colonized islands drowsed timelessly in the embrace of a benevolent if remote imperialism.

All but the most recent historiography has acquiesced to this view of the early twentieth century in the Caribbean. Historians have considered the pre–World War I years formless. The themes so familiar to modern Caribbean history—the rise of trade unionism, black nationalism, ethnic politics, socialism—do not yet fully emerge, but such issues as slavery and abolition have already receded into the past. The 1900–1914 period seemed anomalous to scholars who envisioned it as only transitional, lacking distinctive characteristics of its own. Among the consequences has been the portrayal of events in Haiti and the Dominican Republic as "largely the history of American interventions." Two American social scientists, writing about Haiti, bundled together ninety-five years of Haitian history in a single chapter on the 1820–1915 epoch called "The Lost and Chaotic Years," and in 1975, North American scholars still saw Latin America's "role throughout the colonial period and during the first century of independence [as] largely passive."[1]

1. J. H. Parry and Philip M. Sherlock, *A Short History of the West Indies* (London,

1

A closer examination of the period, however, reveals an enormous ferment in every part of the hemisphere. The Caribbean region fully participated in it. Cubans, Panamanians, Dominicans, Haitians, and Nicaraguans experienced burgeoning nationalism, wrote epic self-criticism, engaged in civil wars, and struggled with neocolonial economies during the early years of the century. In Jamaica, indigenous ideologies battled with British imperialism for the allegiance of the subject people. In Trinidad and Guyana, East Indians began their entry into mainstream society.[2]

The rapidity of change in the Caribbean is apparent from a survey of the period between British emancipation in 1838 and the year 1900, a period that spans a single lifetime. The second half of the nineteenth century transformed the islands. The widespread decline of sugar and other plantation crops, the transition to steam transport, and alterations in the commercial credit system helped create a society that, though still marked by vestiges of the past, could not return to that vanished world. Slave labor gave way to contract labor imported from Asia, Africa, and Europe.

The ingress of contract laborers obscured another, less fully documented international movement of labor. British West Indians went to Panama to build the Panama Railroad and later the Canal; they traveled to other Central American countries to harvest tropical produce. Nineteenth-century Jamaicans settled in Haiti, preferring a black sovereign state to British rule. Persons from the smaller islands of the Lesser Antilles gravitated to the more populous, prosperous centers. Population movements also involved members of the middle classes and the small commercial stratum; migrant French Antilleans were assimilated into the Haitian bourgeoisie, Jews of Dutch West Indian descent were absorbed in the Dominican Republic, Corsicans moved into both French-speaking and Spanish-speaking territories, and Syrian and Lebanese traders were increasingly represented in many countries.[3] This demographic movement needs more study. Ignorance of

1956), 260; Robert I. Rotberg and Christopher Clague, *Haiti, the Politics of Squalor* (Boston, 1971), 65–108; Graham H. Stuart and James L. Tigner, *Latin America and the United States* (6th ed.; Englewood Cliffs, N.J., 1975), vii.

2. Leslie F. Manigat, *L'Amérique Latine au XXᵉ Siècle, 1889–1929* (Paris, 1973); Philip D. Curtin, *Two Jamaicas: The Role of Ideas in a Tropical Colony, 1830–1865* (Cambridge, England, 1955); Gordon K. Lewis, *The Growth of the Modern West Indies* (New York, 1968), 257–288; Donald Wood, *Trinidad in Transition: The Years After Slavery* (London, 1968).

3. David Lowenthal, *West Indian Societies* (New York, 1972), 193–202, 208–10; Eu-

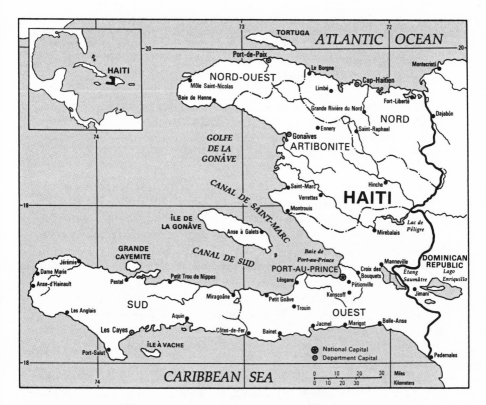

these movements underscores the persistent invisibility of the early twentieth century as a focus for Caribbean historical research.[4]

Agricultural, commercial, and technological change did not stand alone in influencing the direction of Caribbean developments in the early 1900s.

gène Aubin [Léon E. A. C. Descos], *En Haïti* (Paris, 1910), xxii, xiin1; Suzanne Comhaire-Sylvain and Jean L. Comhaire, "Urban Stratification in Haiti," *Social and Economic Studies,* VIII (1959), 179–89; Harry Hoetink, "The Dominican Republic in the Nineteenth Century: Some Notes on Stratification, Immigration, and Race," in Magnus Mörner (ed.), *Race and Class in Latin America* (New York, 1970), 108–14.

4. Hoetink, "The Dominican Republic," in Mörner (ed.), *Race and Class in Latin America*; Lancelot S. Lewis, *The West Indian in Panama: Black Labor in Panama, 1850–1914* (Washington, D.C., 1980); David Nicholls, *Haiti in Caribbean Context* (New York, 1985), 135–64; Franklin Knight, "Jamaican Migrants and the Cuban Sugar Industry, 1900–1934," in Manuel M. Fraginals, Frank M. Pons, and Stanley L. Engerman (eds.), *Between Slavery and Free Labor: The Spanish Speaking Caribbean in the Nineteenth Century* (Baltimore, 1985), 94–114.

A natural disaster in 1902 precipitated unforeseen dislocations. The eruption in Martinique of Mont Pelée destroyed that island's premier city, where the white population was concentrated. The death of half the Europeans spurred emigration and promoted the establishment of a colored bourgeoisie as a leading factor in French Antillean society. The year 1902 was also noteworthy as the year in which Cuba received its nominal independence and the United States and Germany created Caribbean fleets designed to respond quickly to disturbances in the independent republics that might endanger foreign life and property.[5]

Against the backdrop of war, revolution, migration, and natural disaster in the Caribbean, Haiti experienced its own tumultuous changes, belying the depictions by travel writers and humorists. To the notion of changelessness Haiti posited its burgeoning population of restless youth and dissatisfied peasants. To the idea of tropical opulence it contrasted the grim destitution of its countryside, the noisome filth of its cities, and the meanness of its economy. Most of the lurid accounts of the Haitian past that emanated from the West during this period were intentionally malicious. Their object was to discredit the idea of black political autonomy. A long-established precedent for pejorative writing on Haiti existed in the nineteenth-century texts that warned that slave liberation in the West Indies meant only anarchy and dissolution.[6]

The planters' outlook shaped foreign perspectives on the Black Republic during the slavery era. Even after Cuban slavery was eliminated in the late nineteenth century, racism and a relish for forced labor continued to dominate Western discourse on Caribbean subjects. By 1900, reportage on Haiti was linked to an exoticism derived from popular ideas about declining races and nations. In a letter to his nephew, Theodore Roosevelt gave his fleeting impressions of Cuba, Haiti, and the Dominican Republic while on a 1906 cruise. He described "green, jungly shores and bold mountains" and "great, beautiful, venomous tropical islands." Simul-

5. Franklin W. Knight, *The Caribbean: Genesis of a Fragmented Nationalism* (New York, 1978), 169–72; Richard D. Challener, *Admirals, Generals, and American Foreign Policy, 1898–1914* (Princeton, 1973), 22, 122; Parry and Sherlock, *A Short History of the West Indies*, 250.

6. Charles Mackenzie, *Notes on Haiti, Made During a Residence in That Republic* (London, 1830); Spenser St. John, *Hayti, or the Black Republic* (London, 1884); James Anthony Froude, *The English in the West Indies* (London, 1888); Hesketh Prichard, *Where Black Rules White* (New York, 1900). Also of interest is the twentieth-century work by Lothrop Stoddard, *The French Revolution in San Domingo* (Boston, 1914).

taneously attracted and repelled by the lushness, Roosevelt beheld a poisonous Eden and reconstructed the violence of the islands' history: "The desperate fighting, the triumphs, the pestilences, all the turbulence, the splendor and the wickedness, and the hot, evil, riotous life of the old planters and slaveowners." This dark past doomed the Caribbean to an unhealthy present in "the decay of most of the islands, the turning of Haiti into a land of savage negroes, who have reverted to voodooism and cannibalism."[7]

These lurid themes pervaded even the more sympathetic literature. In 1902, John S. Durham, a former American minister to Haiti, had used them in a novella published in *Lippincott's Monthly Magazine*. "Diane, Priestess of Haiti" combined the political, magico-religious, and erotic in the person of a young girl. Diane, the central character, is a transparent metaphor for Haiti; despite her addiction to the drums and the gods and her tawdry affairs with scheming merchants and politicians, she retains a rare and striking beauty. At the end of the story, Diane is redeemed when she accepts conversion and marriage.[8]

Durham's Diane intrigues her admirers with her mysterious charm. She can never be truly possessed. Similarly, foreign observers often perceived Haiti as an inscrutable, closed society. In 1908 the British traveler Harry Johnston wrote of his experiences there and in other New World communities. While the Dominican Republic, Cuba, and Mexico were reaching beyond their borders, Johnston noted, "Haiti remains aloof . . . a little black China in the midst of the Antilles, regarding all the rest of the world, except the far-off France, as uninteresting barbarians."[9]

Outsiders' views of Haiti were also conditioned by two other widely held beliefs: the myth of great hidden wealth and the myth of Haitian exceptionalism. The myth of El Dorado can be traced to Spanish times and proved quite enduring. Early twentieth-century commentators pointed to the fortune that the French had extracted from the colony of Saint-Domingue and compared it to independent Haiti's modest output. They invariably invoked the revolutions and civil wars, black rule and peasant laziness as causes, refusing to consider that French colonial achievements had come about only by means of slave labor and at the cost of innumera-

7. Theodore Roosevelt to Kermit Roosevelt, November 14, 1906, in Elting E. Morison (ed.), *The Letters of Theodore Roosevelt* (8 vols.; Cambridge, Mass., 1952), V, 495; Lowenthal, *West Indian Societies*, 14–16.

8. John S. Durham, "Diane, Priestess of Haiti," *Lippincott's Monthly Magazine*, LXIX (1901), 387–466.

9. Harry Johnston, *The Negro in the New World* (New York, 1910), 190, 193.

ble lives. The prosperity thus generated, moreover, had benefited only a small fraction of the population. The notion that Haiti could become fabulously wealthy did not recognize that its people had never been rich. Reactionaries who desired the resurrection of the old order through the application of external force always assumed that the beneficiaries of the newly recreated bounty would be foreigners. [10]

Like the colonial apologists, some writers of the period persisted in seeing Haiti as impervious to general patterns of social development. They did not base their idea of Haitian exceptionalism on the linguistic and cultural differences that separate it from much of Latin America; rather, they based it on an irrational racial mystique. [11] Racism obscured parallels between Haitian history and society and those of other American states. The idea that Haiti could fit no paradigm prohibited the development of any but the most conservative policies and helped retard the emergence of solid scholarship in the area of Haitian society and politics. Haitian writers share some of the blame for this state of affairs, and their contribution to the mystique will be discussed in a somewhat different context. Genuine knowledge suffered, but sensationalist literature thrived in such a climate. Much of this masqueraded as scientific writing and included works published as late as the 1970s. [12]

Although reactionary work continued to appear, the decade of the 1970s witnessed substantial progress in Haitian studies. Haitians pioneered it, for the most part, with some distinguished contributions by American and European scholars. [13] Several of these writers have explored the roots

10. Knight, *The Caribbean*, 140–42; George M. Fredrickson, *The Black Image in the White Mind: The Debate on Afro-American Character and Destiny, 1817–1914* (New York, 1971), 53, 54, 229, 254.

11. Johnston, *The Negro in the New World*; Rotberg and Clague, *Haiti, the Politics of Squalor*.

12. William B. Seabrook, *The Magic Island* (New York, 1929); Edna B. Taft, *A Puritan in Voodooland* (Philadelphia, 1938); John H. Craige, *Black Bagdad* (New York, 1933); Craige, *Cannibal Cousins* (New York, 1934); Robert Debs Heinl, Jr., and Nancy Gordon Heinl, *Written in Blood: The Story of the Haitian People, 1492–1971* (Boston, 1978).

13. These include George Corvington, *Port-au-Prince au Cours des Ans, La Métropole Haïtienne du XIXᵉ Siècle* (5 vols.; Port-au-Prince, 1976); Roger Gaillard, *Les cent-jours de Rosalvo Bobo* (Port-au-Prince, 1973); Benoit Joachim, *Les racines du sous-développement en Haïti* (Port-au-Prince, 1979); Leslie F. Manigat, "La substitution de la prépondérance américaine à la prépondérance française en Haiti au début du XXᵉ siècle: la conjoncture de 1910–1911," *Revue d'histoire moderne et contemporaine*, XIV (1967), 321–55; David Nicholls, *From Dessalines to Duvalier: Race, Colour and National Independence in Haiti*

of underdevelopment in Haiti, implicitly or explicitly using a dependency model.[14] In recent years, dependency theory has been extensively criticized and has undergone revision by some of its major proponents. The most pertinent objection to dependency theory from the historical viewpoint has centered on its determinism and lack of specificity.

Critics claim that dependency theorists have attached inordinate importance to the external factors that retard the progress of developing countries—for example, colonial conquest and declining terms of trade. They claim that dependency theory does not sufficiently consider the internal dynamics that functioned in concert with imperialist forces to generate underdevelopment. Dependency theory thus denies oppressed peoples the role of actors in their own history. Some commentators believe the empirical foundation of dependency literature insufficiently developed to sustain the level of theoretical generalization that has emerged.[15] At least one writer suggests that emphasis on the nation as the unit of analysis is misplaced: while it conceals the need to more fully examine class relations as a function of imperialism, it highlights the latent bourgeois nationalist pretensions of both dependency theory and the world systems analysis that evolved from it.[16]

With regard to the nation, however, we should remember Dale L. Johnson's assertion that nation-states, no matter how subordinated within international relations of dependency, remain repositories of power. They continue to be "expressions of class relations, and classes socially coalesce, from their consciousness and interests, and carry on struggles within territories."[17] There is yet another reason to adhere to the nation as a unit of analysis, which is equally compelling for our purposes.

(Cambridge, England, 1979); Gérard Pierre-Charles, *L'Economie haïtienne et sa voie de développement* (Paris, 1967); Hans Schmidt, *The United States Occupation of Haiti, 1915–1934* (New Brunswick, N.J., 1971).

14. Joachim, *Les racines du sous-développement*; David Nicholls, *Economic Dependence and Political Autonomy: The Haitian Experience* (Montreal, 1974); Pierre-Charles, *L'Economie haïtienne*; Michel S. Laguerre, *Urban Life in the Caribbean* (Cambridge, Mass., 1982).

15. Tony Smith, "The Underdevelopment of Development Literature: The Case of Dependency Theory," *World Politics*, XXXI (1979), 252, 271; Ahmad Aijaz, "Imperialism and Progress," in Ronald H. Chilcote and Dale L. Johnson (eds.), *Theories of Development* (Beverly Hills, 1983), 40.

16. Carlos Johnson, "Ideologies in Theories of Imperialism and Dependency," in Chilcote and Johnson (eds.), *Theories of Development*, 83, 86, 92.

17. Dale L. Johnson, "Class Analysis and Dependency," in Chilcote and Johnson (eds.), *Theories of Development*, 241.

The enigma of Haiti that so impressed Harry Johnston and John S. Durham lies precisely in its national tradition, a tradition that, despite the articulation made possible by the ideas of the *philosophes* and the praxis of the French Revolution, remained persistently Afro-American. This is not to suggest an irreducible racial mystique but simply to indicate that the sources of Haitian society were heterogeneous and that European culture and ideology were not decisive influences. As Cedric Robinson writes:

> Nowhere, not even in Russia, where a rebellious urban proletariat was a fraction of the mobilized working classes, had a bourgeois social order formed a precondition for revolutionary struggle. Revolutionary consciousness had formed in the process of anti-imperialist and national struggle and the beginnings of resistance had often been initiated by ideological constructions remote from the proletarian consciousness which was a presumption of Marx's theory of revolution. The idiom of revolutionary consciousness had been historical and cultural rather than "the mirror of production." The oppositions which had struck most deeply at capitalist domination and imperialism had been those formed outside the logic of bourgeois hegemony.[18]

The charges of determinism leveled against dependency theory are the most potent. The theory does posit hypothetically balanced societies that create and employ adjustable mechanisms to generate and regulate production, consumption, and trade. Equilibrium in these societies is set askew by capital penetration, and most intensely by monopoly capital. There is no clear sense of a prior class structure and dynamic relations of production before this contact.[19] Historical evidence does not support the existence of such an equilibrium point in Haiti. Only continuing adjustment to change can be located as a response to the momentum generated by the interface of external and internal sources of cohesion and disintegration.

World systems analysis, a related theory of development, treats the dominant Western capitalist economy and its political and social relations with the rest of the world. In Immanuel Wallerstein's *Modern World System*, the "core-state" emerges as a response to favorable historical conditions and, as a specific geopolitical entity, moves temporally in and out of positions of global supremacy. At their zenith, metropoles control the raw materials of "peripheral" states even when they do not control

18. Cedric J. Robinson, *Black Marxism: The Making of the Black Radical Tradition* (London, 1983), 324.
19. Smith, "The Underdevelopment of Development Literature," 249, 252, 257–58; Ahmad, "Imperialism and Progress," 40.

these states politically. By the late Middle Ages, core-states had developed insular Atlantic colonies for the purposes of agricultural exploitation. Lying at the base of the global economy, such colonies enjoyed the least prestige. Closest to them in sociopolitical valuation were the peripheral states, which were politically autonomous but economically dependent on larger imperial systems. Closed empires, like those of the Asiatic states, enjoyed greater prestige. At the apex of the system lay the core-states themselves.[20]

According to Wallerstein, these social relations largely continued to define the "modern world-system." However, the emphasis on the organizational power and attraction of the metropolis fails to adequately recognize the potent forces that were pulling in the opposite direction in the colonial world. The most celebrated of these were the settler revolution in North America and the slave revolution in Saint-Domingue. To argue that the North Americans were simply another wing of the international mercantile bourgeoisie or that the rebel slaves of Haiti would in time reveal their affinities to a socially conservative, bourgeois political order is to ignore the fact that neither group neatly corresponded to an existing Old World counterpart. Both had partners in Europe and in the Americas, but both maintained separate and irreducible political interests. The overshadowing of their respective independent mercantile interests by the realities of superior European economic power was never willed and often actively resisted. Their principal allegiance remained to their own way of life.[21]

The independent market economy in the Caribbean developed before the end of slavery as a response to the failure of European mercantilism to address the needs of island residents. It operated from the very beginning as a countereconomy and opposed the Caribbean development policies initiated by metropolitan authorities. After the abolition of slavery—in Haiti's case, after independence—the relationship between the countereconomy and European mercantilism changed as the majority of the people came increasingly to participate in a money economy. Historical

20. Immanuel Wallerstein, *The Modern World System: Capitalist Agriculture and the Origins of the European World-Economy in the Sixteenth Century* (New York, 1974), 301–302.

21. On Creole nationalism, Francisco A. Encina, "The Basis of Spanish American Independence," in R. A. Humphreys and John Lynch (eds.), *The Origins of the Latin American Revolutions, 1808–1826* (New York, 1965), 243–49; Sergio Villalobos R., "The Creole Desire for Office," *ibid.*, 250–55; Gordon K. Lewis, *Main Currents in Caribbean Thought* (Baltimore, 1983), 69–76.

action did not therefore revolve around imperatives emanating from the metropoles alone. To the degree that motion in the world systems model is centripetal only, it is deficient for the study of Caribbean history, in which centrifugal forces are strong.

Ironically, both Haitians and their critics have sought a determinism in the national decay of the early twentieth century. To romantic racists, it consisted of inevitable military rule, weak civil institutions, superstition, the constancy of poverty, tyranny, and corruption. Only imperialist control could end these problems, which were interpreted as racially inherent. White rule would certainly come, they believed, as Haiti succumbed to its contradictions. For particular nationalist members of the native intelligentsia, the very cycle of revolutionary activity gradually carved out the rough shape that reform must take. Insurgency would end once fundamental political institutions had fully matured. By arresting the revolutionary process, critics of the American occupation of 1915–1934 argued, the United States aborted the embryonic hopes of the Haitian people for meaningful development.[22]

The cure for the Haitian malaise was not to be found in foreign military occupation or in peasant mercenary movements. American domination did not revitalize native institutions nor did the *cacos* in the 1902–1915 period transcend warlordism and social banditry. These facts owe nothing to racial eccentricity but rather stem from unacknowledged cultural and political factors. Within the narrowing options available to most Haitians of the 1902–1915 era, the behaviors they evinced, seen in the context of their cumulative experience, were supremely logical.

This judgment includes the leadership classes, whose activities dominate this study. The work at hand focuses in detail on groups that were in many ways only tangential to the mainstream of Haitian society and culture. They did not represent the majority, with whom many lacked the slightest sympathy. The significance of the elite, both foreign and indigenous, rested in their very marginality, which gave them singular interests to define and preserve, a task they achieved with great skill and intelligence.

In studying the behavior of nations and ruling classes, one must retain an awareness of the autonomy of the political actors and their ability to

22. Examples of the racist view include Prichard, *Where Black Rules White;* and Archibald R. Colquhoun, *Greater America* (New York and London, 1904). An early formulation of the thesis that Haiti was fumbling toward a solution of its problems through social and political upheaval is found in Charles Emmanuel Kernizan, *La République d'Haïti et le gouvernement démocrate de Woodrow Wilson* (Paris, 1919).

effectively control their own sphere to a substantial degree. At the same time, it is important to keep in view the general pattern of control exercised over dependent countries by the imperialist powers. To do otherwise is to invite an analysis that hardly perceives such exploitation and is ready to defend current global policies of abusive retrenchment in economic aid.[23]

Imperialist domination of Haiti began with Columbus. One of the first loci of Spanish colonialism, the western part of the island of Haiti, later passed into the hands of the French, who turned it into a sugar-growing slave colony.[24] The successful rebellion of the slaves ended the French mercantilist empire in the Americas. Within fifty years, slavery was extinct in most of the Caribbean. Imperialist powers subsequently devoted their energies to arresting the regional development by local peoples of alternative economic sectors that the metropoles could not control.[25] They continued to operate an antiquated mercantilism in the islands while their capital—and that of islanders—flowed into larger and more recently acquired colonies on the other side of the Atlantic.

The advent in the twentieth century of the long-anticipated interoceanic canal gave new life to mercantilism and drew attention to the Caribbean region as a strategic center. For Europeans, the worth of the promised commerce would far outstrip that of the few economically depressed plantations they possessed in the area. For Americans, the borders of the Caribbean Sea now stretched to the Pacific, the gateway to Asia.[26] The visionary gaze of advocates of the global market was impeded, however, by upheavals in the independent Caribbean republics, over which they had no formal control. The imperialist states responded to Caribbean unrest through naval exercises and police action. These interventions ensured the continuity and security of metropolitan interests. The great powers disliked what they considered anarchy in the Caribbean and exerted diplomatic and economic pressure to curb it. They demanded that the republics contain the popular movements, the insurrections, and the financial disarray that made it difficult to exploit Caribbean resources,

23. Mats Lundahl, *Peasants and Poverty: A Study of Haiti* (London, 1979).

24. *Española* will be used here to differentiate the island as a geographic entity from the name of the Republic of Haiti.

25. For aspects of the struggle between independent, indigenous economies and planter and metropolitan mercantilism, see Sidney W. Mintz, *Caribbean Transformations* (Baltimore, 1974); Ken Post, *Arise Ye Starvelings* (The Hague, 1978), 30–67; and Curtin, *Two Jamaicas*.

26. William Appleman Williams, *The Tragedy of American Diplomacy* (2nd rev. ed.; New York, 1972), 42–43, 45; Walter LaFeber, *The New Empire* (Ithaca, N.Y., 1963), 147.

including strategic location, efficiently. The metropoles tolerated and encouraged many repressive regimes in the name of political stability. [27]

The United States led the turn-of-the-century effort to revitalize mercantilism. It formed a naval fleet, the Caribbean Squadron, to meet long-range needs as well as undertake police actions in the islands. The Theodore Roosevelt administration, greatly interested in an isthmian canal, aided the Panamanian Revolution of 1903. Soon after the Panamanian declaration of independence, work began on the Canal. [28]

The formation of the squadron, the Panamanian Revolution, and the beginnings of Canal construction occurred within months of one another. The rapid pace was not, however, due exclusively to American initiative. The traditional face of colonialism in the region began to change long before the empires themselves faded from view. The reasons had much to do with extrahemispheric issues. The rising eminence of the United States as a power in the area is contrasted to the gradual decline of France and Britain, both preoccupied with European, African, and Asian affairs. French and British surrender to the Americans was voluntary to the extent that a Pax Americana could guarantee security for European trade and investments. In contrast, Germany had emerged as a minor but ambitious Caribbean power by 1900. German commercial houses competed vigorously for island trade, and German banks began exporting capital to the independent republics during the first decade of the twentieth century. The sovereign states of the underdeveloped world were significant trading partners for Germany, which had only a small colonial market for its manufactures and few guaranteed tropical suppliers. [29]

Germany's activities in the Caribbean were viewed with concern by the other metropoles and particularly by the United States. The commercial and political rhetoric of the era painted a picture of a German trade juggernaut, militantly supported by the Imperial Navy and an army of highly disciplined German immigrants. The threat of German preemi-

27. Challener, *Admirals, Generals, and American Foreign Policy,* 61; Warren G. Kneer, *Great Britain and the Caribbean, 1901–1913: A Study in Anglo-American Relations* (East Lansing, 1975), 1–66; Holger H. Herwig, *Politics of Frustration: The United States in German Naval Planning, 1889–1941* (Boston, 1976), 67–68.

28. Malcolm J. Proudfoot, *Population Movements in the Caribbean* (Port-of-Spain, 1950); Edwin P. Reubens, *Migration and Development in the West Indies* (Mona, Jamaica, n.d.); Lancelot Lewis, *The West Indian in Panama.*

29. L. Abrams and D. J. Miller, "Who Were the French Colonialists? A Reassessment of the *Parti Colonial,* 1890–1914," *Historical Journal,* XIX (1976), 685–725; Kneer, *Great Britain and the Caribbean,* ix; D. C. M. Platt, *Latin America and British Trade, 1806–1914* (London, 1972), 98–135; Herwig, *Politics of Frustration,* 95–96.

nence was greatly exaggerated, however, for Germany could not have made conquests in the Americas without allies, and an increasingly isolated Germany postponed confrontations with great powers in the Caribbean after 1904.[30]

The clear inability of any metropole to seize territory led to a more determined concentration of energies on pacific means of aggrandizement. This effort underlay the resurgence of metropolitan rivalry in the West Indies of the 1900s. The imperialist states exerted strong pressures on the independent republics to let contracts and concessions to their respective nationals. Anxieties and uncertainty about the progress and preferment of competitors further heightened the tension and the jockeying for favors. The metropoles influenced independent countries through their formal representatives as well as through informal brokers and contributed substantially to local governments' problems.[31] Like the Caribbean imperial contests of the seventeenth and eighteenth centuries, the new competition was overwhelmingly mercantile in nature, preserving certain traditional characteristics of Caribbean trade while disguising the fundamental innovations that were under way.

Changes also occurred in the nature and style of conventional diplomacy. Paul G. Lauren locates their origins in the depressed economy of the late nineteenth century:

> After the strain of the Great Depression of 1873–1896, proponents of laissez-faire capitalism were less dogmatic and less enthusiastic than formerly. Those deeply involved in foreign trade and investment increasingly asked the state to assume the role of their defender. They alternately pleaded softly and demanded vociferously that the Ministries for Foreign Affairs venture upon new and expanded responsibilities for international commerce. . . .
>
> Trade associations, chambers of commerce, industrial groups, shipping firms, consular agents, and private citizens [all wanted] active and aggressive state support for securing markets, safeguarding investments, and promoting trade overseas.[32]

As the oldest and most experienced state in the region, Haiti confronted the newly assertive metropolitan drive for markets by pursuing a multilateral foreign policy as a prerequisite to national survival. Each

30. Herwig, *Politics of Frustration*, 39, 91.
31. Manigat, "Substitution"; W. E. Aughinbaugh, *Selling Latin America* (Boston, 1915), 8; Joachim, *Les racines du sous-développement*, 188–92.
32. Paul Gordon Lauren, *Diplomats and Bureaucrats: The First Institutional Responses to Twentieth Century Diplomacy in France and Germany* (Stanford, Calif., 1976), 158, 159–60.

major power represented in Haiti tried to undermine its multilateralism. A study of Haitian relations with the great powers therefore cannot rely exclusively on the abundant store of American documents without incurring the risk of accepting the Americans' self-assessment as guardians of hemispheric security and losing sight of the objectives of other interested states. Perceptions of West Indian countries as actors rather than pawns in the international arena have been rare. The reluctance to examine multilateralist strategies in Caribbean foreign policies has often prevented North Americans from developing fresh perspectives on national behaviors.

I

State and Society in Haiti

Nous c'est nanchon la guè! Ou pas tendé canon' m tiré?
We are a nation of war! Don't you hear my cannon firing?
—Haitian proverb

THE HISTORICAL experience of a nation determines its self-con-
sciousness. It shapes the attitudes, beliefs, and values of statesmen and
the foundation of public policies. Among the most important events in
national history are those that surround the origin of the state, and the
beliefs that evolve from these often serve as the core ideology that molds
the political behavior of individuals and groups. J. G. A. Pocock writes:
"Since so large a part of men's consciousness of environment and time is
gained through consciousness of the frame of social relationships which
they inhabit, the conceptualisation of tradition is an important source of
their images of society, time and history. The importance of these visibly
transcends the political; we are looking at one of the origins of a distinctly
human awareness."[1]

The Haitian conceptualization of tradition was linked profoundly
to the Haitian Revolution. This in turn sprang from slave revolt and
the disaffection of the free nonwhites in the French island of Saint-
Domingue. The French noted the fearlessness of their enemies in this war
for national liberation: "But what men these blacks are! How they fight
and how they die! One has to make war against them to know their
reckless courage in braving danger. . . . I have seen a solid column, torn
by grapeshot from four pieces of cannon, advance without making a
retrograde step. The more they fell the greater seemed to be the courage
of the rest."[2] The bravery of the blacks, their ferocity in battle, and their

1. J. G. A. Pocock, *Politics, Language and Time: Essays on Political Thought and
History* (New York, 1971), 235.
2. Cited in C. L. R. James, *The Black Jacobins: Toussaint L'Ouverture and the San
Domingo Revolution* (2nd rev. ed.; New York, 1963), 385.

willingness to burn and destroy everything rather than yield to the enemy became an important part of the national tradition.

The chronic warfare of the revolutionary era profoundly affected political values. The consequent exaltation of martial virtues, later incorporated into political rhetoric, derived from continued reliance on militarism as a means of social control. The founders of the nation were militarists, and by early in the twentieth century, "General" had become a title of respect for any man of wealth, status, or extraordinary power in Haitian society.[3]

The foundation of the state was intimately connected to territorial self-determination. Haitians knew that the predominance of a European power on the island of Española compromised their own independence. They therefore took a firm stand against the alienation of any part of the national domain to foreigners. The inviolability of the land became a civil axiom, and few administrations ever publicly dared be associated with an attempt to sell or lease part of the soil.[4]

In sum, the most cherished national beliefs arose from the circumstances of the revolution. The tradition of military valor, a rugged republicanism, and the fierce insistence on territorial integrity were the main political principles that Haitians brought with them into the twentieth century. Although other factors entered into their statecraft, militarism and republican nationalism formed the basic consensus that lent a national character to Haitian society and legitimized those who held power.

The rise of Haiti had profound implications for the nascent anticolonial movements of Latin America. The Black Republic provided an ideological link to the French Revolution and lent its soldiers to Simón Bolívar's struggle for self-determination in Venezuela and other rebel colonies. Quickly assuming a position of leadership of the oppressed races of the New World, Haiti also extended automatic citizenship to persons of African and Amerindian origin, who were invited to settle in the country.[5]

3. Hesketh Prichard, Where Black Rules White (New York, 1900), 39–47; Léon Audain, Le Mal d'Haïti, ses causes et son traitement (Port-au-Prince, 1908), 81, 82; Patrick Bellegarde-Smith, "Haiti: Perspectives of Foreign Policy: An Essay on the International Relations of a Small State," Caribbean Quarterly, XX (September–December, 1974), 28.
    4. J. N. Léger, Haiti, Her History and Her Detractors (New York, 1907), 246–47n2; Frederick Douglass, The Life and Times of Frederick Douglass (1892; rpr. New York, 1962), 607.
    5. Magnus Mörner, Race Mixture in the History of Latin America (Boston, 1967), 87–88; Léger, Haiti, 169–72, 290; David Brion Davis, The Problem of Slavery in the Age of Revolution (Ithaca, N.Y., 1975), 80–81, 90, 557.

That Haiti granted civil status to persons deemed unworthy by whites was only part of the problem that it posed for slaveholders and imperialists. The country could not be diplomatically recognized, lest such a gesture imply fundamental acquiescence to the manner in which its people had dispensed with slavery, an institution still unchallenged virtually everywhere. Even the great Latin American revolutionaries had doubts about the capacity of nonwhites for self-rule.[6] The revolts in the Spanish empire, though a shock to the Spanish crown, were generally as conservative as the successful rebellion in North America. Landed settlers and the urban bourgeoisie resisted imperial political and economic domination, but as owners of human property, they could not accept the implications of the Haitian Revolution. The Black Republic, despite its Pan-American ardor and revolutionary militance, found itself virtually isolated in the hemisphere by the mid-1820s. Feared and shunned in the international community, Haiti turned inward, drawing on its internal strengths.

The Haitian state emerged in the context of struggles among the great powers following the French Revolution. The development of Haitian civil society owed much less to European events. The slaves who were brought to the harsh environment of Saint-Domingue came from the culturally rich Yoruba, Fon, and Congo regions of West Africa. Moral, spiritual, and aesthetic values, though affected by the planters' culture, had the authoritative stamp of the black majority's creativity and innovative power.[7]

Haitian civil society was also greatly influenced by *marronage*. During the slavery era, groups of runaway slaves, called maroons, created autonomous settlements in the mountain or forest wildernesses of many colonies, including Saint-Domingue. Maroon communities governed themselves, but colonial authorities often withheld formal recognition of these entities because of the impetus they lent to slave revolt elsewhere. Legally the maroons were outlaws, but in many instances the colonialists honored their de facto independence in exchange for territorial concessions, assistance in recapturing other fugitives, or commercial privileges. Trade and diplomacy with these groups assumed a pragmatic character. The maroons' tenuous strategic position moreover forced on them a general policy of political and social conservatism. The Haitians' reaction to the

6. Mörner, *Race Mixture*, 87–88.

7. Harold Courlander, *The Drum and the Hoe: Life and Lore of the Haitian People* (Berkeley and Los Angeles, 1960); George Eaton Simpson, *Black Religions in the New World* (New York, 1978), 62–70; Robert Farris Thompson, *Flash of the Spirit: African and Afro-American Art and Philosophy* (New York, 1984), 163–91.

political quarantine they suffered during the first half of the nineteenth century bears striking resemblance to the maroon experience.[8]

Some students of maroon communities perceive them as traditionalist societies. Eugene Genovese extends the characterization to the postrevolutionary era in Haiti, which he regards as a consequence of a "counterrevolution of peasant property." Genovese errs when he maintains that Haiti had no national bourgeoisie that could have forced the country to create the conditions for capitalist development. There was indeed a bourgeoisie, and the rise of peasant production represented not simply a restorationist attempt to recreate a "primitive-communalist" society but a rejection of the advanced form of exploitation with which the bourgeoisie was identified.[9]

Contemporary scholarship, perceiving the roots of the Haitian state and civil society in the revolutionary period, has frequently assumed that Haitian energies were exhausted by the upheavals of that era and consequently were incapable of further political elaboration. It depicts a society that had congealed around certain key events and characteristics—an institutionalized revolution, a posture of militant self-defense, the ideal of peasant proprietorship.[10]

There were agencies that served a unifying purpose in the ongoing articulation of civic values in Haiti. Nineteenth-century Freemasonry bridged the gap between an Afro-Caribbean folk culture and the political culture of a modern republic. A white fraternity during the colonial period, Masonry was appropriated by Haitians during the revolutionary years. Secret brotherhoods were not unfamiliar in the Haitian milieu, as West African secret societies found their counterparts in colonial slave communities. The Masons united their members across class and color lines in networks in which merit meant more than ancestry. Freemasonry became popular in the Black Republic in the early 1800s when Haiti was estranged from all Western churches. It simultaneously provided a rational civil religion compatible with the ideals of the revolution and posed an alternative to both Catholicism and voodoo. It helped channel Haitian thought into secular directions and, not surprisingly, found an enemy in

8. Richard Price (comp.), *Maroon Societies: Slave Rebel Communities in the Americas* (Garden City, N.Y., 1973); Jean Fouchard, *The Haitian Maroons* (New York, 1981); Eugene D. Genovese, *From Rebellion to Revolution: Afro-American Slave Revolts in the Making of the Modern World* (Baton Rouge, 1979), 82–91.

9. Genovese, *From Rebellion to Revolution*, 82–91.

10. *Ibid.*; Sidney W. Mintz, *Caribbean Transformations* (Baltimore, 1974), 267–301.

Rome. By 1900, Masonry was identified with Protestant, anticlerical, or freethinking constituencies.[11]

Spacious town houses served as Masonic lodges in the important towns. In 1903, Port-au-Prince boasted five. During the same period, a British traveler estimated that lodge memberships in Haiti comprised as much as 10 percent of the male population. This figure embraced many prominent citizens and key foreigners, such as the two American ministers who served in Haiti from 1898 to 1913. Masons could and did use their fraternal connections to advance individually in politics, but the lodges did not exert an independent force in government, serving instead as political clubs. When they acted as purveyors of republican ideas, perhaps their most significant purpose in the long term, the lodges were important as integrative intermediaries between the social and political facets of civil society.[12]

Haitian civil society thus developed at variance with Haitian polity. The liberal republicanism of Alexandre Pétion and the centralizing despotism of Henri Christophe placed the nation squarely in the camp of modern states. Its bourgeoisie strove to bring the republic even closer to integration with the major metropolitan centers. The civil society, with its roots in a non-European experience, remained hostile to such conformity. Peasant agriculture and Afro-Caribbean traditions did not represent the dead hand of a utopian African past, as Genovese suggests, but a living resistance to the neocolonial tendencies implicit in the form of government Haiti had chosen and in the social stratum that would manage the state. The democratizing and republican elements inherent in Haitian Freemasonry did not succeed in impressing their stamp on the features of government because that secret society remained largely hermeneutic in regard to institutions and instrumental in regard to practical politics. Masons were prepared to understand, come to terms with, and manipulate their world but not to transform it.

11. Wade Davis, *The Serpent and the Rainbow* (New York, 1985); J. T. Holly, "Christian Missions in Haiti," *Missionary Review of the World*, XXVI (1903), 651; David Nicholls, *From Dessalines to Duvalier: Race, Colour and National Independence in Haiti* (Cambridge, England, 1979), 118–19. See the evocative fictional treatment in Frédéric Marcelin, *Thémistocle-Epaminondas Labasterre* (Paris, 1901), 5, 30–31, 71–72; Suzanne Comhaire-Sylvain and Jean L. Comhaire, "Urban Stratification in Haiti," *Social and Economic Studies*, VIII (1959), 183; J. Comhaire, "Religious Trends in African and Afro-American Societies," *Anthropology Quarterly*, n.s., XXVI (October, 1953), 106.

12. Holly, "Christian Missions," 651; J. Montaque Simpson, *Six Months in Port-au-Prince* (Philadelphia, 1905), 128–29.

The endemic revolutionary upheavals of the nineteenth century that so greatly disenchanted foreign observers provide another manifestation of political process in Haiti. To the uninitiated, the street fighting, the gunplay, and the massing of private armies appeared to typify Haitian political immaturity and instability. Racists and colonial apologists needed no further demonstration of black incompetence. What seemed to be anarchic behavior was actually highly patterned, however. In 1902, shots were fired in the Chamber of Deputies during a debate over the interpretation of the constitution. James Theodore Holly, a black American missionary long a resident of Haiti, was not disturbed by the episode.

> It will seem strange to people in the United States when I say that here this is a constitutional proceeding sanctioned by that document. In one of its articles it is declared that the Sovereignty of the nation resides in the *collectivity of all the Haitian people,* and that the safeguard of the constitution is confided to their *patriotism.* Hence, when their representatives betray their trust, the people by such a revolutionary movement take back from them the power that had been confided to those deputies. They do it on the spot. It is a *Supreme Referendum,* so to speak, that has passed into *common law usage* here.[13]

The indisputable fragility of Haitian democracy in the early twentieth century meant that it could be and often was crushed by strong-willed despots. Its significance lies partly in its form. The conviction that tyrannies might rightfully be toppled by popular revolutionary action never disappeared in Haiti.

The Haitian bourgeoisie led the nation in trading freely with the metropoles. Commerce nevertheless did not lessen European and American hostility until 1838, when France recognized the Black Republic as part of an unequal arrangement in which Haiti agreed to pay a staggering indemnity to the former planters. Britain and Germany made their recognition of Haiti contingent on a reconciliation with the French. The United States conducted a profitable provisioning trade with the republic but did not enter into normal diplomatic relations with it until 1862, when the American slaveholders had left the Union.[14]

Fears about the future of chattel slavery prompted general white anxiety about Haitian intentions in the early nineteenth century. Nervous

13. James T. Holly to the Rev. Dr. Joshua Kimber, May 19, 1902, in Papers of the Domestic and Foreign Missionary Society, Record Group 68–4, Archives of the Episcopal Church, Austin.

14. Rayford W. Logan, *The Diplomatic Relations of the United States with Haiti, 1776–1891* (Chapel Hill, 1941), 198–208, 218–22, 231–32.

Colombians believed that Haiti had three hundred agents in their country in 1823, fanning the flames of servile revolt. In the United States, the Denmark Vesey slave conspiracy of the previous year, organized by a free black of Haitian origin, aroused similar alarm. American laws proscribed Haitian entry and included early attempts to limit the immigration of French West Indian coloreds into the newly acquired Louisiana Territory. Barred from normal international contacts, the Black Republic nevertheless became a cosmopolitan crossroads of trade.[15]

National survival in an antagonistic environment bred a concern for security that, combined with a military predisposition and a pride in maintaining the patrimony, helped to create a veritable fortress mentality in nineteenth-century Haiti. During an age when fortifications became increasingly obsolete in warfare, King Henri Christophe built a massive stone citadel, La Ferrière, on the north coast of the island that was designed to withstand lengthy sieges. Maroon thought triumphed in the conception of La Ferrière.[16] After the death of Christophe and the consequent destruction of the northern monarchy, President Jean Pierre Boyer feared a French or British recapture of Española via the sparsely populated and politically weak eastern side of the island, the Spanish colony of Santo Domingo. Motivated by national security concerns, the Haitians since revolutionary times had mounted successive invasions of Santo Domingo in an effort to keep it out of imperialist hands. Boyer went a step further when he sought to base a navy on the northeast coast and made arrangements to bring thousands of black American farm laborers, shipwrights, and other artisans to the area. Such people, adhering to the Haitian government as the agency of their liberation from American slavery, would serve, Boyer thought, as a buffer between Haiti and foreign invasion. As settlers in an area of scanty development, their industry and agriculture could advance the material interests of the state.[17] The Dominican campaigns, which ended slavery entirely on Española and drove

15. Mörner, *Race Mixture*, 83n2; Robert S. Starobin, "Denmark Vesey's Slave Conspiracy of 1822: A Study in Rebellion and Repression," in John H. Bracey, Jr., August Meier, and Elliott Rudwick (eds.), *American Slavery: The Question of Resistance* (Belmont, Calif., 1971), 70–74, 80–85, 92–93; Donald E. Everett, "Emigrés and Militiamen: Free Persons of Color in New Orleans, 1803–1815," *Journal of Negro History*, XXXVIII (1953), 380; Logan, *Diplomatic Relations of the United States with Haiti*, 156, 167–85, 193–97.

16. Frédéric Marcelin, Haitian novelist and politician, called La Ferrière "the thought of an entire people erecting its mausoleum in preference to outliving freedom" (*Au Gré du Souvenir* [Paris, 1913], 111).

17. Loring Dewey (ed.), *Correspondence Relative to the Emigration to Hayti of the Free People of Colour in the United States* . . . (New York, 1824).

out the Spanish elite, continued into the 1850s. The invasions aroused resentment in the neighboring country, which sloughed off Haitian rule in 1844. Frontier warfare made it even more difficult for Haiti to emerge from political isolation. In 1904 a Haitian diplomat confided his concern over border problems to the American secretary of state, John Hay. "You have a Monroe Doctrine too," Hay concluded. The Haitian replied that Haiti had had one before the United States did.[18]

The problem of national security could not be separated from the question of the economic viability of the state, which rested on a modest income from coffee, the single most important crop after the revolution. Coffee had been a colonial plantation commodity but later assumed importance as a peasant crop. Peasants gathered the cherries from half-wild shrubs rather than cultivating them. This practice proved most compatible with the subsistence agriculture that characterized their economy. The coffee, sold in small quantities, arrived at market unsorted and uncleaned. Buyers passed the cost of processing back to the producers, and the export duties levied against coffee by a government constantly in need of ready funds further devalued it.[19]

Haitian coffee grew near the small settlements in the plains, hills, and mountains that were home for most peasants. Country people farmed land that they professed to own, but few could produce certificates of title. The state nominally held all unclaimed real property. As a result, peasant proprietors could be evicted from public lands. Dispossession occurred when the government awarded contracts to concessionaires or land grants to the powerful and the politically faithful. When the peasants were not evicted, they remained on the land and served as vassals to new proprietors. They sometimes outlasted the landlords, for good luck in Port-au-Prince could be ephemeral. In any event, the peasants continued to produce an average of 29,400 tons of coffee a year from 1900 to 1911.[20]

18. Emilio Rodriguez Demorizi, *Invasiones haitianas de 1801, 1805 y 1822* (Ciudad Trujillo [Santo Domingo City], 1955); Bellegarde-Smith, "Haiti: Perspectives of Foreign Policy," 29–31; Haitian Minister to Secretary Murville Férère, March 21, 1904, in Kurt Fisher Collection, Schomburg Research Center, NYPL.

19. Paul Moral, *Le Paysan haïtien* (Paris, 1961), 263–75; Mats Lundahl, *Peasants and Poverty: A Study of Haiti* (London, 1979), 40, 62.

20. Moral, *Le Paysan haïtien*, 45–54; Perceval Thoby, *Dépossessions* (Port-au-Prince, 1930); Candelon Rigaud, *Promenades dans les campagnes d'Haïti, 1789–1928* (Paris, 1928), 124; Louis Janvier, *Les Affaires d'Haïti (1883–1884)* (Paris, 1885), 140–55; J. B. Romain, *Quelques Moeurs et Coutumes des Paysans haïtiens* (Port-au-Prince, 1969), 32–33;

The state relied on the coffee crop not only for operating expenses but as the basis of credit and as a guarantee of the currency. In order to support the price, it raised or lowered the export duties in response to fluctuations in the French market. There was no effective program of crop diversification, but individual planters diverted land into sugar and other tropical commodities as a hedge against losses during periods of falling prices.[21]

The significance of coffee was not limited to the government's needs. General cash flow depended on the purchasing power of the peasants, the principal national consumers. The urban bourgeoisie imported small quantities of luxury goods, chiefly from France, but the peasants bought the bulk of provisions and cloth, which came primarily from the United States. Provision merchants in the towns depended heavily on rural liquidity, which could easily dry up as a result of crop failure. Merchants therefore minimized their risks by passing higher prices on to consumers. The dollar, not the gourde, formed the basis of all foreign transactions, and the exchange rate was subject to speculative fluctuations, as traders and bankers manipulated it for their own purposes.[22]

Merchants doubled as financiers, buying and selling currencies and regulating the daily rate of exchange. When Haiti was selling gold, the premium declined. When the state needed money, it rose.[23] The Haitian government made periodic attempts to circumvent the local business community by searching elsewhere for funds. In the summer of 1899, for example, it reached the limits on pledging its revenues. Local bankers demanded 36 percent interest on any loan, so officials in Port-au-Prince tried to secure money in Germany. Rebuffed there, they approached American bankers of the Morgan group for five million dollars. The Americans refused but offered instead a plan whereby the Haitian debt

---

Spenser St. John, *Hayti, or the Black Republic* (London, 1884), 320; Robert Dudley Longyear, "Haitian Coffee: Its Cultivation and Preparation for Shipment," September 9, 1922, DF, 838.61333/47; Vito Tanzi, "Export Taxation in Developing Countries: Taxation of Coffee in Haiti," *Social and Economic Studies*, XXV (1976), 66–76; William F. Powell to John Hay, June 10, 1901, CD.

21. Pan American Union, *Proceedings of the Pan American Commerce Conference, February 13–17, 1911* (Washington, D.C., 1911), 78; Pierre Carteron to Minister of Foreign Affairs, July 30, 1908, and Alphonse Cillière to the Minister of Foreign Affairs, November 14, 1912, QDO, Vol. 30.

22. J. B. Terres, Annual Report, 1906, in U.S. Department of State, *Consular Reports*, August, 1907, pp. 96–97; Powell to William Day, July 18, 1898, CD.

23. Powell to Hay, August 1, 1899, CD; New York *Times*, June 29, 1899, Sec. 5, p. 14.

would be consolidated and customs revenues, to be controlled by the financiers, put up as collateral. The Haitians in turn rejected the proposal as an affront to their independence. Officials of the French-owned Banque Nationale d'Haïti also insisted on a debt consolidation program that the Haitians would not at first accept.[24]

These frustrated attempts to gain needed capital indicate the character of the government's difficulties. The state was thrown on the mercy of local resident bankers who, as speculators, exerted an invidious influence on the economy. Periodic cash shortages triggered economic crises and political unrest, particularly when, as often occurred, the military and civil service had not been paid, and there was no other source of revenue before the harvest. Small merchants failed as exchange rates behaved erratically. Typically, the Banque Nationale tried to make use of these crises to increase its leverage and that of France in Haitian finances.[25]

Compelled to rely on local private bankers by the refusal of the Banque Nationale or foreign financiers to agree to its terms, the Haitian government could exert pressures on resident foreigners that it could not exercise in negotiations with metropolitan lenders. Forced loans and partial reimbursements were a common method of handling debt obligations. Another was the issue of long-term bonds, a practice that ensured that the administration contracting the loan would not be the one to repay it. Merchant-bankers had to cooperate with official requests for funds if they wished to continue conducting business unhindered, but they were frequently rewarded for their pains by favors at the customhouses.[26]

By the turn of the century, Haiti was locked into a primitive and inefficient banking system and often lacked access to foreign capital. Operators inside the country manipulated the money market. The Banque Nationale, chartered as the official fiscal agent, competed rather than cooperated with the government, much to the general detriment of the economy. During "dead season" in 1904, when crops were not yet ready for export, exchange rates were 540 percent at 9 A.M. on August 1 and 710 percent at 7 P.M. the same day. The consequent hardships of

24. Powell to Hay, August 1, 1899, CD; Benoit Joachim, *Les racines du sous-développement en Haïti* (Port-au-Prince, 1979), 181–83.

25. Powell to Hay, July 20, 1904, and enclosure, CD; Leslie F. Manigat, "La substitution de la prépondérance américaine à la prépondérance française en Haïti au début du XXᵉ siècle: la conjoncture de 1910–1911," *Revue d'histoire moderne et contemporaine*, XIV (1967), 339; Louis R. E. Gation, *Aspects de l'économie et des finances d'Haïti* (Port-au-Prince, 1944), 191.

26. Powell to Hay, August 1, 30, 1904, CD; Jacques C. Antoine, *Jean Price-Mars and Haiti* (Washington, D.C., 1981), 47; Joachim, *Les racines du sous-développement*, 184–85.

ordinary people contributed to a suspicion and hostility toward businessmen, especially foreigners, in the capital and the larger towns.[27]

These sentiments were an intrinsic part of Haiti's troubled relations with the metropolitan powers. Resident aliens, who owned the major commercial establishments and the transportation and communications systems by 1902, effectively controlled Haiti's intercourse with the outside world. Administrations in power frequently played on native feelings of resentment to facilitate their control over aliens and citizens alike and to camouflage unpopular public policies. This political exploitation of an inflammatory issue does not mean that the problem of foreign influence was not real, however. Expatriates could be controlled to some degree, but the Haitian government's dealings with them could not be separated from its disadvantageous position vis-à-vis the United States, France, Germany, and Britain. As a consequence, Haiti's conduct of foreign policy came to resemble a balancing act in which it attempted to pit the great powers against one another to avoid being engulfed by any one of them.[28]

Undeniably dependent on the vagaries of the foreign commodity and capital markets, Haitian policy makers realized that their sovereignty remained purely political. This meant "a right of initiative, even though a limited one, and the opportunity to use it."[29] The governing class consequently elaborated standard policies in international relations: the non-alienability of the soil, prohibition of foreign investment, an Españolan "Monroe Doctrine," and multilateralism. These canons had been applied to diplomacy since the earliest years of the republic. By the late nineteenth century, however, it was evident that a clear foreign policy did not suffice to shore up Haiti's eroding position. Critics began to turn their attention to the domestic causes of the nation's predicament. It is beyond the scope of this work to treat the voluminous literature of Haitian political commentary in depth. This task has already been successfully undertaken by such scholars as David Nicholls, Michael Dash, and Gordon K. Lewis.[30] A few examples will suffice to illustrate the tenor of this literature during the 1902–1915 period.

27. Frédéric Marcelin, *Bric-à-brac* (Paris, 1910), 53–56; Carteron to Minister of Foreign Affairs, March 24, 1908, QDO, Vol. 7; Elihu Root to Secretary Metcalf, March 26, 1908, NF, 2126/184–85; A. G. Vansittart to Foreign Secretary, March 11, 1904, FO 371, Vol. 180.

28. Manigat, "Substitution," 322, 323.

29. *Ibid.*

30. Nicholls, *From Dessalines to Duvalier*; J. Michael Dash, *Literature and Ideology in Haiti, 1915–1961* (London, 1981); Gordon K. Lewis, *Main Currents in Caribbean Thought* (Baltimore, 1983).

The extensive Haitian polemical literature became especially significant in the early twentieth century, when indigenous institutions began to falter. This period coincided with the 1904 centennial celebration of independence, a time for reflection and evaluation of the progress that had been made in the course of one hundred years. The view from that perspective was melancholy. Other countries in the hemisphere quickly outdistanced Haiti in development. The Haitians could not reasonably compare their small island nation with such continental giants as Mexico, Brazil, and Argentina, but the legacy of being the first republic in Latin America made inferiority hard to accept. For the intellectuals who realized that Haiti had not sufficiently progressed, the first century, a period studded with civil wars and depressions, was especially troubling. In critiques of national society, commentators analyzed the causes of the distress and suggested remedies. Most of them traced Haitian difficulties in foreign relations to internal problems. They generally regarded diplomatic controversies as products of Haiti's internal debilities. "Since the epoch of our heroic liberation we have been at war against each other," a politician, Joseph Jérémie, told the Centenary Association in 1892.[31]

The most important polemicist of the early 1900s was Anténor Firmin, a statesman, scholar, and revolutionary who played a major role as an advocate of reform and a practitioner of insurgent politics. Firmin's repeated direct challenges to incumbency made his influence felt during the era as an activist as well as an intellectual. He advocated civilian government and favored a judiciously administered liberal capitalism accompanied by modernizing foreign investment. Firmin was "intellectually omnivorous," a student of German philosophy, the physical and social sciences, and the humanities. He belonged to the American Academy of Political and Social Science and edited the *Messager du Nord*, which became the organ of the Liberal party. As a Haitian apologist, he confronted the steady accretion of racist thought in the infant social science of the age. His *De l'Egalité des Races humaines* challenged the pretensions of classical Egyptology in arguing an African origin for the Nile civilizations. Firmin's intellectual interests were comparable to those of W. E. B. Du Bois in the United States, a man whose work the Haitian knew through membership in the American Negro Academy, a black scholarly association of wide scope.[32]

31. Joseph Jérémie, *Haïti Indépendante* (Port-au-Prince, 1929), 37.
32. Léonce Viaud, *La Personnalité d'Anténor Firmin* (Port-au-Prince, 1948), 51–58; Furcy Chatelain, *Résumé des Considerations sur la Politique extérieure d'Haïti à propos du 15 janvier 1908* (Fort-de-France, 1908), 9–10.

Firmin became minister of finance, commerce, and foreign relations under Florvil Hyppolite, who assumed the presidency in 1889. A U.S. steamship company with intimate ties to ranking American navalists had bankrolled Hyppolite's campaign. In the burst of enthusiasm for large navies that characterized the period, the U.S. government empowered an admiral to aggressively demand from Haiti the Môle St. Nicolas, a promontory with a deepwater harbor. Repayment of Hyppolite's political debt was implicit in the brusque request. Firmin, as minister of foreign relations, turned aside the attempt to acquire part of the Haitian domain with the assistance of the American minister, the black abolitionist Frederick Douglass. Douglass resented being superseded in the negotiations and moreover considered the bid imperialistic. At the end of Hyppolite's term, Firmin resigned the ministry and returned to Cape Haitian, where he briefly practiced law. Perceived as dangerous by the military establishment surrounding the new president, Firmin was soon packed off to Europe as a diplomat. He returned at the head of an insurgency in 1902.[33]

After the failure of the revolution of 1902, Firmin escaped to exile and wrote a number of books, tracts, and apologies. One of them was a lengthy history of Haiti and an exegesis of its foreign policy entitled *M. Roosevelt, Président des Etats-Unis et la République d'Haïti*. Firmin admired what he judged to be the wholesome austerity and virility of Theodore Roosevelt's approach to international relations. He agreed with Roosevelt's insistence on rectitude in international behavior.[34] If Haiti would make certain necessary reforms, there would be no danger of American intervention. Firmin noticed that Roosevelt, unlike his predecessors, had not tried to seize Haitian land. The United States had since secured a naval base at Guantánamo in Cuba. Now that the Panama Canal figured in America's Caribbean policy, Firmin reasoned, the United States merely wanted assurance that Haiti would alienate no territory to a foreign power. The Americans feared the European interloper, he believed, and consequently wanted a friendly, independent, and stable Haiti.[35]

In accord with these views, Firmin proclaimed a community of interest among the Latin American states based on hemispheric security. He

33. Roger Gaillard, "Firmin et les Etats-Unis à travers un document inédit," pt. 1, *Conjonction* (June, 1975), 124; Viaud, *La Personnalité d'Anténor Firmin*, 15–16; Frederick Douglass, "Haiti and the United States: Inside Story of the Negotiations for the Môle St. Nicolas," *North American Review*, CLIII (1891), 337–45, 450, 459.

34. Anténor Firmin, *M. Roosevelt, Président des Etats-Unis et la République d'Haïti* (New York, 1905), 493.

35. *Ibid.*, 477.

argued that the maintenance of Haitian liberty hinged on the reform of Haitian politics and society. "Even after my death," he prophesied in *L'Effort dans le Mal,* "either one of two things must happen: either Haiti undergoes foreign domination, or she adopts resolutely the principles I have always fought for; because in the twentieth century, and in the Western hemisphere, no people can live indefinitely under tyranny, in injustice, ignorance, and poverty."[36]

Firmin's scholarship addressed the history and politics of the entire Caribbean region. His *Lettres de Saint-Thomas,* essays written in exile, discussed the sociopolitical and economic unification of the Antilles and described his friendships with the Puerto Rican nationalist Ramón Betances and the Cuban revolutionary leader José Martí. Firmin advocated a West Indian federation, though he realized the practical difficulties of consolidating such geographically far-flung and linguistically diverse populations, whose consciousness of a Caribbean identity remained undeveloped. Firmin's Pan-Americanism was well in advance of its time in the Caribbean, as was his case for more thorough regional data collection to allow for rational economic planning.[37] His surprisingly contemporary ideas and interests appear to have more in common with the generation of Caribbean scholar-politicans that matured during the World War II era than with the rustic generalissimos who ruled the Caribbean republics at the turn of the century.[38]

The modern sensibility in Firmin's thought is reflected in his support of opening the country to foreign investment. Desirous of retarding imperialist penetration, Haitians had constitutionally barred aliens from owning real estate, but foreigners circumvented this law. Firmin argued that, in any case, prohibition was obsolete and Haiti badly needed the additional capital that outsiders would bring.[39]

During the first decade of the twentieth century, a reform movement coalesced around the charismatic personality of Anténor Firmin, and numerous educated and reflective persons joined the Firminist ranks. They participated in the ongoing critique of Haitian society and institutions as well as in the political and military aspects of the Firminist movement. Alcius Charmant, a politician from Jacmel, represented this group. He could lay no claim to being an intellectual like Firmin, but he

36. Quoted in Viaud, *La Personnalité d'Anténor Firmin,* 34.
37. Anténor Firmin, *Lettres de Saint-Thomas* (Paris, 1910), v, viii, 109–30, 131, 164–68, 172.
38. *Ibid.,* viii.
39. *Ibid.,* 4, 39–86.

had thought deeply about Haitian problems and interpreted them as based in great part on class and racial conflict.

In *Haïti, vivra-t-elle?*, Charmant asserted that color prejudice and conflict between blacks and mulattoes were the greatest national problem. Like many literate Haitians, he admired the nation-building and modernizing achievements of the Japanese and derived from their experience the lesson that the theory of racial inferiority had no basis in empirical observation. Charmant maintained that color consciousness had always been a tool to mislead the masses and noted that a number of politicians widely identified as black militants were simply caretakers for mulatto power brokers. To the charge that his own rhetoric resounded with racial bias, Charmant responded that he did not object to mulattoes per se and looked forward to the day when a wider public education would banish color prejudice entirely.[40]

Haïti, vivra-t-elle? also treated the graft, authoritarianism, and ignorance that Charmant found rampant throughout Haitian history. He traced these vices to the criminal irresponsibility of the ruling class. A group of career politicians and speculators, he believed, deliberately created confusion and incited passions to conceal its profitable use of the state. Charmant's indictment of this group was essentially an attack on an elite class rather than a racial minority. He viewed color prejudice in Haiti, an ideological "virus that has corrupted everything," as carried out on behalf of the ruling class. Because his book contained an open attack on President Pierre Nord Alexis, Charmant was forced to go into hiding.[41]

Firmin and Charmant, though united for a time through politics, did not emphasize the same issues. Firmin approached the questions of reform and development as an administrator, whereas Charmant looked at them as a social commentator. The thread that joined their work was the scope and depth of their critiques. Firmin's Pan-Americanism challenged Haiti's elapsed commitment to hemispheric affairs. His desire to cultivate foreign capital flew in the face of the prohibition against white investors. Charmant's analysis was brutal. He poured vitriol over the social myth of race and its purveyors, finishing the job with a scurrilous cartoon of Nord Alexis, which denied the respect, if not admiration, traditionally sought by and granted to chiefs of state. Charmant's devastating language and his historical chronicle of betrayals were not intended only as black na-

40. Alcius Charmant, *Haïti, vivra-t-elle?* (2nd ed.; Le Havre, 1905), xxi, 12–14, 273, 357.
41. *Ibid.*, xxiii, 262.

tionalist, or *noiriste*, statements, for he understood the complementary relationship between class and race in Haitian society.

Firmin's and Charmant's analyses met their counterparts in works published during the era by conservatives. Perturbed by the reformers' radicalism but realizing that Firminism had addressed the undeniable need for change, these writers took what they perceived as moderate positions. One such writer was Léon Audain, a physician and veteran observer of Haitian society, whose *Le Mal d'Haïti, ses causes et son traitement* was published in 1908. Audain opposed Firmin but recognized the vitality and popularity of Firminist ideas. He attacked the top-heavy police and army bureaucracies and the local abuses of authority characteristic of a national security state, whose needs could not be made consonant with the objectives of social development.

At this juncture, however, Audain, a member of the Port-au-Prince elite, parted company with Firminism. He did not break with personalism, authoritarianism, or oligarchy but instead opted for a system of "reform" in which these political characteristics remained an intrinsic part of the structure. Audain envisioned the salvation of Haiti in a revolution from above, led by a virtuous and courageous chief, whose program would be modeled after Japan's Meiji Restoration. Like Charmant, he greatly admired Japan and the effect on world sensibilities of its victory over the Russians in the recent Russo-Japanese War. He attributed Japanese progress to the abolition of feudalism and the introduction of Western education and constitutional government.[42]

Audain believed that all peoples were perfectible, but he accepted the racist social science of his day. This compelled him to view Haitian problems as due in part to hereditary deficiency. Paradoxically, he de-emphasized the conflict between blacks and mulattoes as a theme and stressed instead the growing gap between the town and countryside caused by maladministration and militarism. He nevertheless made generalizations about particular nations that were based on racial characteristics. *Le Mal d'Haïti* identified Anglo-Saxonism with enterprise, initiative, and individualism and the Latin temperament with emotionalism and aesthetic refinement. Audain judged national policy a reflection of the collective personality of a people.[43] His work was implicitly racist. He said little about color in the Haitian context, but his belief in mulatto superiority

42. Audain, *Le Mal d'Haïti*, 29–43.
43. *Ibid.*, 45–47, 48, 62–63, 78, 119, 120.

can readily be inferred from the ascriptions he accorded various ethnic groups. Audain's adoption of Darwinian formulas prepared the ground for later writers to indulge in mystical treatments of racial personality in their attempts to describe and analyze Haitian society and culture.

The memoirs of Frédéric Marcelin, finance minister in two cabinets, bear examination as polemic. Marcelin, scion of a Port-au-Prince merchant family, had studied law and, like Firmin, served Presidents Florvil Hyppolite (1889–1896) and Nord Alexis (1902–1908). Rumors of corruption shadowed Marcelin's career.[44] Aside from his alleged gift for fiscal legerdemain, Marcelin wrote competent novels, memoirs, political diaries, works on finance, and social criticism.

His memoirs, *Au Gré du Souvenir*, published in 1913, noted the changes that had occurred in recent Haitian politics. In the past, coups d'état had been accompanied by the dissolution of the bicameral legislature, a body generally perceived as the creature of presidential power. More recently, Marcelin believed, the Chamber of Deputies and the Senate had come to remain the same as executives came and went. Marcelin did not interpret this as a sign of health. Lamenting the demise of strong leaders, he held that the president should be empowered to dissolve the legislature. Marcelin's faith in authoritarian leadership partially reflected the ephemerality of conventional politics in an arena where personal gain often outstripped principle in the race for power. Marcelin expressed little sympathy for politicians. "Exactly like those they claim to impose peace on, they themselves are the representatives of private interests, family and kinship interests. Is that truly sufficient to constitute authority?" he demanded. "Is one well qualified to impose one's self when, in the end, the views of one and the other side of the barricades are identical?" Marcelin called for a powerful leader, a statesman above common politics, to shoulder Haiti's problems. He preferred civilian rule, he said, but remained skeptical that the republic could shed its reliance on military government.[45]

Audain and Marcelin looked to generalissimos who would impose modernization on the country without unduly disrupting social relations within it. They abhorred revolution and thought little of the classes that would most profit from it. These polemicists placed great faith in charismatic leadership. Political authority lay in a personalist tradition, which

44. Henock Trouillot, *Les Origines sociales de la littérature haïtienne* (Port-au-Prince, 1962), 290, 291, 295; *Le Moniteur*, August 5, 1905, p. 475.
45. Marcelin, *Au Gré du Souvenir*, 184–85, 197–98.

fully accepted the autocratic and the dictatorial. Indeed, critics called for even stronger chiefs and failed to challenge the undiluted power of the presidency. The generalissimo, backed by an elite cadre, appeared to be the most competent administrator. The official cadre was supposed to be devoted to service to the nation.[46] National service, however, remained a matter of little priority for the elite, an attitude deeply rooted in the evolution of Haitian class structure.

Firminists shared many of these faults. Early twentieth-century Haitian writers understood that their society was undergoing a crisis and were able to diagnose the causes. In prescribing remedies, however, they proved to be prisoners of their cosmopolitan outlook. As members of the educated class, they looked abroad for models of development. In their search for a philosophy or technique that would transform Haiti, they talked considerably of Teutonic values, Japan, wise rulers, and the use of mass education to inculcate industrial behaviors. They rarely appreciated the qualitative differences between Haiti and the advanced nations they sought to emulate and believed that imitation could effect substantive change.[47]

Class divisions in Haiti were intimately connected to the general crisis at the turn of the century. Social conventions suppressed class mobility and created conflicts among sectors of the community. Caribbean societies had inherited social relations from the colonial period. At the top of the pyramid stood the planter or merchant from Europe; at the bottom, the slave or peon, African or Indian. When the European element gradually declined after emancipation, or was defeated, as in Haiti, the second group on the social ladder displaced it: the mestizos in Amerindian-Hispanic societies like Mexico and Peru or the mulattoes in places where a significant African element existed. The fundamental hierarchical relationships remained the same. The postcolonial upper class enjoyed wealth, authority, and prestige. In Haiti, a black and mulatto elite inherited the power of the planter class.[48]

The mulattoes, who maintained a strong loyalty to the French language and culture and to Roman Catholicism, did not constitute the only privileged group. Throughout the course of Haitian history, exogamy

46. Lewis, *Main Currents*, 262, 263; Nicholls, *From Dessalines to Duvalier*, 141.

47. Nicholls, *From Dessalines to Duvalier*, 108–41; Lewis, *Main Currents*, 261–64.

48. Harry Hoetink, *Caribbean Race Relations: A Study of Two Variants* (New York, 1967), 26, 37, 103–104, 180–82; Marvin Harris, *Patterns of Race in the Americas* (New York, 1964), 44–53, 43; Mörner, *Race Mixture*, 56–62.

continued between blacks and mulattoes of all strata. Like the mulatto elite, black ruling-class descendants of the colonial freedmen of Saint-Domingue or the hereditary, landed nobility created early in the nineteenth century by King Henri Christophe maintained their authority. Others had acquired wealth and standing through the army, rising in the ranks, serving—and sometimes becoming—presidents. Not all blacks, therefore, were among the masses, and not all mulattoes were privileged, though color strongly correlated with socioeconomic status.[49]

Some writers have emphasized a historic mutual antagonism between blacks and mulattoes because of the often divergent French and African elements in Haitian culture and because of strong preferences for exogamy within the mulatto group.[50] Upper-class standing and color were never completely coterminous, however, and color often served to confuse rather than elucidate Haitian politics. The phenotypic variety characteristic of black, white, and Amerindian admixtures in the Western Hemisphere is so great that colonial typologies recognized the consequent ambiguities by creating a new vocabulary to classify somatic variations. Many persons could be categorized as *either* black or mulatto; thus socioeconomic referents were utilized so that these individuals could be placed in their proper hierarchical slot. In Haiti, the confusion was sometimes deliberately created. Ambitious politicians appealed to color prejudice to win adherents. The nineteenth-century mulatto president Sylvain Salnave, for example, sent his dark-skinned son to the countryside to enlist peasant support for Salnave's campaign against "the yellow people." The most definitive statement on the syndrome was penned by Anténor Firmin in *Roosevelt et Haïti*: "The truth is that the color question is at the service of all who want to perpetuate the darkness that reigns in the popular mind in Haiti, in order to derive personal advantages from it."[51]

Racial caste also obscured the penury in Haiti on all levels of society. The very poor slept in marketplaces and considered themselves lucky to have a packing crate to call home. Claims of gentility often disguised privation among the upper classes as well. "Are there fifty truly rich Haitian families?" Louis-Edouard Pouget, a minister of finance, asked the

49. James, *Black Jacobins*, 37–44; Léger, *Haiti*, 165; Hoetink, *Caribbean Race Relations*, 50.

50. Charmant, *Haiti, vivra-t-elle?*, xxi; James G. Leyburn, *The Haitian People* (New Haven, 1966), 88–98.

51. Frédéric Marcelin, *Le Général Nord Alexis, 1905–1908* (3 vols.; Paris, 1909), I, 30; Sténio Vincent, *En posant les jalons* (4 vols.; Port-au-Prince, 1939–45), I, 154–56; Firmin, *Roosevelt et Haïti*, 390.

Haitian Chamber of Deputies. "Do you know in the Republic ten men whose fortune is assured for ten years?"[52] A former French minister to Haiti made similar comments to Frédéric Marcelin: "You know what I think of your country? I've never known any—and I've travelled a lot—where the inhabitants are so poor. I don't believe that in the whole island there is one Haitian who possesses one hundred francs . . . in hard, redeemable cash. I'm not talking about your real estate, which you assess as the fancy strikes you, and which is, besides, unsaleable and unredeemable. . . . It's inconceivable. In France, our cooks, very often, have a hundred francs."[53]

Elite status rested inordinately on traditional prerogatives in a society that clung to honor and to patterns of deference. Members of the bourgeoisie made their living as professionals, businessmen, rentiers, and high-ranking civil servants. State employment remained an important livelihood during this period, and a hardened pattern of bureaucratic management emerged. Combined with transient but autocratic executive authority, this system allowed little room for badly needed reforms and innovations.[54] Haiti also boasted an urban middle class devoted to retail commerce, civil service, the lesser professions, and clerical vocations.

Evidence suggests that frustrated elements unable to rise socioeconomically in the stratified Haiti of the epoch accounted for much of the political unrest in the cities. The Port-au-Prince mob—composed of market vendors, beggars, the underemployed, and the unemployed, an assortment of people frequently perceived as dissatisfied—may not have been the only disaffected group.[55] The mob did, however, serve an almost symbolic function. A ready source of manpower for political intrigues, it also meted out street justice to those viewed as political wrongdoers. The same crowds that enthusiastically welcomed victorious presidential candidates violently attacked them on their way to exile.[56]

The cities and larger towns contained blue-collar workers, some of whom had migrated from other islands. Jamaicans, French West Indians, and others came to Haiti after emancipation to live in an independent black country and helped relieve the perennial shortage of skilled labor.

52. Antoine Bervin, Louis-Edouard Pouget (Port-au-Prince, n.d.), 51.

53. Marcelin, Le Général Nord Alexis, II, 35–36.

54. Maurice de Young, "Class Parameters in Haitian Society," Journal of Inter-American Studies, I (1959), 449; Joachim, Les racines du sous-développement, 137–61.

55. Joachim, Les racines du sous-développement, 134; Domenick Scarpa, Memorandum, July, 1916, DF, 838.00/1404; Jean Price-Mars, Anténor Firmin (Port-au-Prince, n.d.), 54.

56. Joachim, Les racines du sous-développement, 134.

They also found employment as domestics, market sellers, drivers, factory workers, millhands, loggers, and sailors.[57]

Most Haitians of the period were rural peasants. The average Haitian, an illiterate country person, knew little of the world outside his or her particular locality but formed the backbone of the economy. The peasantry, though it did not enjoy political power commensurate with its demographic and economic importance, was not inarticulate in the early twentieth century. No administration could long withstand widespread rural disaffection, a phenomenon that occurred when the level of economic exploitation and its attendant distress became unbearable.[58]

The problems of the peasantry were centrally related to the mercantilist enterprise undertaken by the cosmopolitan strata. In the absence of a means to valorize agriculture, and consequently real estate prices, peasants remained on the margin of subsistence and gradually lost their power as political actors. The inability of successive Haitian administrations to endure long enough to undertake and effect change in the agrarian sector postponed indefinitely any serious social and economic investment in agriculture. The state then came to rely on the peasantry as a source of forced taxation while it increasingly based its support on shaky urban coalitions. Haiti experienced this phenomenon, generally characteristic of the underdeveloped states of the Southern Hemisphere in today's world, long before social science was equipped to recognize it.[59]

Haitian agriculture also suffered from built-in constraints to both innovation and productivity increases. Social conservatism played a major constraining role. This was not exclusively the conservatism of illiterate peasants, as has been claimed.[60] As managers of peasant unrest, proprietors could moreover ill afford the political and economic risks that failures of social experiments might incur. The prohibition against white landownership, so frequently cited as a cause of Haiti's underdevelopment, is immaterial here. What was in question was not the color of capital but its function.

57. *Ibid.*, 58, 134–37; Edmond Lauture, *Jacmel, Grandeur et Décadence* (Port-au-Prince, 1955), 11, 26; Madison Smith to Secretary of State, February 2, 1914, DF, 838.00/829; Pierre Carteron to Louis Borno, July 9, 1908, QDO, Vol. 2.

58. Discussions of peasant life and the peasantry's role in Haitian history are found in Janvier, *Les Affaires d'Haïti*; Moral, *Le Paysan haïtien*; and Lundahl, *Peasants and Poverty*.

59. Philip Raup, "History of Agriculture and the Rise and Fall of Nations" (Address delivered at Hamline University, St. Paul, Minn., June 10, 1985).

60. Lundahl, *Peasants and Poverty*, 28–29, 557–618.

Rural Haitians had rebelled against the French during the war against slavery and colonialism. Later, they refused to participate in the revival of the plantation system under the auspices of the state. They remained active participants in Haitian politics to the mid-nineteenth century. By the late 1800s, however, peasant discontent no longer expressed itself as populist revolt, because its energies had been diverted into another form of political expression: the private mercenary army. Peasants recruited in the service of a landowning general, the *cacos*, had no political objectives other than the election of a particular presidential candidate. The most intense *caco* activity nevertheless corresponded with periods of the greatest peasant unrest. The political economist Gérard Pierre-Charles asserts: "Behind the almost daily exactions of the *cacos* . . . is concealed the tragedy of those peasants without land, ready to give their life to any general who offers them in return a shot of *clairin* and carte blanche to pillage. Also concealed is the revolt of a whole class of disinherited and exploited men who want vaguely, without knowing how, to change the order of things. The *caco* is the peasant consciousness brutalized and deformed, looking for a road, a guide, a cause."[61]

Parallels to the unarticulated political yearning that Pierre-Charles describes can be found in the experience of other societies in which social banditry thrived in a milieu marked by weak central government. A connection between banditry and kinship networks is also found, a link that extended to interaction and interdependence with local political figures.[62]

Government power resided in the capital but faced constant challenge throughout the epoch by local groups in outlying departments that could not be adequately controlled. State hegemony per se remained unquestioned. At stake was the legitimacy of a particular regime. Local power figures and their private armies maintained a tactical autonomy and, with their military strength, forced compromises and concessions from the government. Officials in Port-au-Prince had to find means to neutralize the military *délégués*, the independent strongmen who controlled provincial troops and private armies.[63]

61. Gérard Pierre-Charles, *L'Economie haïtienne et sa voie de développement* (Paris, 1967), 45.

62. Barrington Moore, Jr., *Social Origins of Dictatorship and Democracy* (Boston, 1966), 458–59; Roderick Aya, *The Missed Revolution: The Fate of Rural Rebels in Sicily and Southern Spain, 1840–1950* (Amsterdam, 1975), 44; Eric Hobsbawm, *Primitive Rebels* (New York, 1959), 1–29.

63. Pierre-Charles, *L'Economie haïtienne*, 45; Aya, *The Missed Revolution*, 12; Suzy

The generals superintended their soldiery in several ways. Allegiance was based not only on blood kinship but on patronage, especially the godfather relationship. "An injustice done to a godparent wounded two families solidly united," Joseph Jérémie wrote. "The more godsons one had, the more influential one was. . . . All quarrels that severed the bond of the solidarity created by baptism were fatal." Jérémie noted that in the North, family feuds were often so bitter that persons from outside the region had to hold local office in order to maintain peace. He might have added that bringing in outsiders to administer such areas was also a way for the government in Port-au-Prince to check the formation of rival power centers.[64]

Loyalty to a locality also cemented the bonds of *caco* society. To the provincial soldier, economic distress and political upheaval could be readily assigned to the machinations of urban politicians. Once they were removed from office and replaced with familiar patrons, life would return to a peaceful normalcy interrupted only by the seasonal rhythms of agrarian life. Regional and familial allegiances thus substituted for a developed class consciousness. Citizenship obligations were those of the classical figure Cincinnatus, a fearless soldier when needed; at other times, a peaceful cultivator.[65]

Finally, the rugged populism of the *cacos* was supported by the soldierly tradition, as glorified in national political culture. In some areas, only an army post demonstrated the government's presence. Forced labor and press-gang recruitment interfered with agriculture, however, and many peasants avoided it by escape to less accessible mountain areas. Some joined private regional armies and operated as irregulars, a procedure less likely to disrupt planting.[66]

Some recent Haitian students of the period have assimilated the leaders of *caco* armies into descriptive models of Haitian class structure. They identify two ruling classes, a feudal aristocracy and a commercial bourgeoisie. The commercial class is seen as deeply antagonistic to the land-

Castor, *La ocupación nortéamericana de Haití y sus consecuencias* (Mexico City, 1971), 13–14; Moral, *Le Paysan haïtien*, 58; Mme Celestin Jacquet, interview with author, July 31, 1979.

64. Joseph Jérémie, *Mémoires* (Port-au-Prince, 1950), 50; Antoine Pierre-Paul, *La première protestation armée contre l'intervention américaine et 260 jours dans le maquis* (Port-au-Prince, n.d.), 31, 43–44; New York *Herald*, March 12, 1908, p. 3.

65. Jérémie, *Mémoires*, 57; Livy, *The Early History of Rome* (Baltimore, 1960), 197–200.

66. Castor, *La ocupación nortéamericana*, 16; Moral, *Le Paysan haïtien*, 57–61.

owners, whose caudillismo had created unfavorable conditions for capitalist development. At the same time, many of these feudal militarists were generous with offers of concessions to foreign entrepreneurs while suppressing the ambitions of their business-minded compatriots.[67] These scholars see the nineteenth-century Liberal and Nationalist parties, which had ceased to reflect sharp differences by 1902, as the political expressions of the two ruling classes. The Liberals favored constitutional government and liberal capitalism. Adherents of civilian rule, they were traditionally identified with the towns and the mulatto elite. The Nationalists, on the other hand, claimed to uphold the most venerated principles of the nationalist ideology. Associated with the black military and with personalism in government, they sought to limit native entrepreneurial development and showed an anti-urban bias.[68] Other students have questioned the validity of any rigorous categorization of Haitian political groups. Jean Price-Mars claimed that the Liberal and Nationalist parties substituted personalities for programs of substance. He maintained that color and social identification determined partisan allegiance more accurately than did ideology, though there were enough individuals crossing over to cause confusion about the nature of these party formations.[69]

The historical evidence does not support the contention that the Haitian ruling class consisted of two warring factions. The great landowners and the commercial bourgeoisie, often linked through marriage ties, also shared vocations. Landowning by wealthy urbanites and entrepreneurship on the part of landed proprietors were so common that the elite actually stood quite solidly as a unified class.[70] The blockage of foreign capital penetration associated with the commercial bourgeoisie cannot, in fact, be legitimately ascribed to it. As we shall see, this segment was among the most enthusiastic champions of that cause. Opposition to foreign capital penetration, as a policy of the united ruling class, had clear political objectives. The elite had to avoid destruction at the hands of an

67. Castor, *La ocupación nortéamericana*, 13–14.

68. Pierre-Charles, *L'Economie haïtienne*, 34–37, 40–43; Leslie F. Manigat believes the Haitian formations correspond to a Latin American typology, *L'Amérique Latine au XXᵉ Siècle, 1889–1929* (Paris, 1973), 44, 45–47, 146–48; Joachim, *Les racines du sous-développement*, 137–45.

69. Price-Mars, *Anténor Firmin*, 84–85.

70. *Livre bleu d'Haïti/Blue Book of Haiti* (New York, 1920); Semextant Rouzier, *Dictionnaire géographique et adminstratif d'Haïti* (Port-au-Prince, 1928); Rigaud, *Promenades dans les Campagnes d'Haïti*; Marc Pean, *L'Illusion héroïque: 25 ans de la vie capoise, 1890–1915* (Port-au-Prince, 1977); Gil Martinez, "De l'ambigüité du nationalisme bourgeois en Haïti," *Nouvelle Optique*, IX (January-March, 1973), 1–32.

indignant black nationalist civil society and simultaneously guard its role as a broker of Haitian trade and resources with the metropoles. Only a rhetorically antiforeign stance would satisfy these two aims at once.[71]

The Haiti of 1902–1915 was slowly being strangled by the contradictions in its national life. Held at arm's length by other powers, Haiti remained dependent on the European coffee market for its continued autonomy. Isolationism as a national policy did not constitute insulation from external political and economic forces that the Haitians could not control. They had fought and won a profound social revolution. They were rhetorically committed to the Rights of Man, but their intellectuals could not square this with the rank militarism and authoritarianism that characterized their politics. The tradition of revolutionary valor might serve two purposes. On the one hand, it could legitimize popular democracy. On the other, it could perpetuate tyranny.

The contradictions in Haitian life ceased to be latent as the international order gradually changed in the second half of the nineteenth century. Industrial states pulled ahead of agrarian states in the struggle for development and began to organize their more backward neighbors as sources of supply. It became increasingly difficult for small countries to maintain the fiction that they were miniature replicas of the metropoles and could match the great powers in the diplomatic arena.

Haitian intellectuals and policy makers responded to the need for redefinition by developing a literature of self-criticism. Two basic assumptions can be found in most of the work they produced. They held that Haiti's problems with foreign powers stemmed from the country's domestic infirmities and that Haitian society ought to be reformed through greater integrity in public administration and judicious cultural borrowing from abroad. Haitian writers were unprepared to abandon European models of progress and view Haiti as an American nation with a different past and present. Linked to this failure was an elitist differentiation, based on class as well as color, between paternalistic rulers and submissive subjects.

The elites faced few challenges to their power. They were nevertheless hostages to their own leadership position. The national ideology, which shaped the thinking of the majority, defined permissible political behavior. Peasant nationalism did not admit foreign intervention or its advocates, and harbored a latent resentment of the cosmopolitan towns, no less

71. Martinez, "De l'ambigüité," 3, 8–9, 21, 31.

real if compromised by the contrast between wealth and poverty in both urban and rural areas. To be a member of the Haitian ruling class, then, was to engage in a delicate balancing act. The great landowners and commanders of mercenary armies did this adeptly in their co-optation of peasant unrest. For the commercial bourgeoisie, trade and culture served as the balance beam. By opposing cosmopolitanism to the dominant nationalist ideology, merchants created additional social space for themselves.

Cosmopolitanism in Haiti derived in part from the multinational character of its trading community, the enclave character of mercantile commerce, and the traders' considerable independence from local traditions and beliefs. Cosmopolites are by definition at home anywhere in the world without being bound to and absorbed by the strictures of host societies. In underdeveloped countries, aided by their ties to international commerce, they could do much to configure social relations. As representatives of a technologically advanced West whose cultural superiority was also assumed, they were virtually guaranteed a status above that of the ordinary Haitian. The years 1902–1915 legitimated cosmopolitanism more deeply than had been the case in any previous era and temporarily held nationalism in check. The equilibrium collapsed early, however, as the imperialism ushered in by the worldly elites tipped the balance against nationalism and ultimately overturned Haitian autonomy.

II

Merchant Capital

Fourmi pas jam' mouri en bas barrique suc'.
The ant never dies under a barrel of sugar.

—Haitian proverb

WHILE HAITI'S economic dependency and poverty are shared by other Caribbean nations, its history of underdevelopment serves as a prototype for them. Haiti's political independence, achieved in 1804, set the stage for an increasingly difficult struggle to survive among imperialist states. Haiti prefigured the modern Latin American experience and thus provides a classic example of how national aspirations can be derailed. Equally significant, it illustrates the manner in which foreign trade, rather than plantation agriculture, can foster socioeconomic decline.

Trade relations, conducted by an elite that was socially and culturally wedded to the values and institutions of the metropolitan powers, created a continuing pattern of economic dependency and cultural imitation in Haiti. These commercial relations have not been accorded full scholarly recognition. The social and political role of elite groups in Haiti has been studied by numerous social scientists, but the commercial aspects of class privilege require more historical examination. An elite composed of the foreign-born and their children by Haitian spouses emerged early in the 1800s and reached the height of its influence as agents of metropolitan power in the early twentieth century, before World War I. The European and Europeanized merchant communities of Haiti's port cities provided both cultural and commercial links to the outside world but ushered the Black Republic along on a journey to underdevelopment.[1]

1. The Haitian bourgeoisie's commercial role is being increasingly recognized. See, for example, Gil Martinez, "De l'ambigüité de nationalisme bourgeois en Haïti," *Nouvelle Optique*, IX (January-March, 1973), 1–32; and Robert K. Lacerte, "Xenophobia and Eco-

Haiti's dependency, like that of most Latin American societies, originated in the colonial era when land and human resources were diverted from food production to the raising of crops for export. The resulting need for staples and the growing disparities in the world market for agricultural exports imposed economic inequalities on the colonies. The mercantile structures that facilitated the skewed exchange remained in place after the demise of colonialism. As Europe and North America began programs of rapid industrial and economic expansion in the latter half of the nineteenth century, Haiti remained relatively backward—its ties with the great powers aiding their advancement but not its own.[2]

The Haitian elite played a significant intermediary role. As brokers and interpreters for foreigners, members of the elite assisted actively in trading. As consumers par excellence, members of this small bourgeoisie helped weave import-dependency into the fabric of society. Because of their relationship with the metropoles, they strongly identified with external cultural norms. Education and wealth gave the elite a role to play at home analogous to that performed abroad by the metropolitan bourgeoisie. A satellite of the foreign class, the local leadership took Haiti's rural hinterland as its own colony, where its modest power could be exercised.[3]

nomic Decline: The Haitian Case, 1820–1843," *The Americas*, XXXVII (1981), 499–515. For the political and social roles of these groups, see Jean Price-Mars, *La Vocation de l'élite* (Port-au-Prince, 1919); Maurice de Young, "Class Parameters in Haitian Society," *Journal of Inter-American Studies*, I (1959), 449–58; Suzanne Comhaire-Sylvain and Jean L. Comhaire, "Urban Stratification in Haiti," *Social and Economic Studies*, VIII (1959), 179–89; David Nicholls, "Idéologies et mouvements politiques en Haïti, 1915–1946," *Annales, Economies, Sociétés, Civilisations*, XXX (1975), 654–79; and David Nicholls, *From Dessalines to Duvalier: Race, Colour and National Independence in Haiti* (Cambridge, England, 1979).

2. Celso Furtado, *Economic Development of Latin America* (London, 1976), 14, 33, 43, 94–95; Andre Gunder Frank, *Capitalism and Underdevelopment in Latin America* (New York, 1969), xii, 3, 8–12, 281–96; Stanley J. Stein and Barbara H. Stein, *The Colonial Heritage of Latin America* (New York, 1970), 124–55; Susanne Bodenheimer, "Dependency and Imperialism: The Roots of Latin American Underdevelopment," *Politics and Society*, I (1971), 333; James D. Cockcroft, Andre Gunder Frank, and Dale L. Johnson, *Dependency and Underdevelopment* (New York, 1972), xvi–xviii.

3. Cockcroft, Frank, and Johnson, *Dependency*, xvi–xviii; Furtado, *Economic Development*, 72–74; Frank, *Capitalism*, xii. Specific criticism of Haitian upper-class behavior is found in Price-Mars, *La Vocation de l'élite*, 4, 19–22; Sténio Vincent, *En posant les jalons* (4 vols.; Port-au-Prince, 1939–45), I, 346–51; Edward Beach, "Caperton in Haiti" (MS in NR), 26; de Young, "Class Parameters," 449–51, 452–54; Martinez, "De l'ambigüité," 31; and Patrick Bellegarde-Smith, "Haitian Social Thought in the Nineteenth Century: Class Formation and Westernization," *Caribbean Studies*, XX (March, 1980), 17.

This authority did not endure. As a result of changes in international price structure, technological innovation, and acculturation to foreign values, the indigenous bourgeoisie failed to conserve its status. By 1900, Haitian merchants and entrepreneurs were gradually disappearing as foreigners committed to their own national economies replaced Haitian businessmen. The manner in which this process occurred, and the backdrop of import-dependency against which it was enacted, reveals much about the subsequent problems of disincentive to productive investment, deferment of economic diversification, and chronic trade imbalance.

Haiti was not self-sufficient in food. In 1900 an American journalist noted its considerable reliance on imports.

> Here is an island surrounded by millions of the best fish in the world, . . . yet tons on tons of salt codfish and mackerel are imported from St. John, New Brunswick. Nowhere in the world would you expect better native tobacco than here, yet hogshead after hogshead goes ashore, packed with tobacco from Virginia. Salt pork and smoked hams from Chicago, corned beef and barrels of wheat flour swing out over the ship's side and down over the lighters, . . . not a barrel of which would be imported if the full resources of the island were developed as they should be.[4]

Imports even included sugar, the chief crop of the old colony. Machinery and tools, luxury goods, lumber, prefabricated houses, textiles, medicines, paints, and chemicals also came from overseas.[5]

Class determined Haitian consumption habits. The peasantry bought only necessities, whereas the bourgeoisie regarded foreign merchandise as a lifeline to the "civilized world." Its purchases were typical of the upper middle classes in developed countries, a conformity made possible through conscientious imitation. Gentility required French brandies and perfumes, German drugs and eyeglasses, British shirts and linens. Fernand Hibbert, a leading Haitian writer of the period and a keen observer of elite mores and attitudes, satirized the dependence of fashionable society on these luxuries in his novel *Séna*. One character, a Madame Henger, the Haitian wife of a German banker, subsisted on an imported diet. "If we did not send for these provisions from abroad," she asserted, "we would die of hunger in this uninhabitable land of Haiti."[6]

---

4. New York *Times*, May 6, 1900, p. 23.

5. William F. Powell to John Hay, June 10, 1900, CD; République d'Haïti, *Statistique générale de la République d'Haïti* (Port-au-Prince, 1908), 54, 57.

6. Fernand Hibbert, *Scènes de la vie haïtienne: Séna* (Port-au-Prince, 1905), 98, 99. Sténio Vincent wrote: "Mr. Fernand Hibbert's novels have an unquestionable documentary value. . . . By the quality and choice of their quite trenchant observations, Hibbert's novels reveal to us the total spirit of the social sphere, yield up to us the souls of citizens who are

The spirit of conspicuous consumption also permeated the political underworld of concessionary jobbing. Foreign speculators and their Haitian allies trafficked in bids for infrastructural projects. For the edification of the public, they equated expensive American equipment with progress, using consumption as an index of advancement. By the mid-1920s, the plains and harbors of the republic were littered with railroad cars in various stages of disrepair, defunct mills, rusting yachts, and other artifacts derived from years of impulse buying.[7] Pecuniary motives aside, the purchasers' behavior foreshadowed the current belief that accumulated hardware from the West will of itself deliver underdeveloped countries from backwardness. A Pandora's box of secondary assistance, unemployment, and capital outflow thus opened for Haiti during that era.[8]

The Haitian import market was primarily supplied by the United States, Britain, Germany, and France. Sixty-five to 70 percent of the goods that arrived in the republic's ports came from North America. Britain's share was approximately 9 percent. France supplied 10 to 12 percent of all imports during the pre–World War I years. Germany's 3 percent, though modest, did not reflect the substantial profits that the Germans made from shipping. By 1909 the German-owned Hamburg America Line had absorbed 75 percent of the carrying trade, with the rest divided between the Dutch Royal West Indian Mail and the French Compagnie Générale Transatlantique. Minor powers accounted for the remainder of Haitian trade.[9]

The recorded volume of traffic in Haiti, a nation of 1.5 million in 1910, was small. Annual dutiable trade averaged about $20 million for the 1900–1915 period. If it were possible to adjust this figure for the rampant smuggling of the era, however, commerce would demonstrate a greater

cogs in the political machine. The types presented are not fictional characters. They are living. We meet them in the street" (*En posant les jalons,* I, 206).

7. Charles Cowan to State Department, July 19, 1915, DF, 838.00/1208; Henry W. Furniss, Dispatches to Secretary of State, September 15, 1910 (DF, 838.602501/7), October 27, 1910 (DF, 838.304/1), April 4, 1911 (DF, 838.602), July 25, 1911 (DF, 838.34/29).

8. *Le Moniteur,* March 2, 1910; Furniss, Dispatches to Secretary of State, October 27, 1910 (DF, 838.304/1), August 6, 1910 (DF, 838.602), May 13, 1913 (DF, 838.77/76); R. D. Longyear, "Railroad Mileage and Operation in Haiti," July 22, 1925 (DF, 838.77/336). For a general discussion of the problem, see Frank, *Capitalism,* xii–xiv; Furtado, *Economic Development,* 303–304; and Cockcroft, Frank, and Johnson, *Dependency,* 365–75.

9. Pierre Benoit, *Cent cinquante ans de commerce extérieure d'Haïti* (Port-au-Prince, 1954), 12; Bureau of Foreign and Domestic Commerce, *Commercial Relations of the United States,* 1900–1915, Haiti, *passim*; Alexander Murray, Annual Report, 1901, FO 371, Vol. 914; Roger L. Farnham, Testimony, in SI, 110.

vitality. Clandestine illegal activity explains why metropolitan-oriented traders remained interested in Haiti and solidly entrenched there, despite ostensibly small profits.[10]

Metropolitan firms traded in the Caribbean through commission houses. The commission house paid cash for factory goods and took charge of shipment, sales, advertising, credit, and maritime documentation. In exchange for these services, it received sales commissions from manufacturers and interest on loans extended to buyers. The home manufacturer's advantage in using the commission house was that the latter best knew the markets and tariff regulations of specific countries. It therefore could trade more profitably and efficiently than could the producers, who did not orient their overseas marketing departments toward the smaller Latin American republics. Commission agents were regarded by the business community as expert traders in the markets these brokers claimed to know. Organized along national lines, and representing national manufacturers, commission houses inspired confidence among merchants in the exporting countries. They felt that home enterprises were more responsive to their needs than were foreign ones.[11]

Each nation had its own networks and target areas. The Germans, for example, cut off from large areas of Asia and Africa by French and British imperialism, concentrated on developing spheres of influence in such weak but independent states as Haiti.[12] The Germans successfully supplied cheap duplicates of popular European products. Their inventories also reflected the home industry's achievements in metallurgy and pharmaceuticals. They had the largest number of showrooms and the greatest amount of government subvention. German sales representatives were carefully trained in the language and customs of the host country. German traders often came to Haiti as clerks, later succeeding their superiors, who retired to Germany after amassing a hundred thousand dollars or

10. Extrapolated from Bureau of Foreign and Domestic Commerce, *Commercial Relations*, 1900–1915, and U.S. Bureau of Foreign Commerce, *Foreign Commerce and Navigation*, 1900–1915. Powell to Hay, February 15, 1905, CD; Harry Johnston, *The Negro in the New World* (New York, 1910), 204.

11. L. C. Ford and Thomas Ford, *The Foreign Trade of the United States: Its Character, Organization and Methods* (New York, 1920), 86, 87, 91, 92. On American marketing and management in the early twentieth century, see Robert H. Wiebe, *The Search for Order, 1877–1920* (New York, 1967), 19–22.

12. E. P. Lyle, "What Should Haiti's Future Be?" *World's Work*, XI (1906), 7151–62; Francis Mairs Huntington Wilson, *Memoirs of an Ex-Diplomat* (Boston, 1945), 195, 196, 252; Hans Schmidt, *The United States Occupation of Haiti, 1915–1934* (New Brunswick, N.J., 1971), 36.

two.[13] Hamburg buyers purchased large quantities of Haitian coffee. Their home market absorbed only 29 percent of the coffee, but the merchant marine conveyed much of it to other Western countries. Germany also bought Haitian logwood and other dyewoods.[14]

The French consumed most of the coffee produced in Haiti and supplied luxury goods for the bourgeoisie. France provided none of the staples that the peasantry required, however, and did not enjoy a "mass market." French commerce remained static, but France boasted an active merchant marine, overshadowed only by that of Germany. Few other European countries had interests in the Black Republic. The Belgians financed one plantation. A handful of British companies were located in Haiti, but British goods depended on German carriers.[15]

Haiti offered a number of tropical exports in exchange for foreign merchandise. Aside from coffee, it produced fluctuating quantities of cotton, cacao, lignum vitae, beeswax, honey, and hides. These goods derived from peasant cultivation rather than from plantation production. The Haitian government levied export taxes on native commodities, but the widespread evasion of the duties through smuggling prevented the government from realizing all the revenues these taxes might have produced.[16] Americans, unlike Europeans, did not drink Haitian coffee, and they had alternative sources of supply for other Haitian commodities. The inaccessibility of the United States to Haitian exporters illuminates another dimension of Haitian import-dependency and subsequent balance-of-trade problems during this era. Coffee remained the country's only real bargaining chip, and a small one at that.[17]

13. Powell to Hay, May 26, 1900, CD; Leslie F. Manigat, "La substitution de la préponderance américaine à la préponderance française en Haïti au début du XXᵉ siècle: la conjoncture de 1910–1911," Revue d'histoire moderne et contemporaine, XIV (1967), 335–36; Stephen Bonsal, The American Mediterranean (New York, 1913), 396–98.

14. Manigat, "Substitution," 335–36.

15. Franco-Haitian commercial treaty, in Alexandre Battiste to State Department, August 20, 1900, CD; Selden Chapin, Monograph on Haiti, 1935 (MS in the Collection of the U.S. Embassy, Port-au-Prince), Pt. 4, Chap. 3, pp. 6–7; L. Abrams and D. J. Miller, "Who Were the French Colonialists? A Reassessment of the Parti Colonial, 1890–1914," Historical Journal, XIX (1976), 685–725; Bureau of Foreign and Domestic Commerce, Commercial Relations, 1901, p. 567; A. G. Vansittart to Lord Lansdowne, March 16, 1905, FO 35, Vol. 182; Shue to Lansdowne, June 16, 1902, FO 35, Vol. 178.

16. Robert Dudley Longyear, "Haitian Coffee: Its Cultivation and Preparation for Shipment," September 9, 1922, DF, 838.61333/47; Powell to Hay, June 10, 1901, CD; Battiste to State Department, August 23, 1900, CD.

17. Powell to Hay, June 10, July 29, 1901, CD; Furniss to Secretary of State, February

The first merchants to organize Haiti's unequal commerce with Europe and North America were descendants of the free people of color and the civil and military officials of the revolutionary, imperial, and early republican eras (1791–1843). Indigenous merchants owed their original preeminence to the emperor Jean-Jacques Dessalines (1804–1806), who banished foreign traders. King Henri Christophe (1806–1820), Dessalines's successor and ruler of northern Haiti, permitted a few Britons to reside on the coast, but most of the import-export sector remained in the hands of Haitian *compradores.*[18]

The Haitian government attempted to regulate foreigners' penetration of commerce through restrictive laws. Limiting aliens to seaboard cities, barring them from retail trade, and forbidding them to ply the coast were policies aimed at preserving a sphere for the native businessman. Foreigners could not purchase coffee or other cash crops except through a Haitian broker, and they had to buy expensive licenses in order to trade at all.[19] Despite the good intent of these measures, they did not secure a permanent place for Haitian entrepreneurs, for several reasons. The first had to do with changes in commercial practice brought about by the transition to steam transport in the late nineteenth century. Steam permitted more frequent shipments of goods, which therefore could be ordered in smaller quantities by persons with less capital, thus cutting out the distributor. Formerly, consignment merchants ordered large amounts of stock for sale to retailers. By 1900, retailers had begun to import merchandise on their own account. In a 1903 dispatch, the U.S. vice-consul, Alexandre Battiste, noted that no one in Haiti had sought a consignee's patent in years. All had acquired importers' licenses.[20] Frédéric Marcelin described the impact of these changes in his 1913 memoirs.

> My father was one of the biggest sellers of French and English cloth, as there were many of them fifty years ago in our principal ports. This type is no longer encountered. It disappeared as a result of fires, revolutions that ruined families,

23, 1910, DF, 874/68; Alain Turnier, *Les Etats-Unis et le marché haïtien* (Washington, D.C., 1955), 287–88; Joseph Chatelain, *La Banque Nationale, son histoire, ses problèmes* (Port-au-Prince, 1954), 71.

18. Lacerte, "Xenophobia," 511; Eugène Aubin [Léon E. A. C. Descos], *En Haïti* (Paris, 1910), xxi.

19. Lacerte, "Xenophobia," 509. Early twentieth-century examples of such laws appear in *Le Moniteur*, August 25, 1900; and Hannibal Price, *Dictionnaire de législation administrative haïtienne* (Port-au-Prince, 1923), 505–506.

20. Furtado, *Economic Development*, 43; Paul Moral, *Le Paysan haïtien* (Paris, 1961), 270–71; Battiste to Hay, November 10, 1903, CD.

and also because of the change created by steamboats in navigation. Formerly, large sailboats brought full cargoes consigned to the principal houses. This did not happen often. It was necessary to have considerable capital or good credit to fully load those sailboats. Today, thanks to steamers that allow stocks to be replenished rapidly, and by small shipments, importation is no longer the privilege of a few.[21]

Direct importation was easiest for those who could engage in high-volume trading and establish links with overseas firms. Foreigners thus had an important advantage, especially as aggressive and sometimes patriotic promoters of a particular nation's wares.[22]

The second cause of Haitian business decline was the worldwide drop in agricultural prices in the 1890s. Haitian purchasing power rested on the sale of a small amount of tropical produce, which faced considerable international competition. These exports could not underwrite native business development. The Sansaricq family, for example, closed its consignment house in the wake of litigation with French and British creditors in mid-decade. Other traders, such as the Jérémies and the Geffrards, liquidated their businesses when European backers became dissatisfied with their poor showing and began refusing them credit. Forced to contract, and often failing themselves, metropolitan lenders cut off Haitian borrowers. The representative firms Phillips and Laforest of Port-au-Prince and the import-export house of Aux Cayes entrepreneur Malherbe Pressoir suffered this fate in 1895. Like many of their peers, the principals pursued alternative careers in politics.[23]

Civil strife joined technological change and poor economic conditions as a third cause of commercial failure. Such crises as the persecution of segments of the bourgeoisie by President Louis Etienne Félicité Salomon in 1883 and the burning of the town of Petit-Goâve during the revolution of 1902 crippled Haitian business efforts. Petit-Goâve, a coffee port, boasted a population of twelve thousand before fire destroyed everything

21. Frédéric Marcelin, *Au Gré du Souvenir* (Paris, 1913), 20–21.

22. David Nicholls, *Economic Dependence and Political Autonomy: The Haitian Experience* (Montreal, 1974), 18–25. On diminishing Haitian entrepreneurial capability, see Dana G. Munro, *Intervention and Dollar Diplomacy in the Caribbean, 1900–1921* (Princeton, 1964), 246–47; Manigat, "Substitution," 326–27, 329; and Marcelin, *Au Gré du Souvenir*, 20, 21, 107–108.

23. Léonce Bernard, *Antoine Sansaricq, l'homme, sa vie, ses idées* (Port-au-Prince, n.d.), 8; Joseph Jérémie, *Mémoires* (Port-au-Prince, 1950), 95–96; J. Geffrard, "Ce que j'ai entendu et vecu," n.d. (MS in Louis McCarty Little Papers, U.S. Marine Corps Historical Museum, Washington, D.C.); *Livre bleu d'Haïti/Blue Book of Haiti* (New York, 1920), 75, 201.

in town except two houses and the French-owned coffee processing mill.[24]

Finally, foreign competition reduced Haitian trade. The expatriate community had gradually developed after the government's policy on resident aliens became less restrictive in 1843. Frenchmen soon joined the tiny British group in the port cities. French Antilleans figured prominently among the newcomers and, by 1910, constituted a colony of fifteen hundred. Corsican immigrants were also strongly represented, especially in Cape Haitian. In the 1860s, Germans from the Hanseatic cities entered the country as employees of French mercantile houses. Syrians, Lebanese, and Italians arrived in Haiti thirty years later. Figures on the number of Syrians in Haiti range from fifteen hundred to a few hundred. The widely varying estimates reflect the political sensitivity of the question at the time. The Syrian and Lebanese community peaked at six thousand in 1903; the Italian group numbered three hundred in 1914.[25]

Settlement in late nineteenth-century Haiti followed the general trend of European migration to the Americas. The number of aliens never exceeded ten thousand persons, including those who claimed dual citizenship. Drastic fluctuations in the census of certain groups reflected considerable foreign transience. For some aliens, Haiti was only a way station on a journey to other parts of the Western Hemisphere.[26] Although many did not stay, some remained and prospered through trade.

Foreign merchants did not restrict their operations to ordinary commerce. They engaged in a substantial amount of smuggling, a practice believed by contemporary observers to involve virtually the entire foreign community. A common method of smuggling entailed evasion of customs and

24. On 1883, see Louis Janvier, *Les Affaires d'Haïti (1883–1884)* (Paris, 1885), esp. 57–60, 128; Marcelin, *Au Gré du Souvenir,* 107; David Nicholls, "The Wisdom of Salomon: Myth or Reality?" *Journal of Inter-American Studies and World Affairs,* XX (1978), 377–92; for Petit-Goâve, Powell to Hay, August 15, 1902, CD.

25. Descos, *En Haïti,* xxi–xxii, 337–38n1; Marc Pean, *L'Illusion héroïque: 25 ans de vie capoise, 1890–1915* (Port-au-Prince, 1976), 73–74; Madison Smith to Secretary of State, February 2, 1914, DF, 838.00/829; Schmidt, *The U.S. Occupation of Haiti,* 35.

26. Powell to Hay, June 10, 1903, CD; Carl Kelsey, Testimony, in SI, 1282–83; Smith to Secretary of State, February 2, 1914, Enclosure No. 4, DF, 838.00/829; David Nicholls, *Haiti in Caribbean Context* (New York, 1985), 135–64; Frederick Douglass to James Blaine, February 15, 1890, CD; Louis Audain père, *Du changement de nationalité parmi les Haïtiens* (Port-au-Prince, 1903), 14; Consul's Annual Report, 1906, FO 371, Vol. 266; John Terres to Furniss, December 17, 1908, in U.S. Department of State, Post Records, Letters from Consuls to Ministers, Record Group 84, NA; Descos, *En Haïti,* xxi–xxii, 263–72.

export duties through failure to register freight. Ships bound for Europe accordingly loaded up far offshore, with the knowledge and complicity of government officials. Another ploy, one that excluded Haitian functionaries, utilized false rumors of impending revolution. The "revolution" invariably began the day the steamers arrived in port to pick up cargo. Nervous customs officials, the appointees of the incumbent administration, would absent themselves. The exporters could then fill the ships from their own warehouses, thus saving thousands of dollars in duties.[27]

The import-export merchants also made false declarations. The British consul, Alexander Murray, estimated that some exports were worth four times the declared value. Merchants retained half of the resulting profits, with the rest divided among various Haitian officials. Murray confessed that his own countrymen were deeply involved in this corruption but sadly noted that the same Britons made the most efficient consular agents.[28] Murray's ambivalence suggests that the business acumen required for legitimate trade equally served the purposes of organized fraud.

Consuls and consular agents were most often chosen from the resident alien community, regardless of citizenship. Haitians and Germans served as American consular agents during this era, and other European powers farmed out their agencies to persons of various nationalities. The ordinarily routine paperwork and the comparatively small traffic did not compel the adoption of a better system. The popular consular posts were not highly paid, but they granted the trader considerable immunity from Haitian civil and criminal prosecution and provided opportunities for the expansion of profitable personal contacts.[29]

Merchants engaged in various forms of financial speculation in Haiti. Until the multinational reorganization of the Banque Nationale de la République d'Haïti in 1910, merchant-bankers, most of whom were foreign, held the largest proportion of the national currency. By hoarding, dumping, and collaborating, a small group of financiers controlled the monetary structure of the country. They consolidated their position

27. Powell to Hay, February 15, 1905, CD; Johnston, *The Negro in the New World*, 165–66, 204; Captain Fred E. McMillen, "Some Haitian Recollections," U.S. Naval Institute, *Proceedings*, LXII (1936), 526; Moral, *Le Paysan haïtien*, 270.

28. Furniss to Elihu Root, November 20, 1908, NF, 2126/332; Murray to Foreign Secretary, November 20, 1908, FO 371, Vol. 468.

29. Henry M. Smythe to W. W. Rockhill, January 30, 1897, Smythe to State Department, February 6, 1897, Battiste to David Hill, July 18, 1900, Terres to Francis Loomis, April 27, 1903, all in CD.

through friendships with powerful Haitians. The British firms of Lyon Hall and Roberts Dutton, for example, made shrewd use of such techniques. These concerns received advance warning of the Haitian government's decision to halve the interest on the domestic loan in 1905. The tip gave them a chance to quickly sell their own certificates at the going rate and then buy them back cheaply after devaluation.[30]

Lending, another traditional activity, took on added luster in the Haitian milieu. Merchant-bankers charged rates of up to 50 percent on government loans. The Haitian scholar Gérard Pierre-Charles conjectured that in the 1875–1910 period, Haiti borrowed 166 million francs, of which more than half reverted to the lenders under various pretexts. Merchant-bankers argued that the government forced them to make loans, and because some Haitian administrations were short-lived and reluctant to assume their predecessors' obligations, financiers required high interest rates to protect themselves.[31] Smaller Haitian concerns might receive loans from the bankers, but these lenders more often used their capital to compete with local firms that had acquired rewarding franchises or clienteles.[32]

Merchant capital in Haiti during the 1902–1915 period can best be understood if we realize that it functioned within the context of a dual currency system. The gourde served as the unit of domestic trade, whereas foreign transactions, debt payment, and customs duties were payable in American gold dollars. Exporters required gourdes to buy produce from the peasants, and they needed them quickly when crops flooded the market in an economy unable to regulate agricultural production. Gourde values rose during the harvest season, from November to May, and remained strongest during the best crop years.[33]

After the harvest, the gourde typically began a slow decline in value, for producers did not make many market purchases while their own stock of homegrown provisions lasted, and their visits to town were infrequent

30. Chatelain, *La Banque Nationale*, 46; Louis R. E. Gation, *Aspects de l'économie et des finances d'Haïti* (Port-au-Prince, 1944), 191; Murray to Foreign Secretary, December 3, November 11, 1910, FO 371, Vol. 915.

31. Gérard Pierre-Charles, *L'Economie haïtienne et sa voie de développement* (Paris, 1967), 137; Powell to Hay, July 20, 1904, CD; H. P. Davis, Memorandum, n.d., DF, 838.616/75; W. E. Aughinbaugh, *Selling Latin America* (Boston, 1915), 297, 298.

32. For examples, see Powell to John Sherman, May 5, 1898, CD; *Le Matin*, June 17, 1908, pp. 2–3; and Furniss to Secretary of State, February 16, 1912, DF, 838.51/308.

33. Domenick Scarpa, Memorandum, July, 1916, DF, 838.00/1404; John A. McIlhenny, Memorandum, October 5, 1921, p. 3, DF, 838.515/23.

during harvesttime. Eventually the gourde returned to the cities, where its increasing abundance diminished its worth. The amount of gourdes in circulation during the period did not equal the value of an average coffee crop, and only the slowness of the process of bringing coffee to port—four to five months—guaranteed a supply of gourdes sufficient to purchase other agricultural commodities and to effect urban exchanges of goods and services. The supply inelasticity of the currency, combined with the lack of alternatives to agriculture, meant that the demand for gourdes was felt everywhere at once when it was felt at all.[34]

Interest rates did not modify the demand for currency because they had always been abnormally high in Haiti. The fluctuating and manipulated gourde was responsible for this. Merchants who had to place orders and make payments before marketing their goods experienced long-term risks. The manager of the Banque Nationale de la République d'Haïti observed in 1915 that "exchange risk has perverted all Haitian energies from commercial into speculative ones—stunting legitimate enterprise and favoring speculation, from which no public benefit can be derived."[35]

Haiti's other currency, the dollar, did not travel to the countryside. The dollar remained in the major ports, where it paid the salaries of important civil servants, financed imports, provided the basis for the costly interior and foreign loans, and served as a trading medium among the privileged classes. The state did not attempt to abolish the dual currency system because it realized that dollars would raise the cost of living and gradually migrate abroad. Yet some gourde issues had also been expatriated—smuggled out of the country to be melted down for their intrinsic value.[36]

The dollar provided the large indemnities paid to foreign claimants. Damage claims for injuries sustained during civil disorders in Haiti provided a source of income for aliens. Metropolitan governments often supported these frequently inflated demands for reparations with a show of force. The likelihood of gunboat diplomacy lay behind expatriates' willingness to embroil Haiti in disputes with their home country. By

34. Scarpa, Memorandum, July, 1916, DF 838.00/1404; Loomis to Assistant Secretary of State, October 2, 1903, CD; Office of the Foreign Trade Advisor, "The Monetary Situation in Haiti," October 11, 1921, p. 4, DF, 838.51/22.

35. Gation, *Aspects de l'économie*, 176–178; Scarpa, Memorandum, July, 1916, DF, 838.00/1404.

36. Scarpa, Memorandum, July, 1916, DF, 838.00/1404; McIlhenny, Memorandum, October 5, 1921, p. 4, DF, 838.515/23.

1926, claims filed for the years 1899–1916 reached 73,629 and totaled nearly $40 million.[37]

Family ties helped solidify aliens' financial gains. As port city residents, foreigners mingled in a cosmopolitan society. Their children by Haitian mothers shared their privileged status. The practice of registering property in children's names helped to circumvent laws aimed at limiting expatriates' economic activity. Once foreigners entered community life, they were better able to influence the direction of public policy, provide funds for the government, and help shape social and aesthetic standards. The privacy of wealth sheltered them somewhat, but their influence could not be completed disguised.[38]

In 1903, Louis Audain père asserted that eight hundred Port-au-Princiens had renounced their Haitian citizenship in order to claim the protection of another government. France, eager to maintain its influence in peripherally Francophone areas such as Haiti, liberally employed an 1887 law that bestowed French citizenship on all born abroad of a French father or grandfather. By 1890, there were five thousand individuals in Haiti who claimed to be French. Those born at sea or overseas frequently changed their nationality during periods of domestic crisis or returned from foreign travels with non-Haitian identities.[39]

Certain aliens, on the other hand, adopted Haitian citizenship but often did not properly legitimize it. Others kept their status deliberately ambiguous for political or financial reasons. The statesman J. N. Léger accused such individuals of cheating both Haiti and their country of origin. "They escape all the burdens the citizen must undertake," he complained, "while profiting from great advantages." They were exempt from military service, Léger observed, but this exemption did not keep them from making "senseless complaints" against Haiti and "finding foreign ministers to sustain them in so doing." Léger was not alone in this assessment. The British consul in 1904 characterized some resident aliens and dual

---

37. Vansittart to Foreign Secretary, December 31, 1904, FO 35, Vol. 180; British Consul's General Report on the Republic of Hayti, 1906, FO 371, Vol. 266; Nicholls, *Economic Dependence*, 18–19, 27.

38. Frédéric Marcelin, *Les Finances d'Haïti* (Paris, 1911), 38, 39; Marcelin, *Au Gré du Souvenir*, 7; David Lowenthal, *West Indian Societies* (New York, 1972), 197, 198, 210; Leslie F. Manigat, *L'Amérique Latine au XXᵉ Siècle, 1889–1929* (Paris, 1973), 70–71; Gation, *Aspects de l'économie*, 191.

39. Audain père, *Du changement*, 12, 13–14, 15; Douglass to Blaine, February 15, 1890, CD; J. N. Léger, *La Politique extérieure d'Haïti* (Paris, 1886), 21–31, 36–56.

nationals as "professional reclamationists," who expected to be compensated for damages resulting from Haitian revolutions, though most major powers did not make similar awards.[40] Mixed, Europeanized, and foreign members of the Haitian population used ambiguous nationality as a tool to force concessions from a weak government.

The nationality issue further undermined Haitian society in that nationality determined who had recourse to external diplomatic or military force. Haiti could not coerce the great powers, but foreign navies backed up demands on Haiti from the legations. Being Haitian also meant that one lacked protection from the excesses of one's own government, whereas being foreign was insurance against injury and loss. In times of civil war, insurgents usually respected a house or shop that displayed the flag of a major power. An attack on a foreigner invited reprisals or claims. The urban upper class sometimes found it prudent to change citizenship. Occasionally, members of the same family were variously French, German, British, and American. The prestige and security inherent in assuming another nationality contrasted sharply with the risks of remaining Haitian.[41] Léger wrote: "The peaceful Haitian who, never having filled public office and deriving from work only his means of existence, sees his painfully acquired property disappear in flames, and loses in several hours the fruits of several years' labor, cannot fail to have bitter reflections when the State, after a civil war, is generous only to foreigners whose very nationality is often doubtful."[42]

Indeed, this concern was so strong that many bourgeois parents actively recruited foreign spouses for their marriageable daughters. In Hibbert's novel of social mores, *Les Thazar*, Madame Thazar rejects the prospect of a Haitian son-in-law. Chronic political violence, she feels, imperils native men. "What future can a Haitian have in Haiti," she exclaims, "especially a good Haitian?" The young Mlle Thazar rejects a local suitor for a German, realizing that the European's fortunes do not depend on the vicissitudes of politics.[43]

40. Léger, *La Politique extérieure*, 47–53; Vansittart to Foreign Secretary, December 31, 1904, FO 35, Vol. 180; British Consul's General Report, 1906, FO 371, Vol. 266; Ludwell Lee Montague, *Haiti and the United States, 1714–1938* (Durham, N.C., 1940), 245–46.

41. Alexandre Poujol, "De la nationalité dans la République d'Haïti," *Revue du Droit International Public* (1902), 15.

42. Léger, *La Politique extérieure*, 47–53.

43. Fernand Hibbert, *Les Thazar* (Port-au-Prince, 1907), 109; Yvette Tardieu Feldman, "De la Colonie à l'Occupation: les étrangers chez Hibbert," *Conjonction*, No. 122–23 (1974), 24.

In real life as in fiction, the bourgeoisie approved of such marriages because the bride was thereafter sheltered under the French or German flag. The association of light skin color and European features with social mobility also played a role in the preference for European spouses. Léon Descos, France's minister to Haiti in the early 1900s, commented sarcastically on "the German ladies" of Port-au-Prince, whose Teutonic allegiance lasted no longer than their husbands' tours of duty. Descos's remark seemed directed toward common-law or *plaçage* arrangements, but Haitians and foreigners also entered into legal marriage contracts. Widows might also resume their Haitian citizenship after the death of their European spouses. Despite this apparent opportunism, a formal dignity marked marriage brokerage during the epoch.[44]

Genteel Haitians expected reciprocal behavior from aliens, but visitors from abroad did not always represent the cream of metropolitan society. Léger grumbled that Haiti had attracted the refuse of Europe: "Waiters who robbed their bosses, dishonest cashiers, criminals awaiting sentence, escaped convicts. . . . All these people have but one obsession, to get rich. Needless to add that they don't quibble about how. They don't recoil before any evil act, provided that it brings them money." Adventurers could find opportunities for advancement in a country where European superiority was assumed. Frédéric Marcelin observed the aura of distinction that surrounded the white man. "Whether he remains in the cities or goes to the countryside," Marcelin commented, "his title of foreigner, illustrated by his skin, is a prestigious passport for him."[45]

Other evidence corroborates the growing ubiquity of foreigners. In 1891 the Bureau of the American Republics published a handbook, *Commercial Directory of Haiti and Santo Domingo*, from which information about the commercial sector in Haiti can be drawn. The nationality of many firms can be established through various sources. Once Haitian businesses, Haitian partnerships with foreigners, and businessmen of unknown nationality are accounted for, it becomes evident that alien merchants dominated important sectors of commerce.[46]

44. Descos, *En Haïti*, xxiv, xxv; *Le Nouvelliste*, November 5, 1908, p. 2. See Harry Hoetink, *Caribbean Race Relations: A Study of Two Variants* (New York, 1967); Hoetink, *Slavery and Race Relations in the Americas* (New York, 1973); Micheline Labelle, *Idéologie de couleur et classes sociales en Haïti* (Montreal, 1978); and Theodora Holly, "The Haitian Girl: An Analysis," *Negro World*, February 28, 1925, p. 7.

45. Léger, *La Politique extérieure*, 24, 25; Marcelin, *Les Finances d'Haïti*, 38; Montague, *Haiti and the United States*, 245–46.

46. Bureau of the American Republics, *Commercial Directory of Haiti and Santo Do-*

Foreign Participation in Haitian Commerce

	1891	1908	1908	1915
Bankers	75%	93.75%[a]	76.4%	—
Exporters	69.5	51.4[a]	47.3	—
General merchants	60	—	37[b]	75
Importers	33.1	43.9	50	43

SOURCES: for 1891, *Commercial Directory of Haiti and Santo Domingo;* for 1908, *Statistique générale de la République d'Haïti* and "American Export Trade Directory"; for 1915, *Trade Directory of Central America and the West Indies.*

[a]Port-au-Prince only
[b]Excludes Port-au-Prince

In 1908 the Haitian government published the directory *Statistique générale de la République d'Haïti,* which identified the principal importers and exporters. The list of businessmen indicates the remarkable degree of alien penetration in the import-export sector: foreigners now accounted for half the participants in foreign commerce. Haitian merchants persisted in the provincial ports, where their share of trade remained unchanged, but even in smaller towns like Jérémie and Miragôane, which failed to attract foreign enterprise, some Europeans made significant inroads. Port-au-Prince, the capital, experienced the greatest degree of international participation. Ninety-three percent of the merchant-bankers there were non-Haitian, and foreigners led the export trade. Foreigners dominated six out of the seven categories of merchandise listed, leaving Haitians as the principal grocers.[47] The National Business League of America's "American Export Trade Directory," also published in 1908, corroborates the preponderance of foreign merchant-bankers (76.4 percent) and illustrates that alien domination of the export market affected the provincial cities as well as the capital city. Non-

mingo (Washington, D.C., 1891); *Livre bleu d'Haïti/Blue Book of Haiti;* Descos, *En Haïti;* Records of the Gendarmerie d'Haïti (Garde d'Haïti), 1915–34, in U.S. Marine Corps Records, Record Group 127, NA; Georges Corvington, *Port-au-Prince au cours des ans, La Metropole haïtienne du XIXᵉ Siècle* (5 vols.; Port-au-Prince, 1976), IV; Pean, *L'Illusion héroïque.*

47. République d'Haïti, *Statistique générale de la République d'Haïti,* 54, 57.

Haitians were the principal exporters in seven out of ten cities listed and accounted for the bulk of the trade in tropical commodities. The percentage of expatriates in business in Haiti showed a significant increase from 1891 to 1908 in six out of ten towns for which information was available. The U.S. Department of Commerce's *Trade Directory of Central America and the West Indies* further illustrated the erosion of Haitian enterprise in 1915 in its index of leading merchants in the republic. In the nine towns listed, Haitians formed a majority of the traders in only two—Jacmel and Jérémie. None were engaged in significant commerce in Fort Liberté and St. Marc, and of the remaining locations, only in Gonaïves did Haitians constitute as much as 45 percent of the business community.[48]

No figures are available that compare Haitian and non-Haitian business establishments with respect to profits or size, but contemporaries asserted that the most important merchants were aliens. In Port-au-Prince, taxes on foreign enterprises provided the municipality with half its revenues. Europeans did most of the trading in St. Marc and Gonaïves in 1910. One French merchant monopolized more than 50 percent of Jacmel's commerce. By 1911, Germans and Frenchmen conducted 80 percent of the trade in principal Haitian cities and controlled the most powerful and prestigious concerns.[49]

Trade rivalries accompanied foreign commercial expansion in the 1900–1915 period. The increasing competitiveness impinged on local politics. Relationships with a presidential candidate favored by France or Germany, for example, now assumed greater significance. The nationality of a businessman who acquired a concession became a matter of diplomatic concern. American and European merchants could rely on assistance from their respective governments in advancing their interests. They also had at their disposal relatively sophisticated credit, transport, and communications systems.

The foreign build-up in Haiti was part of a global struggle for markets and

---

48. *Ibid.*; "American Export Trade Directory," in National Business League of America, *Practical Suggestions for the Development of American Export Trade . . .* (Chicago, 1908), 61–66; Bureau of the American Republics, *Commercial Directory of Haiti and Santo Domingo* (Washington, D.C., 1891); Department of Commerce, Bureau of Foreign and Domestic Commerce, *Trade Directory of Central America and the West Indies, 1915* (Washington, D.C., 1915), 199–217.

49. Vincent, *En posant les jalons*, I, 218; Furniss to Root, September 24, 1908, NF, 2126/306–307; Descos, *En Haïti*, 234, 264, 272–73; Pan American Union, *Proceedings of the Pan American Commerce Conference, February 13–17, 1911* (Washington, D.C., 1911), 78; Marcelin, *Au Gré du Souvenir*, 182–83.

political influence among the great powers in the early twentieth century. France utilized the ties of language and culture to maintain a stable position for itself in the Haitian market and to cultivate Francophiles for political purposes. Its liberal lending policy encouraged dependence. Germany's self-promotion relied greatly on its efficient enterprises and high-quality manufactures. Britain linked its Caribbean trade to traditional textile exports, which were extensively served by German shipping. The United States, while preserving commercial preponderance in the area, employed the Monroe Doctrine to reduce European challenges to its power, a power it rightly perceived as mercantile as well as strategic.[50]

The American example illuminates the character of the international trade competition. The United States' diplomatic style differed from that of the European nations; however, its relationship to commercial questions in Haiti remained essentially the same as that of its competitors. The Americans dominated the staple commodity market but did not have a significant resident business community before 1915. The reasons for its small representation were partly racial. Deep-seated prejudices, which the British shared, precluded the social mixing that characterized continental European behavior in Haiti.[51]

The predominantly black American legation helped to neutralize the perception of the United States as a racist country. Educated Haitians recognized America's color problems. Some had experienced them first-hand while traveling in North America as representatives of their own government, and their stories of racial discrimination did not improve Haitian-American relations. But the use of black American diplomats accomplished several objectives at once: it fulfilled partisan promises to black politicians at home, it substituted for an absent American resident group, and it partially shielded Haitians from the harsh realities of Ameri-

50. Herbert Feis, *Europe, the World's Banker* (New Haven, 1930), 50; Abrams and Miller, "Who Were the French Colonialists?"; Warren G. Kneer, *Great Britain and the Caribbean, 1901–1913: A Study in Anglo-American Relations* (East Lansing, 1975), ix–xv. Powell to Hay, August 31, 1901, CD; Vansittart to Lansdowne, January 5, 1904, FO 35, Vol. 180; Furniss to Root, January 1, 1908, NF, 2126/39; Alvey Adee to Furniss, September 14, 1910, DF, 838.602/2; Furniss to Secretary of State, December 19, 1911, DF, 838.111/41; William Jennings Bryan to Woodrow Wilson, February 25, 1915, in U.S. Department of State, *The Lansing Papers* (Washington, D.C.. 1939), 465.

51. James Weldon Johnson, *Along This Way* (New York, 1933), 262; James Weldon Johnson, "Why Latin America Dislikes the United States" (MS in James Weldon Johnson Collection, Yale University); Archibald R. Colquhoun, *Greater America* (New York and London, 1904), 118–20.

can prejudice.[52] However, Washington still needed a business community in Haiti. To this end, it supported a Syrian merchant group, despite strong Haitian objections. In order to maintain the preeminence of American exports, the United States confronted Haiti many times over the safety, rights, and privileges of this segment of the population, employing its diplomacy on behalf of commerce with zeal and persistence.[53] American support of the Syrians provides an example of the pressures exerted on Haiti by the great powers in their efforts to strengthen those foreign merchants who sold metropolitan products.

Washington's chief tool in its stewardship of the Syrians and the consequent advancement of its own concerns was the reciprocity treaty of 1864. A product of Secretary of State William Henry Seward's policy of trade expansion in the Western Hemisphere, the treaty resembled other conventions the United States had signed in the same era with various Latin American countries. According to its provisions, Haitians and American nationals would enjoy the same commercial rights in each other's homeland as would citizens. In reality, the treaty did little for the Haitians, who conducted almost no business in the United States.[54]

The treaty's limitations were exposed when the Haitian government resumed taxation on foreign clerks in 1903. The practice of recruiting foreign clerical and managerial assistance created local unemployment and, as many Europeans later became their employers' partners or set up firms of their own, contributed another disincentive for native entrepreneurship.[55] The tax on foreign clerks encountered consistent American opposition. The U.S. minister, William F. Powell, adamantly insisted that American merchants be exempt. Few of the approximately two hundred persons whom Powell defended had ever spent much time in the United States, though some were citizens. In 1904 the U.S. Justice

52. James A. Padgett, "Diplomats to Haiti and Their Diplomacy," *Journal of Negro History*, XXV (1940), 265–330; Vansittart to Foreign Secretary, March 11, June 7, 1904, FO 35, Vol. 180. On racial discrimination against Haitians, see Powell to Hay, May 29, 1904, CD; *Le Soir*, June 14, 1904; Emile Paultre, *Essai sur M. Price-Mars* (Port-au-Prince, 1966), 35; and New York *Times*, January 5, 1910, p. 8.

53. Turnier, *Les Etats-Unis*, 163–95; Nicholls, *Economic Dependence*, 25–27; Brenda Gayle Plummer, "Race, Nationality, and Trade in the Caribbean: The Syrians in Haiti, 1903–34," *International History Review*, III (1981), 517–39.

54. Adee to Powell, October 5, 1903, *FR*, 1903, p. 378; Vansittart to Foreign Secretary, March 17, 1904, FO 35, Vol. 181.

55. Montague, *Haiti and the United States*, 163–72; Powell to Sherman, May 5, 1898, CD.

Department discovered that a number of them held counterfeit U.S. naturalization papers, but this revelation did not deter Powell and the State Department from vigorous support of the largely Syrian group. Even when the Haitian government expelled those who were fraudulently naturalized, the American legation protested. Although these individuals were not U.S. nationals, they, more than any other group, brought American merchandise to Haiti. Because of Powell's intransigence, Haiti ultimately renounced the reciprocity treaty in 1904 in hopes of improving relations with Britain and Germany.[56]

The Americans were not alone in pressing for advantages. By means of a commercial agreement reached in 1900, French goods entered Haiti at very low rates. In exchange, Haitian coffee, cacao, and spices paid the minimum duty in France and Algeria. The treaty also promoted French shipping. French imports became cheaper as a result of these arrangements, but Haitian consumers did not benefit. The price of French goods remained the same, and only the merchant community profited from the changes.[57]

France's commercial policy in Haiti was aimed at preserving, rather than extending, a traditional clientele. In 1907 the French Foreign Office was reorganized—political and commercial affairs were under the same administration—and French officials abroad increasingly served as brokers for French industry. Cultural matters also played an important role in the advancement of French interests. Complaisant Haitian notables were inducted into the Legion of Honor. The French did not limit their pressure on Haiti to the perpetuation of French civilization but also lobbied against the growing contacts with Germany. Their efforts did not dislodge the Germans, however, and in 1905, France canceled the privileged entry status of Haitian coffee and cacao. Haiti then renounced the Franco-Haitian commercial treaty, which by then was of little further value.[58]

France's policies also touched on the Syrian question. Because of

56. Adee to Frederick Van Dyne, March 14, 1905, and Powell to Hay, April 9, 1905, CD; J. N. Léger to Murville Férère, March 18, 1904, in Kurt Fisher Collection, Schomburg Research Center, NYPL.

57. Turnier, *Les Etats-Unis*, 161–95; Plummer, "Race, Nationality, and Trade," 526, 538–39; Léger to Férère, March 18, 1904, in Kurt Fisher Collection; Adee to Van Dyne, November 6, 1905, CD; Vansittart to Foreign Secretary, March 17, 1904, FO 35, Vol. 181.

58. Battiste to State Department, August 20, 1900, CD; Augustus Cohen to Foreign Secretary, May 17, 1901, FO 35, Vol. 176; Powell to Hay, August 31, 1901, CD; Abrams and Miller, "Who Were the French Colonialists?," 687, 706; Feis, *Europe, the World's Banker*, x, xi, 33–59, 129, 134, 158–59.

France's historic interests in Lebanon, some four hundred Syrians in Haiti regarded themselves as entitled to French protection. Haiti disputed the Syrian claim, but the French minister was initially inclined to honor it. Cooperation between the Syrian community and French diplomats allegedly had been so close that one Syrian merchant had illegally expatriated a large quantity of Haitian coin with the complicity of the French legation and under the cover of its seal. This intimacy ended when merchants from Martinique and Guadeloupe, who traded in Haiti, complained about Syrian competition. The Middle Easterners, who had originally placed orders through the larger French commission houses, were becoming independent of French mercantile networks. The French Antilleans then used their greater leverage with the French minister to secure his indifference to the Syrians' problems with the Haitian government.[59]

The British attitude toward twenty Anglo-Syrians was similarly motivated. In a 1904 complaint to the Foreign Office, the Manchester-based Central America Trading Company expressed its concern about the welfare of a Syrian employee in Haiti. The Foreign Office assured the firm that a British gunboat would soon arrive at the island. The reply contrasted sharply to one later made to an independent Syrian, who was told that his British citizenship did not entitle him or his non-British partners to protection. His Majesty's government was prepared to act energetically only when persecuted Syrians represented a home firm.[60]

Two British companies were among the leading foreign enterprises in Haiti but had tenuous ties to the metropole. The British consul considered these firms "merely British in name, but Haytian and German in their interests and sentiments." One concern was "a purely American import house," incorporated in the United States. Many proprietors, moreover, were mulattoes married to Haitian women. Britain's commercial position in Haiti reflected its general Caribbean policy of retrenchment and acquiescence to American diplomatic objectives. It confined its activism to its own colonies and made no effort to draw Britons in the independent countries into strong unions for the purposes of aggressive business development.[61]

59. Powell to Hay, August 17, 1904, and March 13, 1905, CD; Turnier, *Les Etats-Unis*, 160–70.

60. Lawson, Coppock, and Hart to Foreign Undersecretary, August 5, 1904, and appended note, FO 35, Vol. 181. Compare Lucien J. Jerome to Foreign Secretary, November 14, 1905, FO 35, Vol. 182, and instructions to Vansittart, February 23, 1905, FO 35, Vol. 181; Foreign Office to Abraham Shameh, August 29, 1904, FO 35, Vol. 181.

61. Vansittart to Lord Grey, July 18, 1906, and June 6, 1905, FO 371, Vol. 81; Jerome to

In contrast, the German government and its subjects in Haiti enjoyed the closest collaboration of all. As early as 1897, the German minister organized a patriotic society among German residents. Its activities included fund raising for the Imperial Navy, and by 1901 the Germans had collected DM 816,500. Eleven years later, the German community established a school for Germano-Haitian pupils in Port-au-Prince. Subsidized by tuition as well as by gifts from the Hamburg America Line, Hamburg businessmen, and the Kaiser himself, the school gave children of mixed descent a German education.[62]

Germany's dedication to maintaining the metropolitan connection was also reflected in its conflicts with Haiti. The German navy responded to political unrest on the island by demonstrations of force designed to prevent attack on German life or property. Maneuvers in Haitian waters in 1902 and the landing of troops in 1911 both demonstrated to the government in Port-au-Prince the readiness of the Imperial forces. In 1901, Germany began a tariff war with Haiti to secure treaty privileges equal to those acquired by the French. No accord was reached until mid-1908, when a compromise settlement allowed the Germans to significantly expand their shipping and import trade.[63]

Haitian policy makers were not indifferent to foreign penetration, intervention, and pressure. Like other Latin American statesmen, they were sensitive and vulnerable to charges of "selling the country." They were also masters of camouflage and delay when they deemed it necessary to forestall unfavorable action on the part of other powers. "It is worse than useless to enter into a discussion on points of international law with the Haytian Government," British Consul Alexander Murray observed. "There is nothing they like better than such a correspondence in the course of which they make lengthy replies at long intervals interlarded with copious quotations culled from various authorities."[64]

Foreign Secretary, August 23, 1905, and Vansittart to Foreign Secretary, March 16, 1905, FO 35, Vol. 182; Kneer, *Great Britain and the Caribbean*, 119–28, 214–15.

62. Powell to Hay, November 17, 1897, and January 30, 1901, CD; Furniss to Secretary of State, April 30, 1912, DF, 838.42; Schmidt, *The U.S. Occupation of Haiti*, 34; Paul Gordon Lauren, *Diplomats and Bureaucrats: The First Institutional Responses to Twentieth Century Diplomacy in France and Germany* (Stanford, Calif., 1976), 198–99.

63. *Le Soir*, December 6, 1899; Powell to Hay, July 10, 1904, CD; Furniss to Secretary of State, August 19, 1911, DF, 838.00/675; Vansittart to Foreign Secretary, March 1, 1905, FO 35, Vol. 182; Manigat, "Substitution," 336.

64. Manigat, "Substitution," 322–23; Vansittart to Lansdowne, March 11, 1904, FO 35, Vol. 180; Murray, Annual Report, 1910, FO 371, Vol. 915; Patrick Bellegarde-Smith, "Haiti: Perspectives of Foreign Policy: An Essay on the International Relations of a Small

Ultimately, Haiti's attempts to defend its integrity were defeated from within. Foreign influence had penetrated the core of the political and cultural leadership class, and kinship ties as well as outlook now linked these Haitians to external interests. Such prominent families as the Lespinasses, the Lecontes, the Légers, and the Ménos, who together provided a president, diplomats, cabinet officers, and other officials, were related by marriage and blood to powerful foreigners, whose outlook they gradually came to share.[65]

In the business world, the intermarriage pattern facilitated the formation of closely held companies with links to foreign corporations. The classic examples are the Central Railroad of Haiti and the Cul de Sac Railroad. Intrafamilial transfers of stock within these two interlocking bodies are supposed to have baffled their own managers.[66] Marriage ties to foreigners included the diplomatic community. John B. Terres, a black American consul who resided permanently in Haiti, was the brother-in-law of two partners of the banking house of Dejardin, Luders, and Company. All three men had wed Germano-Haitian women and lived in a suburban family compound where they grew and processed tobacco.[67] Lemuel Livingston, U.S. consul at Cape Haitian, also married into a local family. Livingston was later associated with the highly speculative Haytian Pineapple Company, one of many plantation ventures that failed during the American occupation of 1915–1934.[68]

Haitians assigned a high value to family relations. Chronic economic stress and political strife gave weight to the family as a stable, protective institution. Family linkage helped lower the bourgeoisie's resistance to overt foreign intervention. When the United States landed marines in July, 1915, the groundwork for occupation had long since been laid by

State," *Caribbean Quarterly*, XX (September-December, 1974), 21–35; Murray to Foreign Secretary, December 3, 1910, FO 371, Vol. 915.

65. Oliver Wardrop to Foreign Secretary, April 8, 1903, FO 35, Vol. 179; Dantès Bellegarde to Léger, June 12, 1932, in Eugène Maximilien Collection, Schomburg Research Center, NYPL; Powell to Hay, May 17, 1902, Enclosure No. 1, CD; James P. McDonald to R. W. Austin, July 8, 1912, DF, 838.6156M14/1; Furniss to Root, October 13, 1908, NF, 2126/308; Dantès Bellegarde, *Ecrivains haïtiens* (Port-au-Prince, 1947), 146–48; Littleton D. Waller to John A. Lejeune, August 20, 1917, in John A. Lejeune Papers, LC.

66. Furniss to Secretary of State, June 6, 1910, DF, 838.77/1; John Russell, Daily Diary Report, May 5, 1920, DF, 838.00/1641; Munro, *Intervention*, 246.

67. Furniss to Secretary of State, May 30, 1910, DF, 838.6102.

68. State Department Register, 1916, p. 110; Roger Gaillard, *Les cent-jours de Rosalvo Bobo* (Port-au-Prince, 1973), 18n12; Whitefield McKinlay to Furniss, July 18, 1921, in Whitefield McKinlay Papers, Carter G. Woodson Collection, LC.

upper-class Haitian intermediaries who had assisted the extension of the metropolitan market systems.[69]

Women were the bond that cemented the marriage alliances of political, mercantile, and proprietary families. The novels of Hibbert and Marcelin depict marriageable girls as delicately bred pawns, but bourgeois women had not always been helpless dependents. Some, like Marcelin's own grandmother, had been traders themselves fifty years before. Female merchants had traveled on business, and their economic independence had even entailed some freedom from conventional matrimony. *Plaçage*, the institution of cohabitation associated with the peasantry, had also been practiced among the upper classes in the early 1800s. The state's establishment of an accord with the Vatican in 1860 gradually replaced *plaçage* with Catholic and civil marriage within the upper classes.[70]

The progress of marriage accompanied the commercial demise of the bourgeois woman. After 1860 she was increasingly confined to the home, a victim of the same economic forces that diminished Haitian entrepreneurship generally. Society made the relegation of the *bourgeoise* to domesticity more palatable by assimilating it to prevailing French custom, where higher-status women remained relatively secluded. The retirement of women from trade in imitation of a Western model may have been perceived as a modernizing improvement. Frustrated and idle at home, however, some affluent *Haïtiennes* became petty tyrants and tireless consumers of foreign merchandise. Jean Price-Mars, writing in 1919, ascribed many of the failings of the Haitian bourgeoisie to women's problems. As the property of husbands and fathers, wives and daughters became repositories for wealth as manifested in articles of consumption. Luxury remained the limit of their horizons, and they learned to push their spouses into ruinous spending. Before 1915, Price-Mars averred, ladies did not question the source of the largesse that graft bestowed on them. He recalled a conversation with a seemingly innocent girl who candidly admitted that she aspired to marriage with a cabinet official who could steal enough to keep her in style.[71]

69. Frédéric Marcelin, *Bric-à-brac* (Paris, 1910), 53–56; John Russell to Secretary of State, February 13, 1928, DF, 838.00/2442; Nicholls, "Idéologies," 656–57.

70. Marcelin, *Au Gré du Souvenir*, 182–83; Madeleine Sylvain Bouchereau, *Haïti et ses femmes* (Port-au-Prince, 1957). 71–75; Sidney W. Mintz, "Economic Role and Cultural Tradition," in Filomina Chioma Steady (ed.), *The Black Woman Cross-Culturally* (Cambridge, Mass., 1981), 521–23; Antoine Pierre-Paul, *La première protestation armée contre l'intervention américaine et 260 jours dans le maquis* (Port-au-Prince, n.d.), 22–28.

71. Roger Gaillard, "Hibbert: Sexualité des Personnages et Erotisme du Romancier," *Conjonction*, No. 122–23 (1974), 44, 45; Françoise Mayeur, "Women and Elites from the

The decay of Haitian entrepreneurship and the rise of cosmopolitanism and consumerism coincided with the gradual exodus of the bourgeoisie from the coastal cities. Its members had begun leaving the rural areas in the nineteenth century and now found life in the capital preferable to existence in the provincial centers. Evidence suggests that the bourgeoisie's departure from the lesser towns was synchronized with its withdrawal from commerce. As early as 1908, Léon Audain noted the dwindling significance of the port cities, by then visited only irregularly by foreign steamers. The lack of transport, inability to compete with foreigners, and the vicissitudes of revolutionary upheaval spurred emigration. The foreign-owned National Railroad Company established rail contact between Port-au-Prince and the potentially rich Artibonite Valley. In so doing, it paved the way for the decline of the once powerful city of St. Marc, whose gentry began to desert it between 1908 and 1910.[72]

Some cities resisted this process for some time, because of either their independent power or their remoteness and isolation. Cape Haitian and Jérémie provide examples. Cape Haitian, fed by the breadbasket of the northern plains and endowed with its own historic traditions, posed a threat to central government hegemony well after 1915. Aliens controlled the bulk of its commerce, but the economic diversity of the area and its cultural cohesion were great enough to withstand many of the disintegrative pressures.[73]

Jérémie, at the end of the southwest peninsula, owed its self-sufficiency to the exigencies of geography. Members of the bourgeoisie still traded there and in 1908 controlled most of the enterprises, but Jérémie's food supply came from New York. Visitors praised the cleanliness and general appearance of this town, in which the native bourgeoisie, now a *comprador* class, still held undisputed sway. The bourgeoisie also continued to rule in various tiny enclaves, such as the logwood port of Aquin, where one family monopolized the dyewood supply. Even here, foreign firms

Nineteenth to the Twentieth Century," in Jolyon Holworth and Philip G. Cerny (eds.), *Elites in France: Origins, Reproduction and Power* (New York, 1981), 60, 62; Fortuna A. Guery, *Témoignages* (Port-au-Prince, 1950), 69, 70, 76; Price-Mars, *La Vocation de l'élite*, 103, 104, 106, 126–27.

72. Powell to Hay, August 15, 1902, CD; Brigade Commander to Military Governor of Santo Domingo, May 17, 1917, DF, 838.00/1458; Léon Audain, *Le Mal d'Haïti, ses causes et son traitement* (Port-au-Prince, 1908), 106n1; Stephen Leech to Grey, January 13, 1914, FO 368, Vol. 1309; de Young, "Class Parameters," 453.

73. De Young, "Class Parameters," 455.

conducted the shipping, and Haitians depended on imported staples.[74]

The decline of the provincial ports increased the capital's population and its authority over the hinterland. The arrival of comparatively affluent people, who withdrew their wealth from the smaller towns and invested it in Port-au-Prince, enlarged the city's importance. Thus, the United States' occupation did not cause the intensified centralization of power in the Haitian capital, as has been argued.[75] The process was well under way before the marines landed.

The native bourgeoisie contributed to the growth of cosmopolitanism. It embraced foreign behavior, ideas, and commodities. It permitted the efflorescence of a subtle sense of inferiority. A critical consequence was the subsequent debasement of the Haitian identity as the political decrepitude of the country was exposed. Abandonment of Haitian citizenship, so bitterly opposed by Léger and Audain, was a symptom of the bourgeoisie's desire to escape from the burdens of membership in a small, black, impoverished, and beleaguered society. To a large degree, the ruling class had been supplanted. Its successor was a foreign elite, much more powerfully connected.

74. Captain Murdock to Secretary of the Navy, August 24, 1904, NR; Antoine Laforest, *Trente-huit jours de voyage . . .* (Port-au-Prince, 1910), 113–14; Admiral Caperton to Secretary of the Navy, Report, October 31–November 6, 1915, DF, 838.00/1369.

75. John M. Street, *Historical and Economic Geography of the Southwest Peninsula of Haiti* (Berkeley, 1960), 427–28, 429, 464; Michel S. Laguerre, *Urban Life in the Caribbean* (Cambridge, Mass., 1982), 1, 2–3, 145–47.

III

The Instruments of Power

Bois plus rwo dit'l wè loin, graine proméné dit'l wè plus loin.
The tallest tree says he sees far, the migratory seed says he
sees farther.

—Haitian proverb

TRADE COMPETITION in Haiti early in the twentieth century remained
narrowly mercantile during a period when industrial expansion increasingly characterized the economies of North America, western Europe, Japan, and even such larger Latin American states as Argentina and
Brazil. Mercantilism in Haiti was reinforced by a strong traditionalism
that narrowly limited the scope and diversity of Haitian enterprise. Mercantile trade flourished within a rigidly institutionalized commercial
structure, shaped by local usage and preference as well as by metropolitan
imperatives.[1]

The dual Haitian and metropolitan motivation has its counterpart in
other aspects of Haiti's relations with the great powers. Commerce in-
teracted with ideology and culture in shaping the linkages. Among the
most potent instruments at the disposal of all the states concerned was
historiography, which underlay the extensive polemics and travel literature of the late nineteenth and early twentieth centuries on the subject
of the Black Republic.

For many Europeans, the abolition of slavery was identical to the eradica-
tion of the Caribbean from their consciousness. It is no accident that even
today the content of Caribbean historiography is heavily weighted to the

1. Elizabeth Fox-Genovese and Eugene D. Genovese, *The Fruits of Merchant Capital:
Slavery and Bourgeois Property in the Rise and Expansion of Capitalism* (New York, 1983),
5, 7, 8; Norma Stoltz Chinchilla, "Interpreting Social Change in Guatemala: Modernization, Dependency, and Articulation of Modes of Production," in Ronald H. Chilcote and
Dale L. Johnson (eds.), *Theories of Development* (Beverly Hills, 1983), 160–61.

pre-emancipation period. The methodological difficulties associated until recently with the problem of reconstructing the history of disfranchised masses does not entirely explain this persistent focus.

The source of the bias can be located in the European tradition of Caribbean historiography, which began in the sixteenth century. The original European historians concerned themselves with the islands as political and economic adjuncts to the developing mercantile empires. Geographic descriptions and analyses of island life remained auxiliary to colonialist objectives. These historians were writing not insular history but imperial history, and their efforts must be recognized as part of the imperialist enterprise.[2]

Between 1776 and 1803, England and France struggled unsuccessfully with their respective colonies in North America and Saint-Domingue in an effort to keep their empires in the Western Hemisphere lucrative. Their failures contributed heavily to their decision to abolish the slave trade in their own realms and make it difficult for other nations to pursue it. The high cost of plantation production in the islands, the development of new tropical commodity areas in the colonized regions of Africa and Asia, and the growth of a European beet sugar industry assisted the devaluation of the Caribbean. Once gems in the crowns of imperial rulers, the islands rapidly became financial liabilities, more valuable as strategic bases and commercial entrepôts than as producers of agricultural wealth.

Nineteenth-century historiography reflected this change. The status of newly emancipated blacks was problematic in a society that had been consciously organized around their exploitation. "There are no people there," James Anthony Froude wrote of the West Indies, "in the true sense of the word, with a character and purpose of their own, unless to some extent in Cuba." With the islands' largesse exhausted, "there is nothing to fall back on."[3] Nostalgia for a supposedly idyllic plantation past abetted the attempts to squeeze more profit out of the islands.

Even before emancipation, a peasant sector developed in Caribbean economies that provided an alternative to plantation exploitation. Pro-slavery advocates generally condemned this development. Haiti's rich peasant culture and society incurred substantial criticism from conservatives. In 1828, James Franklin wrote that the Black Republic ex-

2. See the general discussions in Eric Williams, *British Historians and the West Indies* (London, 1966); Elsa Goveia, *A Study on the Historiography of the British West Indies to the End of the Nineteenth Century* (Mexico City, 1956); and Gordon K. Lewis, *Main Currents in Caribbean Thought* (Baltimore, 1983), 103–16.

3. James Anthony Froude, *The English in the West Indies* (London, 1888), 183.

emplified the problems attendant on slave emancipation without "moral and religious" preparation. The collapse of chattel slavery in Haiti proved that colonial agriculture and free labor were incompatible.[4] The nineteenth-century myths of progress and amelioration through benevolent colonial tutelage were marshaled in defense of a continued economic and social discrimination against the freedmen. Talk of retrogression masked deeper fears of the consequences of black progress. It is against this background that the diatribes of the late colonial era against black self-rule in the Caribbean must be read.

Haiti served as the example to avoid for both independent republics and colonies faced with the problem of absorbing freedmen. Aside from the immediate political concerns of maintaining the regional status quo, a general racism prescribed a negative attitude toward Haiti and its history. By 1900, racism had come to characterize European contact with non-European peoples. It proved a useful tool in the colonizing mission in Africa and Asia and offered simultaneously a handy explanation for Haiti's difficulties and a rationale for dismissing the republic as an unworthy member of the community of nations.

As might be expected, the Haitians perceived history differently. The Europeans' bloodthirsty slaves and tyrannical despots were their heroes and martyrs. More important, history played a sustained ideological role in the articulation and defense of a Haitian nationality. Gordon K. Lewis writes the following of the nineteenth-century Haitian pamphlet literature.

> It portrays Haiti as a symbol of black dignity and power in a world dominated by the white European nations. Hitherto, the world has thought in terms of white civilization. Now Haiti reveals a black civilization. Colombel tells his fellow Haitians that they are the *regénérateurs de l'Afrique* and that their struggle holds out hope for two-thirds of the human race. Chanlatte dares to believe that the whole colonial edifice is now in ruins and that the nineteenth century will be witness to the liberation of men of all races throughout the world. . . . In all of this, blacks are seen as co-equals with whites and others. Even more, there is presented a theory of citizenship in which all Haitians and Haitian residents are seen . . . as *noirs*; so that in that sense, as Nicholls points out, the word *noir* is used for the first time in an ideological and not a racial sense.[5]

---

4. James Franklin, *The Present State of Hayti* (1828; rpr. Westport, Conn., 1970), 409.
5. Lewis, *Main Currents in Caribbean Thought*, 254.

Haitian and metropolitan historiographies conflicted sharply, but iron-ically they both isolated Haiti from the Western intellectual mainstream and from popular thought. The metropolitan version created a Haiti invulnerable to the modernizing influences of peaceful international con-tacts. In this view, only a determined imperialism could move Haiti out of its rigidity and traditionalism. The Haitian version fed into the global current of black nationalist and Pan-African thought, an underground expression during this colonial age. It became part of the vast canon of tales untold, facts suppressed, truths finally revealed—a literature care-fully preserved and hungrily perused only by the oppressed peoples and denied legitimacy by the dominant academy.[6]

The comparative historiographies of Haitians on one hand and Euro-peans and North Americans on the other demonstrate another dimension of the inequality of the states in question. Ultimately the European and American version prevailed, not because it was sound, but because the metropolitan powers could convince with economic and military force. The Haitian version was necessarily antagonistic to the racist premises on which the European and American perception of Haitian reality was based.

The Haitians' image of themselves as revealed in their writing of history required that Haiti's fin de siècle disarray be explained in terms that honored the Haitian past, a task that few aside from Haitians would perform. The reason transcended questions of race per se and was closely linked to the legitimation of the Haitian experience in more existential terms. "Every society possesses a philosophy of history," J. G. A. Pocock has written, "a set of ideas about what happens, what can be known and what is done, in time considered as a dimension of society—which is intimately a part of its consciousness and its functioning. How these images and ideas of time arise, function and develop may be studied as part of the science of society." As an instrument in the hands of the intelligentsia, history could articulate this philosophy, but it also exposed the divided loyalties of cosmopolites, who, like their metropolitan models and mentors, had great difficulty fully accepting the legitimacy of the Haitian identity.[7]

    6. Cedric J. Robinson, "Coming to Terms: The Third World and the Dialectic of Imper-ialism," Race and Class, XXII (1981), 363–85; Cedric J. Robinson, Black Marxism: The Making of the Black Radical Tradition (London, 1983), 98–106.
    7. David Nicholls, From Dessalines to Duvalier: Race, Colour and National Indepen-dence in Haiti (Cambridge, England, 1979), 92–94; Robinson, "Coming to Terms," 366–68, 374–81; J. G. A. Pocock, Politics, Language and Time: Essays on Political Thought and

Western writers were more at ease with the liberties afforded them by the travel literature genre. Haiti had long been the subject of lurid tales of voodoo rites, bizarre crimes, and capricious customs, none of which the writers of these narratives witnessed. This sensationalism originated in the early nineteenth century, but Americans and Europeans had hardly modified their disparaging tone by 1900 and continued to harp on the themes of black eccentricity and misrule. Books by Protestant missionaries also depicted a Haiti teetering on the edge of perdition, led to the brink by the theological errors and Machiavellianism of Roman priests and pushed out over the abyss by voodoo demons.[8]

A significant characteristic of travel accounts about Haiti was the endless repetition by one author after another of a durable repertory of myths, legends, and simple gossip, which through constant use took on the patina of truth. Most of the stories originated as idle chatter among urban cosmopolites. Passed on to visitors as verities pronounced by seasoned veterans, the tales, which prominently featured voodoo, entered the canon of geographic and political lore. Dispersed throughout this anthology are reports of cannibals who kidnapped, sacrificed, and feasted on young children. Supposedly descended from a savage African tribe, the Mondongue, they allegedly persisted in their habits well into the modern era and remained a shadowy presence in the world of Afro-Christian cults. There is passing reference to them during the colonial period. After independence, when ostensibly the restraints imposed by the French were removed, accounts of the sacrifice of "the goat without horns" proliferate in the historical literature and travelogues.[9]

Spenser St. John devoted two chapters of his *Hayti, or the Black Republic* to voodoo and cannibalism, in which anthropophagy is not confined to ritual purposes but involves the exhumation of corpses and salting

---

History (New York, 1971), 233; Michel-Rolph Trouillot, *Nation, State, and Society in Haiti, 1804–1984* (Washington, D.C., 1985), 6.

8. Hesketh Prichard, *Where Black Rules White* (New York, 1900); Harry Johnston, *The Negro in the New World* (New York, 1910); Harry A. Franck, *Roaming Through the West Indies* (New York, 1920); Mark Baker Bird, *The Black Man, or Haytian Independence* (1869; rpr. Freeport, N.Y., 1971); W. F. Jordan, *Crusading in the West Indies* (New York, 1922); Nicholls, *From Dessalines to Duvalier*, 118.

9. M. L. E. Moreau de Saint-Méry, *Description topographique, physique, civile, politique et historique de la partie française de l'Ile de Saint-Domingue* (Philadelphia, 1797); M. E. Descourtilz, *Voyage d'un naturaliste en Haïti, 1799–1803* (1809; rpr. Paris, 1935); Bird, *The Black Man*, 306.

of human flesh for culinary purposes.[10] St. John's documentation for these assertions rested largely on thirdhand information related by anonymous curés, journalists, and other foreign residents and on conversations with Auguste Elie, a former secretary of state for foreign affairs. In only two instances did St. John provide substantial support for accusations of cannibalism, which he was content to imply rather than prove. The extent to which human sacrifice and cannibalism existed as a cult practice in Haiti cannot be clearly ascertained. There is no reason to believe that they were anything but rare and generally deplored practices. The persistence and ubiquity of the legends is perhaps less important as measures of veracity than as indicators of their purveyors' state of mind. Plainly alienated from the Creole majority, foreigners and elite urbanites used these accounts to discharge fears and psychic tensions that rapidly accumulated in a society in which they remained outsiders.

St. John bequeathed his legacy of rumor and innuendo to subsequent generations of travel writers. James Anthony Froude echoed his claims, and Hesketh Prichard, writing in 1900, asserted that the practice of human sacrifice in turn-of-the-century Haiti was "beyond all question." Tales of anthropophagy were also taken as gospel by F. A. Ober, in his 1908 and 1928 guides to the West Indies, and by Amos Kidder Fiske, whose travel account appeared in 1911. By the 1930s, the legends had become further embroidered. William B. Seabrook's *Magic Island* has the daughter of a Haitian president ordering the heart torn out of a soldier's chest and bearing it away in a silver dish. Richard A. Loederer used a pseudonymous German in *Voodoo Fire in Haiti* to claim that cannibalism underlay the vengeful assassination attempt on the nineteenth-century Haitian president Nicholas Fabre Geffrard. This German, typically an "old coaster," relayed these stories to Loederer after dinner at a country club, as both men fortified themselves with Rhum Barbancourt.[11]

The fascination with the dark potentialities of voodoo, and particularly its orgiastic aspects, continued into the twentieth century and conditioned the moral atmosphere of such works as: Hesketh Prichard, *Where Black Rules White* (1900); Harry Johnston, *The Negro in the New World* (1910); Stephen Bonsal, *The American Mediterranean* (1913); Paul Re-

10. Spenser St. John, *Hayti, or the Black Republic* (London, 1884), 187–257. See J. N. Léger's refutation in *Haiti, Her History and Her Detractors* (New York, 1907).

11. St. John, *Hayti*, 93; F. A. Ober, *A Guide to the West Indies and Bermuda* (New York, 1908), 267–68; Amos Kidder Fisk, *The West Indies* (New York, 1911), 247; William B. Seabrook, *The Magic Island* (New York, 1929), 122–23; Richard A. Loederer, *Voodoo Fire in Haiti* (New York, 1935), 257, 263, 254–55.

boux, *Blancs et Noirs* (1919); Harry A. Franck, *Roaming Through the West Indies* (1920); W. F. Jordan, *Crusading in the West Indies* (1922); William B. Seabrook, *The Magic Island* (1929); Faustin Wirkus and Taney Dudley, *The White King of La Gonave* (1931); John H. Craige, *Black Bagdad* (1933) and *Cannibal Cousins* (1934); Richard A. Loederer, *Voodoo Fire in Haiti* (1935); Edna B. Taft, *A Puritan in Voodooland* (1938); J. Verschueren, *La République d'Haïti*, vol. 3 (1948); Robert Debs Heinl, Jr., and Nancy Gordon Heinl, *Written in Blood* (1978).[12] The picaresque and fantastic titles of many of these books, some of which are illustrated with drawings meant to evoke a sense of the bizarre, indicate their mutual kinship in a literature of condemnation.

Haitian writers constantly refuted work of this genre. Their forays into historiography were extremely effective, but for several reasons they failed to reverse the tide of international opinion concerning their politics and society. In writing history, Haitians drew for moral support on the irrefutable success of their revolution and the confidence that they derived from national sovereignty, no matter how politically fragile their state might be. However, qualitative assessments of internal conditions were another matter.

Haitian historical evolution had formally circumscribed foreigners' contacts with insular society. To a considerable degree, Haitians had remained oblivious and indifferent to international opinion. They sometimes sought French publishers for their texts, but the vast majority of Haitian books were published in Port-au-Prince for domestic consumption. The novels, poetry, histories, polemical tracts, social science texts, journals, biographies, memoirs and eulogies, ably cataloged in the Bissainthe and Laguerre bibliographies, span more than two hundred years of literary history. Unlike much contemporary Third World literature, the Haitian *oeuvre* was traditionally directed inward, and polemics and apologetics also focused on a home constituency. Such works as Edmond Paul's *Les Causes de Nos Malheurs* (1882) clearly aimed to explain Haiti

12. Prichard, *Where Black Rules White*; Johnston, *The Negro in the New World*; Stephen Bonsal, *The American Mediterranean* (New York, 1913); Paul Reboux, *Blancs et Noirs* (Paris, 1919); Franck, *Roaming Through the West Indies*; Jordan, *Crusading in the West Indies*; Seabrook, *The Magic Island*; Faustin Wirkus and Taney Dudley, *The White King of La Gonave* (New York, 1931); John H. Craige, *Black Bagdad* (New York, 1933); Craige, *Cannibal Cousins* (New York, 1934); Loederer, *Voodoo Fire in Haiti*; Edna B. Taft, *A Puritan in Voodooland* (Philadelphia, 1938); J. Verschueren, *La République d'Haïti* (3 vols.; Paris and Wetteren, Belgium, 1948); Robert Debs Heinl, Jr., and Nancy Gordon Heinl, *Written in Blood: The Story of the Haitian People, 1492–1971* (Boston, 1978).

to Haitians.[13] Only with the advent of the twentieth century did Haitians begin to examine themselves in relation to others.

The Haitian response to Western travel literature did not, even after 1900, always address metropolitan opinion, and when it did, short-term, pragmatic considerations were frequently involved. J. N. Léger, in the bilingually published *Haiti, Her History and Her Detractors* (1907), meant to neutralize Western hostility to President Nord Alexis's repressive rule after strong criticism had appeared in the North American press. Anténor Firmin's *M. Roosevelt, Président des Etats-Unis et la République d'Haïti* (1905) had been intended to demonstrate Firmin's worth as a Haitian presidential candidate and to communicate his admiration for Roosevelt and the United States' Caribbean policies.[14]

Aside from its preoccupation with voodoo, Western travel literature espoused the political conviction that Haiti was locked into a downward trajectory of racial, social, and political degeneration. Like a fallen angel plummeting through space, Haiti in these accounts never seems to hit rock bottom. In 1889, a former British consul to Haiti, Spenser St. John, warned in his *Hayti, or the Black Republic* that "the coloured element, which is the civilising element in Hayti, is daily becoming of less importance." He saw prospects for progress ending in mulatto genetic diffusion through intermarriage with darker people. His gloom was deepened by his belief that "in spite of all the civilising elements around the Haytians, there is a distinct tendency to sink into the state of an African tribe." To this Englishman, nurture had done battle with nature and had lost. In an article suggestively entitled "The Passing of the Black Republics," the London correspondent of *Harper's Weekly* assured readers that the independence of Haiti and the Dominican Republic were doomed. The advent of the Panama Canal spelled the end of caudillismo and maladministration. He compared the Haitians to the Boers in their reluctance to open their country to foreign exploitation.[15]

Archibald R. Colquhoun, a geographer and confidant of the American secretary of state John Hay, was more pessimistic than most on the eternal inferiority to which West Indians in general had been condemned

13. Max Bissainthe, *Dictionnaire de la bibliographie haïtienne* (Washington, D.C., 1951); Michel S. Laguerre, *The Complete Haitiana* (Millwood, N.Y., 1982); Edmond Paul, *Les Causes de Nos Malheurs* (Kingston, Jamaica, 1882).

14. Léger, *Haïti*; Anténor Firmin, *M. Roosevelt, Président des Etats-Unis et la République d'Haïti* (New York, 1905).

15. St. John, *Hayti*, ix; Sydney Brooks, "The Passing of the Black Republics," *Harper's Weekly*, May 16, 1908, p. 20.

by nature. "On northern soil," he wrote in *Greater America*, "man is sufficiently master of his fate to break through the bonds woven for him and make a new world for himself, but in the West Indies he must remain forever a slave, not only to his weaker self, but doomed to toil forever, to roll back the stone which his fathers, in ignorant passion, threw down."[16]

For Haitians, the Western belief in a Haitian spiral of degeneration had immediate and alarming implications. Fear of foreign intervention remained justifiably strong. The Haitians' understanding of the role of the press and other publicists in generating opinion and influencing policy decisions made them uneasy.[17]

In general, Haiti lacked the resources to make a sustained response to Western propaganda. By 1900, the United States and western Europe had moved into an age in which technology accelerated access to information while simultaneously empowering those who could employ the innovations. As a consequence, news about Haiti could readily be adapted to particular tastes and prejudices and rapidly disseminated. Lacking the necessary tools to effectively counter unfavorable perceptions of their country abroad, Haitians responded only sporadically. The increasingly unequal exchange between Haiti and the West was not limited to commerce but also made its impact felt in the world of communications and the transfer of cultural information.

The press, more than any other informational resource, based Haitian reportage on the dubious assumption that the Black Republic was about to collapse. Sensational crisis reporting sold newspapers; it also provided opportunities to deplore unrest in unstable countries and to call for disciplinary action on the part of the great powers. Major newspapers sent correspondents to the Caribbean who recirculated old saws but also sometimes gained access to genuine information that interested Foreign Offices. The big metropolitan dailies spent generously for useful news items, and Western reporters in Haiti enjoyed prestige far beyond their status at home.[18]

It is clear that the press executed an important function in shaping

16. Archibald R. Colquhoun, *Greater America* (New York and London, 1904), 179.

17. *Le Nouvelliste*, December 12, 1908, p. 1, and December 14, 1908, p. 3.

18. See, for example, New York *Times*, September 13, 1902, p. 3; Brooks, "The Passing of the Black Republics," 20; "M" to Pierre Carteron, October 30, 1908, QDO, Vol. 8; Captain Potts to Secretary of the Navy, March 26, 1908, NR; Carteron to Minister of Foreign Affairs, February 19, 1908, and Victor Montasse to Carteron, June 20, 1908, QDO, Vol. 2.

public opinion in the advanced countries. Policy makers had realized this by the turn of the century and were already making their own sophisticated use of journalists and publicists. The press could be mustered into service not only in defense of individual policies but also in support of general policy overviews. Aside from disseminating factual information, the international news agencies promoted a particular nation's policies and outlook on current affairs. Reuters did this in Britain, and Havas in France. Under the chancellorship of Prince Bernhard von Bülow in Germany, the German Foreign Office developed its Pressebureau in an attempt to rival the news services of other European countries.[19]

As has been noted, Haitian intellectuals, like others in Latin America, were debating the respective merits of Latin and Anglo-Saxon (or Teutonic) mental training as part of their search for development strategies. The position chosen often reflected a bias regarding particular countries. Fully aware of the debate, metropolitan nations made conscious use of cultural media to project favorable images of themselves. In Haiti, the American, French, and German viewpoints were associated with specific schools, charities, and newspapers, foreign and domestic.[20]

During the Nord Alexis administration (1902–1909), a regime strongly identified as pro-American, Anglo-Saxonism enjoyed increased respectability as an intellectual template for future Haitian progress. A particular foreign newspaper was associated with this: the New York *Herald*. The *Herald*'s Haitian coverage was detailed and well disposed to the regime. It had broken with the stereotypical perspective on Haiti as a country in need of white control and depicted Nord Alexis as a wise leader valiantly struggling to contain the forces of political dissolution. At the same time, the *Herald* sacrificed none of its yellow journalistic style. "It has been said that good journalism consists in 'knowing where Hades is going to break loose,'" the newspaper editorialized, "'and having a man on the spot.'"[21]

The *Herald*'s interest in Haiti supposedly stemmed from a Caribbean

19. Paul Gordon Lauren, *Diplomats and Bureaucrats: The First Institutional Responses to Twentieth Century Diplomacy in France and Germany* (Stanford, Calif., 1976), 180, 185–86, 197; Emily S. Rosenberg, *Spreading the American Dream* (New York, 1982), 35–37.

20. Nicholls, *From Dessalines to Duvalier*, 137–38; Léon Audain, *Le Mal d'Haïti, ses causes et son traitement* (Port-au-Prince, 1908), 111, 112–13; J. B. Moore, Memorandum, December 27, 1913, DF, 711.38/15; Leslie F. Manigat, *L'Amérique Latine au XXᵉ Siècle, 1889–1929* (Paris, 1973), 78–83.

21. *Le Nouvelliste*, December 12, 1908, p. 1; New York *Herald*, March 17, 1908, p. 10.

cruise taken by its publisher, James Gordon Bennett, in his private yacht during the spring of 1907. Bennett met some prominent Haitians, liked them, and admired the beauty of the island. He dispatched a correspondent to Port-au-Prince with orders to write favorably about Haiti. Winning the sympathetic interest of Bennett was a coup for the Nord Alexis administration. The *Herald* had declined somewhat in the competitive American newspaper business, but it remained an important organ. Bennett, "one of the most romantic figures in American journalism," also owned the Paris edition of the *Herald* and the New York *Evening Telegram*. It was Bennett who had hired H. M. Stanley to search for Dr. Livingstone in the wilds of the Congo.[22]

A good press in America, the Haitian government reasoned, could forestall interventions by the great powers. It cultivated the *Herald* correspondent by ensuring that he was royally treated. Accorded privileged interviews, he occasionally upstaged accredited foreign diplomats by receiving favors that they were unable to obtain. The French grumbled about this, particularly since they saw the *Herald*'s position as part of an Anglo-American plan to promote Anglo-Saxonism. They were gratified, however, when the honeymoon period ended early in 1908.[23]

Blandishments could not entirely disguise the repressive nature of the Nord Alexis presidency. Once the *Herald* correspondent began to talk to unofficial sources—opposition leaders, European envoys—it became increasingly difficult for him to soft-pedal daily brutalities in Haiti. During 1908, the *Herald*'s reportage became tangibly less adulatory. By autumn of that year, its correspondent had lost favor with the regime and had been replaced. The *Herald* soon abandoned its sympathy for Haiti and rejoined the regular chorus of doomsaying American newspapers.[24]

U.S. officialdom did not involve itself in the *Herald*'s Haitian venture. The *Herald* had worked itself into a bind; if Haiti indeed possessed a model government, there should be no news to report. If the Haitian government was as bad as reputed, there was no need to alter the standard approach to it. Officials in Roosevelt's State Department viewed the *Her-*

---

22. Frédéric Marcelin, *Au Gré du Souvenir* (Paris, 1913), 168–76; Henry W. Furniss to Elihu Root, September 10, 1908, NF, 2126/297–98; *Dictionary of American Biography*, I, 199–204; New York *Times*, September 11, 1914, p. 9.

23. New York *Herald*, March 19, 1908, p. 3, and March 10, 1908, p. 3; Montasse to Carteron, June 20, 1908, QDO, Vol. 2.

24. Carteron to Ministry of Foreign Affairs, February 19, 1908, QDO, Vol. 2; "M" to Carteron, October 30, 1908, QDO, Vol. 8; Furniss to Root, September 10, 1908, NF, 2126/297–98.

ald episode impassively. A good press for Haiti would protect it from European interventionists and relieve the United States of immediate responsibility for it. A bad press would simply continue the status quo.

Haiti tried but failed to improve its reputation with journalists. The black American press was no more taken with the country than was its white counterpart. T. Thomas Fortune expressed a representative view in the *Voice of the Negro*. Condemning the parasitism of wealthy Haitians, he wrote sarcastically that former presidents, after looting the national treasury, went "usually to Paris,—where all Haytians go while they are living if they can, and where those who fail to do so in the flesh hope to do so when they die." Although some black Americans remained sympathetic, the general ambivalence of informed Afro-American opinion on the Haitian question could not have been reassuring to officials in Port-au-Prince, who realized that, in any event, the black community in the United States was too embattled to exercise much influence on Haiti's behalf.[25]

Unfavorable press coverage worried Haitian policy makers because it could be used to support an invasion. European intervention would be a matter of short-term gunboat diplomacy, a response to an immediate crisis in relations. European circumspection regarding the Monroe Doctrine made it unlikely that France, Britain, or Germany would attempt any lengthy occupation of the country. American journalism, more than any other, interested the Haitian government because of the greater possibility of preemptive action by the United States in a region that it had long regarded as legitimately part of its sphere of influence.

The Haitian official press ironically contains little documentation of an ongoing crisis in Haitian institutions. The remarkable continuity of the official organ, *Le Moniteur*, lends credence to the belief that while revolutions, palace coups, and other power struggles took place in Haiti, functionaries did the real work of running the government. Civil society had learned to accommodate the increasingly ephemeral transitions of executive power, which had become in every sense normal. As the rate at which these transitions occurred accelerated during the 1902–1915 period, how-

25. T. Thomas Fortune, "Haytian Revolutions," *Voice of the Negro*, I (April, 1904), 142, 140; Booker T. Washington to John S. Durham, April 10, 1905, and Washington's lecture, in Louis R. Harlan and Raymond W. Smock (eds.), *The Booker T. Washington Papers* (13 vols.; Urbana, 1979), VIII, 253–54, 458–59; T. G. Steward, "Life in a Negro Republic," *Independent*, LVI (1904), 477–79; *Le Moniteur*, February 3, 1904, p. 74; Moore, Memorandum, December 27, 1913, DF, 711.38/15.

ever, civil society became less capable of withstanding the repeated shocks.

Metropolitan responses to events in Haiti as registered by resident diplomats, Foreign Offices, the international press, and other ideological agencies reinforced the essentially racist and imperialist bent of policy makers and the foreign policy audience. News relayed by ministers and consuls in Haiti drew heavily on these officials' assumptions about race and nation. Most perceived Haiti as a hardship post offering few career opportunities. At best, it afforded a professional debut. The French turnover, for example, was high—three ministers in four years between 1903 and 1906. At worst, Haiti was a dumping ground for alcoholics and the noninfluential. The German minister Eugen von Zimmerer began his Haitian career after governing the dissolute Cameroons colony. British consul-generals openly detested Haiti and bluntly aired their dissatisfaction. The American ministers and consuls, black Republican political appointees, were among the few who did not despise their posts. American blacks had few foreign service opportunities, and heading the legation in Port-au-Prince or Monrovia was as much as they could hope for.[26]

The French mustered little enthusiasm for a higher profile in a sovereign nation over which they could exercise little direct authority. France accordingly maintained a caretaker legation in Port-au-Prince. The French sluggishness evinced in the Americas did not manifest itself elsewhere during these years. The first foreign ministry of Théophile Delcassé (1898–1905) placed France in the forefront of imperialist expansion. An avowed colonialist, Delcassé saw empire as a solution to the problem of overseas markets but looked to the Eastern Hemisphere. His desire to mediate in the Spanish-American War reflected not an interest in regaining power in the Americas but the fear that the United States, in its conflict with a weak Spain, might gain a foothold in the Mediterranean.[27]

26. G. Michahelles, "Im Kaiserlichen Dienste," Nachlasse Michahelles, MSS from Captured Documents from the German Foreign Ministry Archives (Microfilm ed., Washington, D.C., 1958), 87–88; British Consul General's Report on the Republic of Hayti, 1906, FO 371, Vol. 266; A. P. Murray to Secretary of State, July 31, 1908, FO 371, Vol. 468, and May 6, 1910, FO 371, Vol. 466; Petitioners to Lord Lansdowne, n.d., and attached note, February 2, 1905, FO 35, Vol. 183; Foreign Office Memorandum, April 18, 1904, FO 35, Vol. 181; Lucien Jerome to Foreign Secretary, September 15, 1905, FO 35, Vol. 182; Lamar Cecil, *The German Diplomatic Service, 1871–1914* (Princeton, 1976), 14.

27. C. M. Andrew, *Théophile Delcassé and the Making of the Entente Cordiale: A Reap-*

In the early 1900s, France made its greatest efforts to control the resources of underdeveloped areas on its own side of the Atlantic. The French Foreign Office and its official representatives in Port-au-Prince believed it more important to maintain the friendship of the United States than to attempt to establish an unquestioned political and economic hegemony in a country as marginal to their interests as Haiti. They accordingly identified a sphere of traditional concerns that they would strongly defend: collecting the debt, protecting the interests of French residents, preserving their share of that part of foreign trade that catered to the bourgeoisie, and cultivating Haitian Francophones for ideological purposes.[28]

The French consequently viewed the advances of other powers jealously. In 1909 the French chargé d'affaires in Port-au-Prince reported the progress made by the Germans in shipping and the import trade. He noted the newly proposed American railroad contracts. France, in contrast, had only a disorganized bank, monthly shipping connections with Haitian ports, and an overpriced cable service. France's position was not good, he lamented, and the bonds that connected the two countries were superficial.

> Despite the ties of tradition and of language which unite us to this country, despite all the beautiful phrases that have been written on one hand or another on this subject, I believe, indeed, that we have never had here, except for rare exceptions, truly sincere friendships. We have always been considered as former masters, that is, as enemies, and if until this day they have kept good relations with us, it is because Haitian products, notably coffee, sell more and better in France than anywhere else. Such is, in my view, . . . the real basis of our influence in Haiti.[29]

Some officials believed that the American diplomats in Haiti had a special relationship with their hosts because of racial affinity. The British staff felt that William Frank Powell, as a "mulatto," enjoyed more success with the Haitians than did the French and German ministers and had fewer claims to present.[30] In fact, the racial similarity of host and envoy

---

praisal of French Foreign Policy 1898–1905 (New York, 1968), xi, 26–27, 53, 80–81, 256.

28. Paul Desprez to Minister of Foreign Affairs, December 5, 1908, QDO, Vol. 3; Carteron to Minister of Foreign Affairs, August 24, 1908, QDO, Vol. 2; Frédéric Marcelin, Le Général Nord Alexis, 1905–1908 (3 vols.; Paris, 1909), I, 21.

29. E. Jore to Minister of Foreign Affairs, October 8, 1909, QDO, Vol. 22.

30. Foreign Office Memorandum, April 18, 1904, FO 35, Vol. 181; Jerome to Foreign Secretary, September 15, 1905, FO 35, Vol. 182.

did little to improve Haitian-American relations. J. N. Léger complained constantly about Powell, sometimes uncannily echoing the State Department's own criticisms. Haitians received mixed messages from Afro-Americans in general, many of whom harshly criticized political culture in the Black Republic.

Of all the powers represented in Haiti, only the United States seemed friendly to President Nord Alexis. American tolerance for him did not rest, as the British envoys wanted to believe, on the crafty manipulation of racial solidarity. The State Department had found a way to neutralize European ambitions by supporting a vocal but conservative nationalist. Haitian-American cohesion threatened to disintegrate whenever Haitians perceived a threat to their independence. Roosevelt and Elihu Root privately favored an interventionist Haitian policy but could not make it acceptable to Congress. They also thoroughly understood Haitian opposition to such a policy. In a letter to the journalist Albert Shaw, Root summarized his views.

> The Haitians are suspicious of us. They are densely ignorant and really believe that we want to gobble up their country, and we have to be very careful about volunteering any interference in their affairs lest we be met with an outcry of protest. Of course, they have some pretty good reasons for doubting the advantages of too close an association between the United States and a black man's government. I have been watching every move in Haiti for several years very closely in the hope that a situation would arise in which we could give that help in such a way as to establish the right sort of relations. We have done something in that direction, but for any positive step I think we must wait for the "psychological moment."[31]

Early in April, 1904, the U.S. Congress divided what had been the joint accreditation of the minister to Haiti and the Dominican Republic and appointed separate ministers to the two countries. The desire to improve intelligence on insular affairs, the chronic political violence on Española, and the dearth of adequate transportation between the republics influenced the lawmakers' decision. A black American army officer, Captain Charles Young, was added to the legation staff in Haiti as military attaché. No other legation in Haiti had such an official. The U.S. War Department later acknowledged the existence of contingency plans for an invasion of Haiti based on reconnaissance Young conducted. A visit by the assistant secretary of state to the Caribbean in late 1908 further reflected increased American concern about the region. This official would travel to Haiti

31. Philip C. Jessup, *Elihu Root* (2 vols.; New York, 1938), I, 555.

aboard the presidential yacht *Mayflower*. The choice of the *Mayflower* was ostensibly dictated by a shortage of navy vessels, but it subtly communicated Roosevelt's personal interest.[32]

Germany, a nation with few colonial outlets for trade and investment, cultivated underdeveloped, independent states in Asia, Africa, and Latin America. It extended its sphere of influence into areas where it met challenges from other metropolitan powers. In the Caribbean, the Reich realized that it could not successfully compete with the United States as a furnisher of staple commodities and concentrated instead on the development of shipping. It pursued a monopoly in the carrying trade with Haiti in 1901 but failed to secure the Haitian government's cooperation. Local officials had little desire to see Haitian commerce a virtual prisoner of the Hamburg America Line.[33]

Haiti was significant to Berlin as a component of a network of trade, investment, and political influence in the Western Hemisphere. The commerce of other European nations with Haiti, aside from the French in shipping, did not present major obstacles. Haiti's location near major Caribbean maritime routes and its political autonomy held out promising possibilities. It was therefore in the German interest to oppose any annexationist attempts on Haiti and to remain especially sensitive to the activities of the United States.[34]

The Haitians as a people did not impress the German envoys who were sent to live among them or the officials to whom the envoys reported. To Count Adolf von Götzen, special military envoy to Washington, Haitian officials were among the "half-civilized authorities" in the Caribbean who governed "states that are constantly in revolution." A German

---

32. *House Documents*, 58th Cong., 2nd Sess., No. 668, April 5–6, 1904, pp. 1–2; Captain Murdock to Secretary of the Navy, August 24, 1904, and Admiral Sigsbee to Secretary of the Navy, August 30, 1904, NR; Captain Barnardiston to Lord Fisher, August 29, 1904, FO 35, Vol. 181; Vansittart to Foreign Secretary, June 7, 1904, FO 35, Vol. 180; William F. Powell to John Hay, April 5, 1905, in U.S. Department of State, Dispatches from U.S. Ministers to Haiti, 1862–1906; J. N. Léger to Nord Alexis, March 14, 1907, in Eugène Maximilien Collection, Schomburg Research Center, NYPL; Consul Desportes, No. 282, July 27, 1908, QDO, Vol. 2; New York *Herald*, July 29, 1908, p. 3.

33. Vansittart to Foreign Secretary, March 1, 16, and June 15, 1905, all in FO 35, Vol. 182; Leslie F. Manigat, "La substitution de la prépondérance américaine à la prépondérance française en Haïti au début du XXᵉ siècle: la conjoncture de 1910–1911," *Revue d'histoire moderne et contemporaine*, XIV (1967), 336; Holger H. Herwig, *Politics of Frustration: The United States in German Naval Planning, 1889–1941* (Boston, 1976), 5, 9, 27, 30, 71.

34. Herwig, *Politics of Frustration*, 43ff., 70; Lamar Cecil, *Alfred Ballin: Business and Politics in Imperial Germany* (Princeton, 1967), 152–53.

presence was required in the area to protect national interests from their shifting "moods." For G. Michahelles, German minister resident from 1898 to 1900, the dirt, disease, and disorder in Haitian life offered proof that blacks were incapable of self-government. Zimmerer, minister from 1903 to 1911, let his contempt for Haitians be known in diplomatic circles. Haiti's most constant allies in the German community were the German and Germanized merchant-bankers; the official authorities reflected the general prejudice against blacks, and particularly independent blacks, then rife in cosmopolitan society.[35]

These biases may have contributed to several incidents of gunboat diplomacy involving the Imperial Navy from 1897 to 1911. In each instance, the infringements on Haitian sovereignty and consequent injury to sensibilities could have been avoided had more conventional means of conflict resolution been used. The German failure to be conciliatory incurred a long-term cost in the sacrifice of harmonious relations and in an enduring mistrust that characterized Haitian perceptions of Germany for many years.[36]

Germany demonstrated its capacity for aggression in Haitian waters when it felt that circumstances so warranted. The kaiser was contemptuous of the Monroe Doctrine and Roosevelt's amendment to it, but the Germans took high ground in pressuring the United States to make good its claim to be a referee in the Caribbean. Germany remained circumspect in matters in which aggressive action might pose a direct political challenge to the United States. One of these was a proposed Franco-German Panama Canal consortium, first broached in 1899 by the director of the Hamburg America Line and Admiral Alfred von Tirpitz. Even the kaiser viewed such an initiative as too bold, in view of Germany's inability to successfully confront the American navy. Similarly, Germany hedged at and finally rejected the offer of a coaling station in the Dominican Republic from President Ulysse Heureaux because its fleet was not yet large enough to permit it to so thoroughly antagonize the United States.[37]

35. Count Götzen, special military envoy to Washington, quoted in Herwig, *Politics of Frustration*, 70; Michahelles, "Im Kaiserlichen Dienste," 88; Anténor Firmin, *Diplomates et diplomatie* (Cape Haitian, 1899), 9–10; Furniss to Root, April 2, 1908, NF, 2126/235.

36. Michahelles, "Im Kaiserlichen Dienste," 82; *Le Soir*, December 6, 1899, clipping in Powell to Hay, December 7, 1899, CD; Desprez to Théophile Delcassé, March 2, 1903, QDO, Vol. 10; Powell to Hay, July 10, 1904, CD; Herwig, *Politics of Frustration*, 69.

37. Herwig, *Politics of Frustration*, 69, 71, 76; Count Hatzfeldt-Wildenburg to Robert Bacon, August 1, 1908, NF, 2126/289; Furniss to Root, April 2, 1908, NF, 2126/235; Cecil, *Albert Ballin*, 153; Michahelles, "Im Kaiserlichen Dienste," 80.

Germany, like France and the United States, jealously begrudged Haiti's independence. Only the lack of concert among the powers guaranteed the Black Republic's fragile autonomy.

Britain, as the colonial ruler of more than a million Caribbean blacks, had always taken a dim view of Haiti as a political entity, though it had enjoyed an extensive trade with Port-au-Prince since colonial times. British publicists and diplomats rhetorically condemned a nation with which their country's commerce was shrinking and to which they had no cultural affinity. The British generally bowed to the United States' leadership as far as Haitian affairs were concerned. Together, Anglo-American cultural media promoted Anglo-Saxonism, but the British encased it in so hard a racist and imperialist shell that it proved difficult for even the most ardent Haitian Anglophiles to swallow. Despite the anti-Americanism of British envoys in Port-au-Prince, Britain would have liked firmer American control of Haiti and did not believe that Anglo-Saxonism would benefit Haitians without colonialism.[38]

Of the four major powers that maintained ties with Haiti, Britain was the least important. Its trade volume had declined substantially. The British government raised its consulate in Haiti to a legation in 1913, but Britain's political priorities, cultural and racial prejudices, and decreased economic interests ensured that Anglo-Haitian relations would not improve substantially before World War I.[39]

The nature of metropolitan interest in Haiti distressed rather than pleased informed Haitians. Foreign energies could not be absorbed in investment, because aliens could neither own land nor directly invest in Haitian enterprises. More significantly, few expatriates expressed genuine interest in such options. Foreign ministries seemed more concerned with neutralizing potential rivals than moving forward with concrete plans to expand their influence in Haiti. Their attitude nourished certain long-standing characteristics of Haitian diplomacy, which became increasingly evident during this era.

One of these was to disappear in the smoke and thunder generated by disputes among the great powers. "What unfortunately appears to aid the Haytian Government in its hostile attitude," the British Foreign Office observed in 1904, "is the want of cohesion among the Foreign Represen-

38. Warren G. Kneer, *Great Britain and the Caribbean, 1901–1913: A Study in Anglo-American Relations* (East Lansing, 1975), 126–28; Froude, *The English in the West Indies*, 345; Prichard, *Where Black Rules White*, 284.

39. *Statesman's Yearbook, 1913* (London, 1913), 970; Kneer, *Great Britain and the Caribbean*, 119.

tatives." The French and Germans rarely agreed "while the American Legation is in the habit of holding aloof and transacting business in its own peculiar but certainly effective way." The Haitian government's margin of operation was the space left by metropoles holding each other in check.[40]

Other strategies could be resorted to when the powers unified or became adamant. Stratagems of various sorts—pretenses of ignorance, subterfuges, semantic difficulties, or legal technicalities—could be marshaled into service. The German minister Michahelles called bargaining with the Haitian government a war of nerves. Once, exasperated during a meeting with Haitian officials, he pointedly remarked that while Germany was a great power, Haiti was but a small state. "The Minister of Foreign Affairs only laughed," he recalled, "and told me: 'But we have the strength of our weakness.' "[41]

Haitian diplomacy also embraced more conventional approaches to foreign relations. Educated urbanites followed current events abroad with keen interest and kept abreast of changes in metropolitan policies. A representative opinion, expressed by Durinville Pierre in the Chamber of Deputies in 1902, cautioned the Haitian leadership to do nothing that would lead to annexation by the United States, since anti-imperialist and antiracist elements no longer controlled that republic's government.[42] Such admonitions were often taken by Haitian authorities as directives to ruthlessly repress dissent and to prevent the public from becoming aware of problems that might cause unfavorable comment. British Consul Murray interpreted this dourly in an annual report, maintaining that "the general foreign policy of Hayti in 1910 was confined to the usual attempt to keep up appearances and disguise the real state of the people, in order to continue to be treated as a civilised nation."[43] Haitian efforts to "keep up appearances" did not differ markedly from those of other nations. The major distinction lay in the lack of material resources at Haiti's disposal.

During the 1902–1915 period, one of the most important figures in Haitian diplomacy served in key government posts. Jacques Nicolas Léger was the son of an army officer and politician from Aux Cayes. Léger studied law in Paris while serving as the secretary of the Haitian legation from 1881 to 1885. A partisan of President Tirésias Simon Sam, he was

40. Foreign Office Memorandum, April 18, 1904, FO 35, Vol. 181; Vansittart to Foreign Secretary, July 3, 1904, FO 35, Vol. 180; Manigat, "Substitution," 322.

41. Michahelles, "Im Kaiserliche Dienste," 78.

42. *Le Moniteur*, June 27, 1903, p. 404.

43. A. P. Murray, Annual Report, December 16, 1910, FO 371, Vol. 915.

named minister to Washington in 1895 and remained there, serving Sam's successor, until 1909. Léger became foreign minister during the Cincinnatus Leconte regime, and was retained in that position by Presidents Tancrède Auguste and Oreste Zamor. He was a shrewd and gifted statesman and the author of La Politique extérieure d'Haïti (1886), which prescribed broad reform for diplomatic practice in Haiti. Léger deplored the excesses of arrogant consuls, the breaches of protocol, the exorbitant reclamations, and other abuses commonly practiced in the country. He called for drastic changes in domestic programs, which he felt should complement a rational foreign policy.[44]

Léger endorsed the creation of a professional foreign service and urged the Haitian government to improve its communications with envoys at their posts. Most important, he advocated a general policy review. Haiti should not rely on traditional associations, he believed. Much confidence had been placed in European allies, but the Europeans' mutual friendships were more important to them than good relations with Haiti. To Léger, the United States provided a better guarantee of Haitian independence than did the European powers, which in any event would consult the United States before agreeing to any proposals Haiti might make.[45]

Léger's views are important because of the central place he occupied during the 1902–1915 period and the influence he exerted during the Sam, Nord Alexis, Leconte, Auguste, and Zamor presidencies. His assigned task was to "manage" officials in Washington, but he brought to that charge a different perspective on the United States. Léger wanted a rapprochement with the Americans, though he realized that their past anti-imperialist stance in Caribbean affairs disguised ulterior motives.[46] His opinions were originally articulated before the Spanish-American War, during an era of relative American inactivity in the Caribbean. Subsequent events did not substantially change Léger's thinking, and he remained a strong pro-American voice.

For most Haitians, however, the United States' presence in the Caribbean remained a sword of Damocles, and continental Europeans saw it as a double-edged weapon poised against themselves. Content to allow the Americans to do the police work of intervention, they wanted to retain

44. Catts Pressoir, Ernest Trouillot, and Henock Trouillot, Historiographie d'Haïti (Mexico City, 1953), 275; Admiral Caperton, Testimony, in SI, 320; Alcius Charmant, Haïti, vivra-t-elle? (2nd ed.; Le Havre, 1905), 284; J. N. Léger, La Politique extérieure d'Haïti (Paris, 1886).

45. Léger, La Politique extérieure, 133–34, 136, 137, 144–45.

46. Ibid., 137.

rights to consultation and joint action. The United States government opposed such cooperation in what it regarded as its natural domain. The French and German surrender of hegemony was only provisional, for these powers continued to cultivate loyal followings in Haiti, which they hoped would resist American domination. The preservation of their commercial spheres in the island nation rested on continued visibility there.[47]

Visibility sometimes began with "showing the flag." Yet sporadic official visits and "fleet demonstrations" designed to cow recalcitrant Caribbean republics were not sufficient to guarantee the security of trade and facilitate the expansion of political influence in the area. This required a more sustained effort, first made when the U.S. Navy established a Caribbean Squadron within its North Atlantic Fleet in October, 1901. The purpose was to assist in the fulfillment of American treaty obligations to independent West Indian countries and help maintain law and order where unrest threatened the lives and property of American citizens. The official order of October 4, 1902, did not mention an isthmian canal, but the area under the squadron's jurisdiction included those Central American coasts where a canal would be built. The Caribbean Squadron gathered data on navigation in parts of the Caribbean Sea where limited American traffic had resulted in scant knowledge of local hydrographic and topographic features. The navy encouraged officers assigned to the squadron to learn regional languages and customs and pass on valuable commercial, military, and geographic information to their superiors.[48]

This naval initiative reflected renewed State Department interest in Caribbean affairs. The U.S. Navy was very active during this period, but always as an arm of the executive. It did not exercise independent authority in policy making, though communication problems gave individual commanders much freedom to make daily decisions in the field while undertaking assignments in troubled areas.[49]

The squadron planned naval visits to each country. In the summer of 1904 the USS *Denver* sailed to the sleepy port of Jérémie on Haiti's southwest peninsula to verify rumors of political unrest there. The reports proved unfounded, but the ship commander claimed his visit illus-

47. *Le Moniteur*, September 8, 1909, p. 526; André Georges Adam, *Une crise haïtienne, 1867–1869: Sylvain Salnave* (Port-au-Prince, 1982), 209.

48. William Moody to Commander of North Atlantic Station, October 4, 1902, NR.

49. Richard D. Challener, *Admirals, Generals, and American Foreign Policy, 1898–1914* (Princeton, 1973), 45–66; Peter Karsten, *The Naval Aristocracy* (New York, 1972), 172–74.

trated "the certainty with which any outbreak would be investigated." American ships cruised Haitian waters extensively during the months of June, July, and August. The United States moreover appointed a military attaché to the American legation in Haiti. The British consul surmised that the selection of Captain Charles Young, a black officer, while flattering to Haiti, "probably has an ulterior object." It meant that the United States would watch events on the island more closely. Port-au-Prince considered Young's appointment an extremely grave matter and cause for a military revitalization. The defensive buildup could not ward off the Americans; suppressing domestic dissidence was its sole purpose. If the state could contain domestic unrest, no interference from the United States would be forthcoming.[50]

Haitian waters constituted one of the regions about which the United States government lacked geographic intelligence, and the U.S. Navy initiated a project in November, 1903, to fix the positions of the principal characteristics of the north coast of Española. Significantly, the plan coincided exactly with Theodore Roosevelt's efforts to assist the Panamanian Revolution and negotiate an isthmian canal treaty. Española was of special interest to the navy, for the sea lanes through the Windward Passage directed Canal traffic past the northern shores of Haiti and the Dominican Republic. Seizure of Española by a European power would seriously compromise Canal security. The navy considered keeping a permanent warship nearby.[51]

Early in 1903 the Office of Naval Intelligence sent two officers disguised as journalists to report on conditions on the northern border between Haiti and the Dominican Republic. Navy officials regarded the bay area between Fort Liberté and Monte Cristi as especially strategic, since the power that controlled it would dominate the entire island. The General Board of the Navy insisted that the United States prevent the military use of this zone by any other major power and recommended that Fort Liberté be considered as a future base site.[52]

The navy's concern indicated that the Americans did not remain unchallenged in the Caribbean. The German government had never accepted U.S. claims to regional hegemony. The Reich's naval attaché in Wash-

50. Murdock to Secretary of the Navy, August 24, 1904, and Sigsbee to Secretary of the Navy, August 30, 1904, NR; Vansittart to Lansdowne, June 7, 1904, FO 35, Vol. 180; Nord Alexis to Léger, May 26, 1904, in Eugène Maximilien Collection.
51. Léger to Secretary of State, November 12, 1903, in Records of the Department of State, Notes from the Haitian Legation in the United States, NA.
52. Memorandum of Office of the General Board, Navy Department, May 6, 1903, NR.

ington, Hubert von Rebeur-Paschwitz, noting that the United States had made itself a "referee" in Latin American affairs, anticipated an eventual clash over dominance in the area. Kaiser Wilhelm, a notorious scoffer at the Monroe Doctrine, did not plan to defer to American claims of preeminence.[53]

During the winter of 1901–1902, German Admiral Otto von Diederichs requested studies of the military geography of the West Indies. These continued through the next two years and included discussions of American policy and the U.S. Navy, as well as possible bases on selected islands. The Imperial Navy's interest in the Caribbean had originated in gunboat diplomacy. By the turn of the century, however, rivalry with the United States played a far greater role in German activity. The Admiralty even drafted contingency plans for a naval assault on the American mainland and the seizure of Puerto Rico.[54]

Germany badly wanted a Caribbean base, which would give it some control over and access to the proposed isthmian canal. After 1898, it focused on Curaçao and St. Thomas. Realizing the speed with which the United States was pursuing the development of an isthmian project, German naval officers urged their own government to stake its claim. It would have to acquire a base without clashing with the heavily armed United States, now patrolling Spain's former colonies. Theodore Roosevelt had, in his own words, already "succeeded in impressing on the Kaiser, quietly and unofficially, and with equal courtesy and emphasis, that the violation of the Monroe Doctrine by territorial aggrandizement on his part in the Caribbean meant war, not ultimately, but immediately, and without any delay." The Reich surreptitiously secured commercial and naval rights in the Danish Virgin Islands. According to the arrangement, the director of the Hamburg America Line, Albert Ballin, obtained land on St. Thomas that would later be transferred to the German state. The American consul on St. Thomas, ordered to make periodic reports on German fleet movements, noted that Germany had free run of the islands. "Her squadron comes here and stops as long as it pleases and the officers and men are almost idolized by the Danish authorities here."[55]

German power in the Caribbean was exaggerated by publicists who

53. Herwig, *Politics of Frustration*, 71, 69, 76.

54. *Ibid.*, 43, 66.

55. Theodore Roosevelt to Cecil Spring-Rice, November 1, 1905, in Elting E. Morison, ed., *The Letters of Theodore Roosevelt* (8 vols.; Cambridge, Mass., 1952), V, 65; Cecil, *Albert Ballin*, 152–53; Herwig, *Politics of Frustration*, 70, 26, 27, 71; Christopher Payne to Francis Loomis, Enclosure, October 27, 1903, and Payne to Assistant Secretary of State

were impressed by the vigorous discipline the German navy displayed. In reality, the small size of the Reich's fleet hampered Germany's efforts at naval expansion in the region. Germany postponed the expected day of conflict with the Americans until a bigger navy could be developed. It meanwhile hastened to improve relations with Haiti, whose territory might later be needed. The German government began mending its bridges with the Haitian government in the early months of the Nord Alexis administration and sent several German celebrities and dignitaries to visit Haiti in February, 1903, when the German community staged an elaborate celebration of the kaiser's birthday.[56] Germany had opposed the Firminists, political enemies of Nord Alexis, in their failed attempt to seize power the previous year. German identification with anti-Firminism undoubtedly facilitated the Reich's rapprochement with the Nord Alexis administration. Germany perceived Anténor Firmin's reform movement as a hindrance to burgeoning German aspirations to power in the Caribbean. A rationally managed Haiti did not necessarily suit German planners, who sought to use their knowledge of current business and political practices in the republic to their own advantage. German settlers had arrived in the Americas by the hundreds of thousands in the 1880s and 1890s. In most cases, Germany benefited only indirectly from their presence. This was especially true of the German immigrants in the United States, which had nearly three million residents of German descent in the 1890s. In Haiti, on the other hand, national identity would not rapidly diffuse, and German loyalties could be counted on. Empire, formal or informal, continued to be the only answer to Germany's need for growth and development. "The question is not if we want to colonize," Chancellor Bernhard von Bülow remarked in 1904, "but that we must colonize whether we want to or not." Bülow considered colonization no less than the "struggle for one's survival."[57]

The German navy and merchant marine developed rapidly in the 1900s. The Hamburg America Line acquired the British-owned Atlas Steamship Company in 1901 and took over more of the West Indian carrying trade. By 1905 the Hamburg America Line had purchased corpo-

---

Peirce, February 4, 1904, in Records of the Department of State, Dispatches from U.S. Consuls in St. Thomas, NA.

56. Herwig, *Politics of Frustration*, 34; Desprez to Delcassé, March 2, 1903, QDO, Vol. 10.

57. Herwig, *Politics of Frustration*, 5, 7.

rate headquarters in Manhattan's financial district. German merchants now penetrated the British West Indies, where they competed with veteran British traders and established large residential settlements in Jamaica and Trinidad.[58]

Naval proliferation was also a product of German expansion. By 1907 the Imperial Navy outstripped that of the United States in the battleship and cruiser categories. The U.S. Caribbean Squadron found itself matched by Germany's Atlantic American Squadron, similarly charged with the surveillance and policing of tropical American waters. Despite rapid growth, the German navy ultimately failed to earn the Reich a firm foothold in the Western Hemisphere. The Anglo-French Entente Cordiale and Germany's isolation in Europe made the likelihood that Germans could successfully challenge the United States' hegemony in the Caribbean increasingly remote. From 1904 to 1906, Germany focused on creating a bloc of anti-British states in Europe but only consolidated the often ephemeral friendship of two of its most powerful rivals, France and Britain.[59]

The German and American naval buildup in the Caribbean contrasted with the steady withdrawal of Britain and France. The British navy, under the leadership of First Sea Lord John Fisher (1904–1910), sharply reduced its regional presence. Fisher's top priority was to defend Britain against possible German aggression. He accordingly deployed British sea power in the Mediterranean and the North Sea and left to the United States the task of defending British interests in the independent Caribbean republics and challenging rising German ambitions. The Hay-Pauncefote treaty, which acknowledged American supremacy in the construction and management of an isthmian canal, underscored Britain's increasing acceptance of a Pax Americana.[60]

France had declined considerably as a naval power by 1902, ranking third in Europe, behind Britain and Germany. Its small ships had limited value in modern warfare, and a sluggish construction industry retarded its sporadic efforts to bridge the maritime gap. Even the French Admiralty expressed disdain for the fleet. France's armored cruisers handled badly and guzzled fuel. Heterogeneous ordnance of doubtful quality further contributed to French naval problems. Finally, frequent changes at the

58. New York *Times,* May 14, 1901, p. 8, and October 29, 1905, Sec. 5, p. 18; London *Times,* November 12, 1918, p. 4.

59. Herwig, *Politics of Frustration,* 82, 83, 90–91.

60. Kneer, *Great Britain and the Caribbean,* 100, ix–x, 170.

ministerial level and a consequently erratic policy undermined the navy.[61]

France increasingly concentrated its naval strength in the Mediterranean as part of an arrangement with Britain whereby the latter would guard the northern coasts of France in exchange for a larger French presence in southern Europe, where Britain also had interests. The two powers put the smaller fleet where it could most advantageously repel German, Italian, or Russian aggression. After 1909 a renewed construction program under the vigorous leadership of Minister of the Marine Boué de Lapeyrère (1909–1911) somewhat improved the quality of the French navy, which continued to be most visible in the Mediterranean. It did little in the Caribbean, where the French Foreign Office mandated cooperation with local German interests in the independent republics.[62]

Weakened commercial power accompanied the naval reduction. The price of coffee fell sharply between 1895 and 1899, when many French residents left Haiti for Madagascar and other more promising territories. "French commerce has almost entirely abandoned this market," the French minister reported in 1900. The French Antilles and the continental colony of Guyane experienced the same slump. The continued price decline in sugar and the Mont Pelée volcanic disaster of 1902 stymied the resurgence of commerce in the French West Indies. Official lack of interest in the islands led to a prolonged period of drift marked by economic depression, caste and class conflict, and public corruption.[63]

Naval proliferation in the Caribbean gave impetus to political regimentation in Haiti. Port-au-Prince could not realistically expect to challenge the foreign presence, but it planned to obviate any military demonstrations by clamping down on dissent. Its dissatisfaction with the growing surveillance and patrol could only be expressed through polite remonstration, as when General Labissière asked the commander of a U.S. ship rather conspicuously named City of Washington to leave the port of

61. Arthur J. Marder, From the Dreadnought to Scapa Flow: The Royal Navy in the Fisher Era, 1904–1919 (5 vols.; London and New York, 1961), I, 118.

62. Ibid., 276, 288–98, 304–306.

63. French Minister in Haiti to Minister of Foreign Affairs, February 21, 1900, quoted in Benoit Joachim, Les racines du sous-développement en Haïti (Port-au-Prince, 1979), 214; Franck, Roaming Through the West Indies, 456–59; Stephen Roberts, History of French Colonial Policy (1870–1925) (London, 1929), 503, 506–508; Don R. Hoy, "Changing Agricultural Land Use on Guadeloupe, French West Indies," in Michael M. Horowitz (ed.), Peoples and Cultures of the Caribbean (Garden City, N.Y., 1971), 284–86.

Léogâne in 1908.[64] In any event, the political price of "showing the flag" of great powers in Haitian waters was ultimately paid by Haitian nationals.

As we have seen, conscious attempts to deploy the instruments of cultural, ideological, and political influence to the benefit of the respective powers accompanied commercial rivalries in Haiti. The objective was not solely to impress Haitians but also to dominate them and thoroughly absorb them as satellites into networks of relationships that encompassed the cultural and political as well as the economic. These arrangements held out to Haitians the possibility of a very limited partnership in a modernizing enterprise. The difficulty, of course, lay in the racial and political subjection to which they would consequently expose themselves. "Make no mistake," the legislator Durinville Pierre warned, "the Negro is truly a man only in Haiti."[65]

This concern transcended the self-interest of governing elites. Haiti had emerged as a historical refutation of slavery, racism, and imperialism. Its national identity and purpose hung on that fact and contradicted the Westernizing ambitions of reformers and adventurers alike. The failure of Haitian institutions to achieve complete coherence can be attributed to an inability to reconcile national development with the cultural surrender implicit in modernization. This was not simply a question of backwardness, bourgeois cynicism, or stubborn resistance to change. The temporal and spatial context in which the Haitian polity evolved and the limitations placed on it by historical circumstance prevented it, as they did most Latin American states, from following the lines of industrial development. Forced into economic dependence and bound to increasingly obsolete forms of commercial and social intercourse with the rest of the world, Haiti came to rely on a rigidly unvarying self-perception, which it then presented to the world in response to and in contrast to the full arsenal of ideological responses available to its adversaries.

The distinction between the interests of the small bourgeoisie, a class addressed in part in the preceding chapter, and the masses of Haitians blurs here. Whatever political tyrannies and economic deprivations the

64. General Labissière to Commander of the *City of Washington*, April 27, 1908, Léger to Secretary of State, March 30, 1905, Alvey Adee to Léger, April 3, 1905, all in NR; Léger to Secretary of State, November 12, 1903, and Léger to Adee, July 27, 1905, in Notes from the Haitian Legation.
65. *Le Moniteur*, June 27, 1903, p. 404.

populace suffered, the universal desire for independence was the one genuine consensus the country enjoyed. It was the only legitimating principle for the elite leadership. Given the realities of life for colonized blacks in the early twentieth century, it remained the indispensable foundation of all political and social discourse within the country. Consequently, progress could be discussed only in terms that did not impinge on national sovereignty, a state that involved specific cultural concomitants and commitments.

The rules of the game for Haiti were based on a denial of the very process of domination being rapidly imposed on the world by the imperialist powers. Haiti posed anti-imperialist and antiracist stances to the political, social, and economic systems of organization with which it was confronted. These responses proceeded from Haitians as a collectivity rather than from a single class, and the messages delivered to the metropoles in 1904 had been delivered in 1804. However, the potency of the communication had diffused as Western strategies had changed.

In the course of a century of national history, Haitian ideologues had prescribed the terms in which the Black Republic would meet the West. These did not change, but the internal demands for reform had multiplied considerably by the 1900s. The great contest, then, did not take place in the international arena, where Haitian policy had remained quite consistent for generations, but at home, where events would force the issue. Haiti could valiantly withstand modernizing pressures from without, tinged as everyone knew they were with subversive, ulterior motives. The question remained as to how the desire for change, internally generated, would fare confronted with traditional political forces and ideologies.

IV

Reform and Reaction

Chak noua gan mulat li, chak mulat gan noua li.

Each black has his mulatto, each mulatto has his black.

—Haitian proverb

H AITI IN 1902 had a government comprising a bicameral legislature, an independent judiciary, and a chief executive officer. In reality, the authoritarian president enforced his will through extraconstitutional means, which included stacking the legislature with placemen, buying off political opponents, and ruthlessly repressing citizens. A president was only as effective as his ability to control the opposition and serve powerful commercial and political interests. Any personal agenda had to complement business as usual.[1]

The commonly held idea of the civil service as a sinecure penetrated the highest offices. Government employees were irregularly paid and inefficient. Floods, fires, disease, filth, and general decay blighted city life. No public services existed in rural areas. Demoralized bureaucrats presided over shabby departments. Paid in scrip, junior civil servants had recourse to private merchant-bankers, who redeemed their receipts at 40 percent of face value. Liquidity problems as well as convention dictated this expedient. New administrations, saddled with the debts of their predecessors, were at the mercy of commodity price fluctuations. Private corruption further complicated the problem of civil service organization.[2] A significant part of state revenues flowed into maintenance of the large standing

---

1. Paul Deléage, *Haïti en 1886* (Paris, 1887), 163–64; T. Thomas Fortune, "Haytian Revolutions," *Voice of the Negro,* I (April, 1904), 140; Jacques C. Antoine, *Jean Price-Mars and Haiti* (Washington, D.C., 1981), 9.

2. Report of Secretary of State of the Interior and Police, in République d'Haïti, *Exposé Générale de la République d'Haïti, 1898* (Port-au-Prince, 1898), 38–43; William F. Powell to John Hay, March 3, 1899, CD; Eli K. Cole, Daily Diary Report, July 27, 1917, DF, 838.61351H33/4.

army, but the funds primarily benefited officers, as little was spent on recruits. Peasants aged fourteen to sixty-five were forced into military service. "In the mountain districts," according to one observer, "they are hunted like wild animals, and are driven into the cities like a drove of cattle with the legs tied together with rope." Haitian soldiers often went hungry and ragged and were commonly shot if caught trying to escape.[3]

A strong reforming impulse developed in response to the harsh realities of Haitian life. Firmin as a historical figure and Firminism as a political creed represented the culmination of this process. Firmin, a self-made man, emerged from the Cape Haitian working class in an era in which a nascent popular consciousness began to question the established social order. A gifted youth, Firmin was "promoted" into the lower-middle-class world of poorly paid clerks, teachers, and tutors whose marginal existence, bleak prospects, and grim dissatisfaction made them receptive to demands for change.[4] The timing of the Firminist revolt was particularly significant. Since the early 1890s, Haitians had been preparing for the centennial celebration of their national independence. Steeped in historical lore and imbued with an awareness of the continuity of tradition, many felt a sense of urgency as 1904 approached. Could Haiti make the necessary leap into modernity?

Firminism had ideological roots in the nineteenth-century writings of such pamphleteers as Demesvar Delorme and Edmond Paul. Firmin's agenda for change greatly resembled theirs. His Pan-Americanism and commitment to liberal capitalism were discussed earlier. His domestic program consisted of a reduction in the size of the army, a restructuring of civil bureaucracies, and a reappraisal of the importance of meritocracy in political life. Firmin advocated a lower interest rate, tax law reform, and the creation of reliable statistical data for fiscal use. He adamantly opposed the opportunistic use of foreign nationality and, as minister of foreign relations during the Hyppolite administration, had some fraudulent French naturalizations canceled. Firmin shared his region's customary distrust of Port-au-Prince, an area he considered a parasitic enclave that

---

3. New York, *Herald*, December 1, 1908, p. 4; Henry W. Furniss to Secretary of State, July 29, 1919, DF, 738.915/152; Powell to Hay, September 22, 1902, CD.

4. Léonce Viaud, *La Personnalité d'Anténor Firmin* (Port-au-Prince, 1948), 5; Castera Delienne, *Souvenirs d'épopée* (Port-au-Prince, 1935), 67; Joseph Jérémie, *Mémoires* (Port-au-Prince, 1950), 21.

leeched the resources of the country. For Firmin, the core of the Haitian potential lay in the larger, agriculturally rich North.[5]

President Tirésias Simon Sam (1896–1902) appointed Firmin minister to Paris in 1900, primarily to distance him from domestic politics. A death in the family brought Firmin back to Haiti just days before Sam's resignation on May 12, 1902. The resignation created a power vacuum, which the president planned to fill with a handpicked successor. He had already packed the Chamber of Deputies with relatives and clients. The legislature quickly convened, but Sam's opponents fired shots into the Chamber, breaking up the assembly. In the absence of duly constituted authority, prominent citizens of Port-au-Prince formed a committee of safety to ensure public order during the interregnum.[6]

The formation of committees of safety had become a political ritual. This one, like all others, consisted of Haitian representatives of the capital's business and political circles, who were primarily interested in the security of expensive residential and commercial properties in the city and its environs. The popular violence that could damage or destroy these holdings and trigger foreign intervention had to be contained. Committees of safety typically had a police arm in members who were honorific generals commanding private troops, which on such occasions were paid from public funds. These soldiers maintained order for the urban elite. Once a presidential successor had been chosen through armed conflict or political truce, the committee of safety would resign. Similar committees were formed in provincial cities.[7]

Three presidential aspirants, each with his own personal army, began to rally adherents as soon as Sam went into exile. The principal candidates were Calisthène Fouchard, a southerner with strong regional support; Pierre Sénèque, the son of a famous Liberal noted for his heroism in

5. Viaud, *La Personnalité d'Anténor Firmin*, 9–10, 11; B. Danache, *Choses vues: Récits et souvenirs* (Port-au-Prince, 1939), 22; Anténor Firmin, *Diplomates et diplomatie* (Cape Haitian, 1899), 33–34.

6. Jérémie, *Mémoires*, 21; French Minister to Minister of Foreign Affairs, October 7, 1904, QDO, Vol. 1; Danache, *Choses vues*, 17–19; Powell to Hay, January 26, May 24, 1902, CD; A. Cohen to Foreign Secretary, May 22, 1902, FO 35, Vol. 177.

7. Cohen to Foreign Secretary, May 22, 1902, FO 35, Vol. 177; Georges Corvington, *Port-au-Prince au Cours des Ans, La Métropole Haïtienne du XIXe Siècle* (5 vols.; Port-au-Prince, 1976), IV, 101; Roger Gaillard, "Firmin et les Etats-Unis à travers un document inédit," pt. 1, *Conjonction* (June, 1975), notes, 143–44, 150.

resisting President Salomon's repression of the bourgeoisie in the 1880s; and Anténor Firmin, sustained by intellectuals, "flaming youth" in the capital, and certain powerful northerners with their clients and armies. All these contenders were civilians, but as General Joseph Jérémie shrewdly noted, the generals who provided their military arm had no intention of risking their lives to put others in office without gaining substantial concessions.[8]

Northern Haiti appeared to present a united front around Firmin's candidacy. Nord Alexis, an experienced general in his eighties who had been the military commander of the departments of the North and the Northwest during the Sam administration, headed the Firminist army. Firmin also enjoyed the allegiance of General Jean-Jumeau, *délégué* of the Artibonite, and of Hammerton Killick, admiral of the Haitian navy. Firmin's brother-in-law, General Albert Salnave, commanded the *arrondissement* of Cape Haitian. Within three days of Sam's departure, Firmin's forces, split into several groups, began to march to the capital along alternate routes.[9]

Concerned about the looting and arson that might ensue should unruly peasant armies enter the city, businessmen closed their offices and shops. While military units controlled by local officers patrolled the deserted streets for the committee of safety, the united diplomatic corps sent Firmin and Nord Alexis polite telegrams that asked them to keep their troops out of the capital. The presence of the gunboats HMS *Psyche* and USS *Topeka*, in port to land marines in case of danger to foreign life and property, backed up the diplomats' request.[10]

Firmin and his supporters obligingly came unescorted to the capital, where an uneasy coalition of generals, politicians, and businessmen declared a provisional government on May 26. The chairman of the Port-au-Prince committee of safety, Adolphe Boisrond-Canal, was named president. Boisrond-Canal, an exemplar of the urban elite, had been president of the republic from 1876 to 1879. A headquarters was established in the Ministry of Foreign Relations. Presidential candidates could not be named to the provisional government, but men believed loyal to Firmin were

8. Jérémie, *Mémoires*, 21.

9. *Ibid.*, 14; Commander Patch, Report, September 30, 1902, NR; *Le Moniteur*, July 12, 1902, pp. 433–34; New York *Herald*, March 12, 1908, p. 3; Powell to Hay, May 24, 1902, CD; Anténor Firmin to Hay, May 24, 1908; Gaillard, "Firmin et les Etats-Unis," Pt. 1, notes, 148–52.

10. Powell to Hay, May 19, 1902, CD; Cohen to Foreign Secretary, May 22, 1902, FO 35, Vol. 177.

members. Nord Alexis was appointed minister of war and the navy, a concession that gave this ambitious and powerful man a considerable advantage should he decide to act on his long-cherished presidential aspirations. Relations between Firmin and Nord Alexis remained cordial for several days following the establishment of the provisional government, but the alliance rapidly deteriorated once they returned to Cape Haitian for the June legislative elections.[11]

On the surface, political management of the crisis had proceeded smoothly. The *Topeka* left Port-au-Prince on June 3, its commander satisfied that threats to public order had been successfully contained. The provisional government borrowed money to pay off the northern army and send it back to Cape Haitian. Nord Alexis followed these troops a week later. Once at home, he turned his attention to an open, armed assault on Firmin and Firminists. The election for deputy of Cape Haitian provided the background for bitter struggle. Nord Alexis's ostensible purpose as minister of war was to suppress rioting between factions. Instead, he used his military authority to harass his erstwhile ally, now an obstacle to his plans.[12]

Despite assistance from Admiral Killick and Generals Jean-Jumeau and Albert Salnave, the violence unleashed by Nord Alexis under the pretext of restoring order for the provisional government forced Firmin to leave Cape Haitian. The Haitian flagship *Crête-à-Pierrot* conveyed him to Gonaïves, which declared him its first deputy. Firminists in Port-au-Prince then hurried to Gonaïves to take up arms. The circumstances of Firmin's departure from the Cape—the destruction of his home, the imprisonment and execution of his followers—led to civil war. In the conflict that ensued, many Firminists lost their lives in bloody battles in the principal towns of the departments of the North, the Northwest, and the Artibonite.[13]

The absence of Firminists in Port-au-Prince permitted conservative forces to reassert themselves there. The militarists, businessmen, and politicians that the provisional government represented had little taste for Firmin's intended reforms. Nord Alexis's appointment as provisional

11. Cohen to Foreign Secretary, May 22, 1902, FO 35, Vol. 177; Powell to Hay, May 30, 1902, CD; Admiral Nickels to Secretary of the Navy, June 30, 1902, NR; Firmin to Hay, received May 24, 1905, in Gaillard, "Firmin et les Etats-Unis," Pt. 1. notes, 152–53.

12. Nickels to Secretary of the Navy, June 6, 1902, NR; Gaillard, "Firmin et Les Etats-Unis," Pt. 1, p. 162.

13. Gaillard, "Firmin et Les Etats-Unis," Pt. 1, pp. 154–64; Powell to Hay, June 30, 1902, and enclosure, CD; John A. Rogers to Secretary of the Navy, July 5, 1902, NR.

minister of war gave them a means of subjecting Firmin to their authority. They also realized that without adequate military support, Firmin could achieve nothing. Boisrond-Canal's courtship of Nord Alexis and his silence in the face of the latter's June attacks on Firmin indicated his willingness to see Firminism suppressed. The provisional president dismissed Admiral Killick as insubordinate, thereby depriving Firmin of a naval arm. Killick, however, continued his allegiance to Firmin, absconding with the flagship *Crête-à-Pierrot* and its crew.[14] Boisrond-Canal played on the fears of resident aliens in a letter to the American minister that denounced Killick as a pirate. He knew that metropolitan intervention in favor of the provisional government could be maneuvered into the final destruction of the Firminist insurgency. During the summer of 1902 the remaining Firminists in Port-au-Prince went into hiding. Some scaled the twenty-foot walls of the American legation in search of asylum, and two of the three Firminists in the provisional government resigned to join the rebels at Gonaïves.[15]

On July 26 the Firminists declared their own provisional government of the Artibonite and the Northwest with Firmin as president. As the declaration made the Firminist insurgency official, opponents subsequently argued that Firmin thereby began the civil war. In reality, a war had already been initiated against Firmin and his supporters. The new provisional government simply articulated the Firminist objective of immediate self-defense and eventual consolidation of power in Port-au-Prince.[16]

The capital remained firmly under Boisrond-Canal's control despite the rebel navy's offshore presence. The major urban battle of the war was for Cape Haitian, for if the Firminists could break Nord Alexis's hold on the city, they would dominate the country. Customs collection remained the only continuing governmental function and business in the city's streets and markets ground to a halt. "With the fear of violence and

14. Cohen to Foreign Secretary, May 22, 1902, FO 35, Vol. 177; Lemuel Livingston to Secretary of State, July 21, 1902, in Records of the Department of State, Dispatches from U.S. Consuls in Cape Haitian, NA; Rodolphe Charmant, *La Vie incroyable d'Alcius* (1946; rpr. Port-au-Prince, 1981), 238–40; *Le Moniteur*, July 12, 1902, p. 433; Gaillard, "Firmin et Les Etats-Unis," Pt. 1, notes, 144–45, 156.

15. Adolphe Boisrond-Canal to Powell, July 23, 1902, in Cohen to Foreign Secretary, August 4, 1902, FO 35, Vol. 177; Firmin to Hay, May 24, 1905, in U.S. Department of State, Dispatches from U.S. Ministers to Haiti; Roger Gaillard, "Firmin et Les Etats-Unis à travers un document inédit," Pt. 2, *Conjonction* (December, 1975), notes, 124–27.

16. New York *Times*, August 6, 1902, p. 3.

retribution in the air," the New York *Times* noted sarcastically, "each quaking citizen tries to recall that he is not really a Haitian at all, and that his great-aunt or his wife's cousin came from St. Thomas or Martinique." Yet foreign identities only exacerbated local hostilities. Suspicions that Nord Alexis had deliberately aroused xenophobic sentiments among the poor led a U.S. Navy commander to request that he disarm antagonistic citizens. Nord Alexis denied that he had influenced the street idlers who subjected whites to insult, but he readily complied with the American's request. Resentment of foreigners reflected their nearly invulnerable position. The prosperous town of Petit-Goâve burned to the ground in August, leaving ten thousand people homeless. The American minister, William Frank Powell, estimated that the fire would add $800,000 to the national debt. "Of this sum the Haitian unfortunates will get nothing, all will go to foreign interests." There was no reward in civil disturbances for the vast majority, who could claim no special protection. In another dispatch, Powell noted the destruction of the inland towns of Limbé and Marmelade. "In these interior villages or towns there are no foreign residents, so foreign interests do not suffer."[17]

Foreigners' indifference to bloodshed and ruin in the interior contrasted sharply with their determination to keep warfare out of the port cities. Because of their pressure, the Firminists' hands were tied in the North. Admiral Killick promised to give official notice before he bombarded Cape Haitian. The U.S. government regarded Killick's one-ship blockade as ineffective and refused to recognize it. An American ship was dispatched to northern Haiti to protect metropolitan interests, bearing a warning to Killick that any Firminist boarding of a foreign ship would be regarded as piracy. Killick subsequently abandoned the blockade.[18]

The Port-au-Prince government then used naval blockades against the rebel ports of Gonaïves and St. Marc. Boisrond-Canal asserted that his provisional government thereby intended to protect bondholders, many of whom were foreign. As Haiti used the revenues from duties to pay interest on government bonds, seizure of the customs receipts by insurgents would force the government in Port-au-Prince into default. The United States maintained the position on blockade that it had taken weeks

---

17. *Ibid.*, July 27, 1902, p. 25; Henry McCrea to Secretary of the Navy, July 31, August 9, 1902, NR; Jérémie, *Mémoires*, 21; Nemours Rigaud, *Petit-Goâve* (2nd ed.; Port-au-Prince, 1980), 174; Powell to Hay, August 15, 29, 1902, CD.

18. McCrea to Secretary of the Navy, August 9, 11, August 13, 1902, and McCrea to Admiral Killick, August 12, 1902, all in NR.

earlier when the Firminists employed it: to be recognized, the blockade must be effective. Unlike Admiral Killick, who relied on only one ship, the Port-au-Prince government had three leaky steamers. Of the major powers, only Germany honored this blockade, but its merchant fleet did not conform to diplomatic fiat. The first ship to run the blockade at Gonaïves was a Hamburg America Line vessel. In this instance, trade did not follow the flag.[19]

While civil war proceeded in the North, parliamentary struggle continued between followers of Fouchard and Sénèque in the capital. In September the Sénèquists placed soldiers around the Chamber of Deputies, whose infrequent meetings adjourned in panic and confusion. Boisrond-Canal, increasingly unpopular, narrowly averted a parliamentary attempt to depose him on the grounds of old age. By September 22, only four out of thirty-nine senators had been elected, and the Chamber of Deputies, unable to form a quorum, could not convene. In Powell's view, only the anti-Firminism of the legislative branch drew the deputies together in vacillating support for the provisional government. The mysterious disappearance of $31,000 in connection with a purchase of German arms by the provisional government further discredited Boisrond-Canal. From Washington came the grave news, communicated by the Haitian minister resident, J. N. Léger, that certain American newspapers, most notably the Washington *Post*, were avidly calling for American intervention. Neither side in the conflict had effective modern weapons, and an impasse was reached when they curtailed their activities in the most vital theaters because of foreign pressure.[20]

From the very beginning of the conflict, the urban community put the heaviest pressure on the Firminists to end the fighting. As early as May, long before the establishment of the provisional government of the Artibonite, the *Jamaica Gleaner*, even then a bellwether of conservative Caribbean opinion, suggested that Firmin assume personal risk in order to avoid a war. It gave no such counsel to other presidential candidates or to the generals who actually controlled the use of force. Firmin found his stature as an intellectual held against him when he tried to implement his ideas. Critics decried his recourse to a military solution, even though they

19. Alvey Adee to Powell, September 10, 1902, U.S. Department of State, Diplomatic Instructions of the Department of State, NA; Powell to Hay, September 19, 1902, NR; Powell to Hay, September 12, 1902, *FR*, 1902, p. 653; October 3, 1902, *FR*, 1902, pp. 669–70; S. C. Neale to Adee, October 1, 1902, NR.

20. Powell to Hay, September 13, 1902, *FR*, 1902, pp. 655–58; September 22, 1902; *FR*, 1902, p. 668.

knew that revolutionary succession was the only road to state power in Haiti. Firmin must not take the route of the ignorant militarists he so rightly despised, they held.[21]

These objections ring hollow, not only because they were so pointedly directed to Firmin, but also because they clearly circumscribed the limits that prominent Haitians and their foreign allies would willingly accept in reforming Haitian institutions. Firmin might write all the books he wished—and be warmly praised for them—but the frontier between theory and practice was not to be bridged. The diplomatic community, the foreign press, and even the international Pan-African Association insisted that Firmin lay down his arms. An increasingly pro-annexation tone in the American newspapers accompanied these demands. The New York *Times* claimed to have learned that the "best" Haitians "stand today as one man in open acknowledgment of the impossibility of a successful or even of a decent 'black republic.'" Characteristically, the paper could associate no specific individual with this viewpoint.[22]

In Haiti, the Firminists attempted as best they could to placate Powell and use him as a means of conveying their intentions to Washington. In late summer, Firmin asked him to forward a letter to Theodore Roosevelt. He offered in exchange safe conduct through the port of Gonaïves for an American businessman of dubious reputation. Powell replied to Firmin in an eloquent letter that, appealing to his intelligence and patriotism, begged him to end a conflict that was proving devastating to Haiti.[23]

The United States maintained strict military neutrality during the civil war despite American press jingoism and the anti-Firminism of leading policy makers.[24] England and France followed suit, but Germany openly supported the government in Port-au-Prince. This adherence owed little

21. *Jamaica Gleaner*, May 21, 1902, p. 4; Powell to Hay, May 24, 1902, in Dispatches from U.S. Ministers to Haiti; Alexander Walters to Firmin, September 26, 1902, in Antoine Bervin, *Benito Sylvain, Apôtre du relèvement social des Noirs* (Port-au-Prince, 1969), 86–87.

22. *Jamaica Gleaner*, May 21, 1902, p. 4; Powell to Hay, May 24, 1902, in Dispatches from U.S. Ministers to Haiti; Walters to Firmin, September 26, 1902, in Bervin, *Benito Sylvain*, 86–87; New York *Times*, July 27, 1902, p. 25, and September 13, 1902, p. 3; William Bayard Hale, "The Disorder in Haiti," *Independent*, LIV (1902), 1180–83.

23. Firmin to Powell, August 18, 1902, in Powell to Hay, August 29, 1902, NR; and Powell to Hay, September 4, 1902, in Dispatches from U.S. Ministers to Haiti; Powell to Firmin, August 21, 1902, in Powell to Hay, August 29, 1902, NR.

24. Adee to Secretary of the Navy, July 26, 1902, NR; David Hill to Powell, May 6 and July 30, 1902, in Diplomatic Instructions of the Department of State; Adee, Memorandum, October 2, 1902, in Records of the Department of State, Notes from the Haitian Legation in the United States, NA.

to the sentiments of the local German community, which was bankrolling both sides in the struggle. The German grudge against Firmin could be traced to the Luders incident of 1897, when as foreign minister Firmin had confronted the Reich in a dispute over a German national, and to German resentment of the Firminist blockade.

The Firminists closed the ports they occupied and forbade consular contact with legations in the capital. In September, 1902, they boarded a German vessel forty miles out to sea and removed an arms shipment. In line with his desire to keep the United States uninvolved, Firmin instructed Admiral Killick to be scrupulously courteous to the commanders of two American warships cruising the area. The U.S. government did not view these naval confrontations between German carriers and Haitian rebels with comfort and held that the Firminists could hardly justify their claim to prizes on the high seas as a belligerent right, considering the ineffectiveness of their blockade in port. Under the circumstances, the United States did not contest German reprisals.[25]

Germany retaliated against the rebels on September 6, 1902. The provisional government had declared the *Crête-à-Pierrot* a pirate and asked foreign naval vessels in the area to capture or sink it. The request provided the German navy with a pretext for demanding Killick's surrender. Realizing that a return to Port-au-Prince in irons meant death and dishonor, the Haitian admiral remained aboard and ordered the ship blown up. The destruction of the *Crête-à-Pierrot* and Killick's suicide dealt the Firminist revolution of 1902 a blow from which it never recovered.[26]

The Firminists, in losing the one-ship navy, forfeited $2,000,000 in paper money printed in New York, 800,000 rounds of ammunition, and firearms, all of which had just arrived in Gonaïves the day before the disaster. A former Dominican president had extended Firmin these credits against his hoped-for victory. Without the currency and the weapons, the Firminists could make little progress. They held the customhouses at Gonaïves, St. Marc, and Port-de-Paix, but the provisional government in the South was readying 900 "volunteers" to meet them at Mirebalais. Within two weeks of Killick's death, the government in Port-au-Prince had blockaded Gonaïves and St. Marc, but it allowed commerce to con-

25. Firmin to Admiral Killick, October 2, 1902, in Powell to Hay, October 2, 1902, CD; Adee to Acting Secretary of the Navy, September 4, 1902, NR.

26. Adee to Acting Secretary of the Navy, July 26, 1902, NR; Jérémie, *Mémoires*, 17–18, 20, 21; J. C. Dorsainvil, *Manual d'histoire d'Haïti* (Port-au-Prince, 1925), 279–80.

tinue at Port-de-Paix, where American citizens had substantial logwood interests.[27]

On October 2, 1902, J. N. Léger called on Alvey Adee, acting U.S. secretary of state. Just returned from a vacation, Léger, pleading lack of information from his government, asked for news of Haiti. Adee informed him that the situation was stable; the provisional government had failed to elect a Senate, and the Firminists maintained a steady hold on certain ports. Léger expressed concern about possible American intervention. The United States would not interfere, Adee assured him, except to protect Americans in either government-held or insurgent territory. In a later memorandum, Adee recorded his response to Léger when the Haitian pressed him on the matter. "I answered him that no purpose of that kind existed; that we respected the sovereignty of Haiti, and that our disposition to respect the sovereign rights of our neighbors had been abundantly shown by us in our treatment of Cuba."[28] Léger could hardly have been cheered by reference to that Caribbean satellite, but the knowledge that the United States planned no military action cleared the way for the Port-au-Prince government's October 12 offensive.

The groundwork was laid during the first half of October. Boisrond-Canal remained intransigent regarding peace initiatives. Firmin had started the war, he insisted, and Firmin should be the first to sue for peace. Boisrond-Canal claimed that he had Nord Alexis's written word that the general would not be a presidential candidate, which, if true, in Boisrond-Canal's view rendered the revolt of Gonaïves superfluous. The provisional government in Port-au-Prince was holding its own in the field, but politically it grew weaker daily. Boisrond-Canal alone held six cabinet portfolios. If action was not soon taken, only Sénèque and Fouchard in their feeble candidacies would oppose Firmin's bid for power. The absence of an armed central power meant an inevitable Firminist victory.[29]

Marshaling its energies, the provisional government sent 500 soldiers against the army of the Artibonite. It captured the towns of Limbé and Plaisance and, on October 12, prepared to march on St. Marc. Firmin then indicated his willingness to parley, with Powell acting as an intermediary between Gonaïves and Boisrond-Canal's government. The decision came too late. By the time Firmin's message, conveyed by the USS *Cincinnati*,

---

27. Powell to Hay, September 6 and September 22, 1902, NR.
28. Adee, Memorandum, October 2, 1902, in Notes from the Haitian Legation.
29. Powell to Hay, October 7, 1902, *FR*, 1902, pp. 670–72; Corvington, *Port-au-Prince*, IV, 101–103.

reached Port-au-Prince, Powell had left for the Dominican Republic, to which he was also accredited. Boisrond-Canal's government used Powell's absence as an excuse to delay peace talks until Nord Alexis could be consulted.[30]

Firmin, defeated militarily, could expect no concessions from Nord Alexis and chose exile. He left Gonaïves with 250 supporters on October 15 aboard a Hamburg America Line steamer bound for Inagua in the Bahamas. After the Firminist evacuation, foreign marines promptly took up positions around Gonaïves. The rout of the insurgents left no government in the city, where jails had been opened. The *Cincinnati* landed 21 guards to protect the U.S. consul and foreigners' lives and property in general. The Germans also landed marines. On the evening of October 16, armed men from the French ship *d'Assas* disembarked. When Boisrond-Canal's soldiers arrived the following afternoon, foreigners controlled Gonaïves.[31]

With Firmin now out of the picture, Nord Alexis spent the autumn of 1902 wiping out residual rebel resistance in the North. He came to Port-au-Prince in the middle of December. In the legislature, his soldiers training cannon and rifles on its members, he was quickly elected president.[32] The administration rapidly consolidated its strength as Nord Alexis commissioned new army officers. J. N. Léger, still the Haitian minister to the United States, kept that position and attempted to improve Haiti's bad press in America. The importance of public opinion at home was also recognized. Nord Alexis tried to neutralize growing foreign influence by making shrewd demagogic use of the nationalist sentiments of the Haitian poor and backing a 1903 law that taxed holders of the national debt. This levy fell squarely on the urban community of affluent Haitians and expatriates.[33]

Nord Alexis's conflict with the Banque Nationale d'Haïti, however, constituted one of his most enduring legacies. When *Le Nouvelliste* published a series of articles alleging probable fraud and irregularities in the

30. N. E. Mason to Secretary of the Navy, October 19, 1902, NR.

31. *Ibid.*

32. Corvington, *Port-au-Prince*, IV, 103; Gaillard, "Firmin et Les Etats-Unis," Pt. 2, notes, 135–36; *Le Moniteur*, January 2, 1904, p. 3.

33. J. N. Léger, "The Truth About Haiti," *North American Review*, CLXXVII (1903), 45–46; Powell to Hay, July 2, 1903, CD; Corvington, *Port-au-Prince*, IV, 104–109; A. G. Vansittart to Foreign Secretary, November 19, 1903, FO 35, Vol. 179; *Le Moniteur*, March 21, 1904, pp. 181–82.

debt consolidation of 1900, the regime launched an investigation. The inquest into the so-called consolidation scandal, unprecedented in Haiti, disclosed the issue of certificates that corresponded to no state debt. Some of these featured illegally inflated interest rates. Commissions and coupons were being unlawfully collected. Investigators discovered that a number of Banque Nationale officials and other creditors had collaborated to defraud the state. These included prominent Haitians, an American or two, and some Germans and Frenchmen.[34]

Although Nord Alexis rose to the presidency through naked force, there was nothing irrational, anarchic, or savage about the process. Contrary to the depictions of travel writers, Nord Alexis and other nineteenth-century Haitian presidents were chosen by the cosmopolitan and proprietary classes that governed Haiti. A scion of the northern landed and titled class himself, and a skilled politician, Nord Alexis represented an alternative to Firminism. Firmin might have brought less socially prominent people to power and instituted unpredictable changes in government. Nord Alexis, whatever the heavy-handed methods he used, would not upset the established order.

In making their selection, however, the ruling classes had taken a calculated risk. No intelligent governor would be entirely at their disposal if he wished to survive the vicissitudes of Haitian politics. Nord Alexis, like others before him, could exploit his esteem among the black peasantry and the lower classes of the towns. This is how presidents kept elites at bay. An equilibrium was necessary, and the achievement of balance constituted a key objective of executive politics. Nord Alexis was, for a time, successful at this. Georges Corvington, the historian of Port-au-Prince, describes his regime as one in which high society in the capital sparkled as never before.[35] Apparently the urban upper classes felt sufficiently at ease to turn their attention to the outward expression of gracious living.

Political succession in Haiti thus lacked the arbitrary character often attributed to it. The raising of peasant armies, the marches to the capital, the seizure of executive power as a preliminary to formal inauguration: all of these were meaningful rituals. They served to both contain and direct popular discontent while simultaneously alternating and distributing power among competing segments of the ruling class. As odd as it may

---

34. Joseph Chatelain, *Le Banque Nationale, son histoire, ses problèmes* (Lausanne, 1954), 69–70.

35. Corvington, *Port-au-Prince*, IV, 129.

seem to those acculturated to parliamentarism, the Haitian process also had mechanistic qualities. The chief beneficiaries of the system rarely lost control of it.

The approbation of the great powers was another necessary component in the harmony of interests that Haitian presidents sought. In Nord Alexis, Haitian kingmakers found a leader who was acceptable to an increasingly vigilant and activist United States at a time when European interest was flagging. An uneasy and unspoken truce eventually emerged between Nord Alexis and the Roosevelt administration. Roosevelt's inability to persuade Congress to accept further responsibility in the Caribbean contributed greatly to the peace with Haiti. A Dominican treaty that made the United States the receiver for that republic's customs revenues, for example, did not win Senate approval. It was accordingly instituted as an executive agreement. The Dominican experience indicated the limits of what American executive power could achieve in Haiti without congressional consent. Only under extreme circumstances would the United States intervene in the Black Republic. The Haitian task, therefore, was to see that such conditions did not arise.[36]

Nord Alexis was well suited to the task that circumstances had dictated. That he shared some characteristics with his American colleague, Theodore Roosevelt, may have helped him. Both men were staunchly nationalistic and socially conservative. One led an ascendant nation, the other, one in decline, but both wanted to perpetuate the respective heritages that internal weakness and foreign enemies threatened to destroy. Nord Alexis believed that the society built on the ruins of Saint-Domingue could be protected only through constant vigilance. Roosevelt cautioned against his own country's loss of vigor through decadence and lassitude. Both presidents believed a return to traditional roots essential for national rejuvenation. They distrusted European values and relied on policies of disengagement. The two men were patricians in their respective cultures. Roosevelt, a Hudson River aristocrat of landed Dutch antecedents, moved easily in the European and American high society of the period. Nord Alexis, son of a proprietary family ennobled by King Henri Christophe, had married into another wealthy and titled lineage and had begun a military career early in the nineteenth century.[37]

Nord Alexis and Roosevelt entered political life before the maturation of modern imperialism. For Nord Alexis, the struggle was to prevent

36. Dexter Perkins, *A History of the Monroe Doctrine* (Boston, 1963), 236–43.
37. *Notice Biographique sur le Général Nord Alexis* (Port-au-Prince, 1907), 5, 6, 10.

engrossment of Haiti by the metropolitan powers. Roosevelt, too, sought to avoid the political annexation of Caribbean territory, but at this point, the objectives of the two heads of state diverged and revealed the over-powering differences that their respective situations had carved out for them.

Nord Alexis's nationalism remained defensive. He sought not Haitian aggrandizement but Haitian survival. For Roosevelt, the continued inde-pendence of the United States was not at issue. The great battles to arrest social discontent and dissension had been fought and won in the 1890s. The contest now centered on the imposition of American ideas of order on a turbulent world.

Certain institutional limits confronted the leadership in both coun-tries. In the United States, Congress posed the largest single obstacle to presidential initiative. Roosevelt, while realizing that congressional power could be evaded, also recognized the limits of secret diplomacy and executive agreements. In Haiti, executive fiat was the government. Re-straints on Nord Alexis's power did nonetheless exist. Chief among them were interest groups that competed among themselves for institutional political expression and privileges. No tradition of loyal opposition per-mitted the cooperation of antagonistic elements within the framework of the Haitian state apparatus. Power could be shifted only by the destruc-tion and replacement of the existing government whenever an opening could be found.

Public office in Haiti had traditionally been associated with political patronage. If the president benefited from his place at the summit, he had concomitant obligations to provide for others who were on the top rungs of less important ladders. Friends, partners, relatives, godchildren, and other associates had to be protected. As in many other poor countries, these relationships were avenues for the distribution of benefits. Any important official, civil or military, who neglected them undercut his own position and limited his possibilities. At the same time, this system pro-moted charismatic rather than ideological leadership and militated against reform.[38]

The president of Haiti had sweeping powers, but his ability to effect fundamental change was decidedly circumscribed. The president of the United States, while limited by the machinery of constitutionalism, could accomplish much more at home and abroad. If many Americans of the early twentieth century felt an impulse to move beyond their borders

38. Deléage, *Haïti en 1886*, 163; Jérémie, *Memoires*, 50; Antoine, *Jean Price-Mars*, 9.

through commerce and war, the Haitians turned in on themselves. Their society had imploded, and both domestic and foreign forces clamped shut the safety valves of its growth and developmental potential.

A shifting balance of power in the Caribbean, accompanied by growing surveillance and militarization of Caribbean waters, made governance extremely difficult for small states ridden with debt and plagued by the continual threat of civil war. Nord Alexis responded by attempting to remove irritants that could precipitate domestic insurrection or foreign intervention. The elderly general raised an army alleged to number 24,000 and imprisoned political enemies as well as those accused in the bank frauds. "His palace [is] an arsenal in reality," an American naval officer reported, "with guards at every point and fortified to resist a siege; guns mounted on the walls; and even in the hallway of the house there is a battery of three gatlings."[39] Nord Alexis's show of force was intended to cow domestic enemies and to illustrate to the great powers that he firmly controlled his country. The need to demonstrate unequaled strength reflected the tangible increase in metropolitan influence in Española.

Under Nord Alexis's firm control, no revolutionary outbreak occurred during the January 1 centennial celebration. Yet the costs of defeating the Firminists had left the administration with little money. "People are wondering how the Government intend carrying out their elaborate centenary fêtes," British Consul Arthur G. Vansittart commented, "with an empty exchequer, and bankruptcy staring them in the face."[40]

The regime planned to raise the money by the customary method. It approached the resident foreign bankers late in December, 1903, for a loan. The bankers, including the director of the Banque Nationale d'Haïti, agreed to lend only if the administration promised to drop the consolidation hearings and free those imprisoned in the scandal.[41] Nord Alexis refused, for the celebration required a convincing semblance of probity and order, especially as a growing debt confronted the country, leaving little for the daily operations of government. With only weeks to go before the national holiday, the crisis called for unusual methods.

The Nord Alexis administration's difficulties with resident financiers reflected an institutional problem. Foreign businessmen had come to view Haitian governments as ephemeral and evaluated each one according to its

39. Admiral Wise to Secretary of the Navy, February 21, 1904, NR.

40. Vansittart to Foreign Secretary, December 5, 1903, FO 35, Vol. 179.

41. Frédéric Marcelin, *Le Général Nord Alexis, 1905–1908* (3 vols.; Paris, 1909), I, 43–53.

prospects for survival and the extent to which it could be expected to honor its obligations. They felt strongly that they were above laws imposed by transient officials. Metropolitan policy makers shared this outlook. "These republics to the South, with few exceptions, constantly need to be saved from themselves," asserted a U.S. State Department jurist, John Bassett Moore. "Their evanescent authorities" showed "desperation and weakness" in performing actions that undermined their own national dignity.[42]

After a succession of interim finance ministers had served from 1902 through 1903, Nord Alexis prevailed on Frédéric Marcelin, a veteran of the Hyppolite administration, to raise sufficient funds to observe the hundredth anniversary of the republic. When local bankers refused him also, Marcelin endorsed a previously planned government issue of a nickle coinage and paper money. Marcelin became finance minister on April 10, 1905.[43]

Contrary to John Bassett Moore's assumptions, Haiti's issue of an unsecured currency had been an attempt to restore a blemished national dignity by breaking out of a pattern of reliance on a few expatriate capitalists, whose external allegiances could readily internationalize business disputes. National security interests could best be served by the discovery of a way to control the foreign element. The need grew imperative when increased metropolitan naval activity in the Caribbean, coinciding with the commencement of the Nord Alexis presidency, became evident. An acute historical consciousness, always a characteristic of Haitian ruling-class elements, further heightened the tension that the centennial celebration inevitably produced. Elite groups had just vanquished the forces of reform. Could they sustain their current momentum and regain the equilibrium that had kept Haiti viable in the past?

Mixed joy and fear greeted the centennial. The foreign legations were full of refugees, and principals in an alleged conspiracy stood trial in a courtroom where their attorneys were not allowed to speak. Despite diplomatic pleading, Nord Alexis refused to commute the subsequent death sentences. Criticism focused on the president's "kitchen cabinet," a group of clients and relatives who held lucrative commissions to travel at government expense and mysteriously supported plutocratic life-styles on tiny salaries. Expatriates accused Madame Nord Alexis of engaging in an illicit, and competitive, cloth and coffee trade. The presidential coterie,

42. J. B. Moore to Adee, September 15, 1902, in John Hay Papers, LC.
43. Chatelain, *La Banque Nationale*, 71.

motivated by personal ambition, often cloaked itself in executive authority. The official cabinet had little genuine control over the departments,
and functionaries could be denounced and incarcerated by one of the
president's men.[44]

Election to the Senate also depended heavily on executive approval.
One day, Frédéric Marcelin passed the Legislative Palace and noticed how
shabby it looked. Horses, sheep, a donkey, and a cow grazed on its badly
kept lawn. "Perhaps it's a symbol," he noted in his diary. "It speaks
better than the longest pages about the decrepitude of Haitian parliamentarism, frequented only by beasts. Again, it's the green stuff that draws
them there." The legislature, increasingly supine, exercised no control
over the executive, which permitted it little decision-making power. The
regime used the Chambers primarily to showcase its consolidation scandal
hearings. The investigation soon became a government weapon to stifle
opposition from the wealthy, cosmopolitan sector. Graft and corruption
continued to flourish in the Haitian government, despite the publicity
given to probing the financial irregularities of the urban elite.[45]

Antiforeign sentiment fed on the debt consolidation issue and the
repressive atmosphere of the centennial year. The administration remained vindictive toward expatriate firms it believed implicated in the
scandal or otherwise antagonistic to the president. The wrath of the poor,
in particular, focused on aliens. "What unfortunately aids the Haytian
Government in its hostile attitude is the want of cohesion amongst the
Representatives of the Great Powers," Vansittart opined. "The Haytian
Government is well aware of this and skillfully plays one country against
the other."[46]

Two sets of incidents reveal different facets of the character of Haitians' resentment of foreigners. In the first, expatriates in provincial cities
were targeted for attack. In Jacmel, the most prominent European businessmen received anonymous threats of arson and assassination. Aux
Cayes and Jérémie experienced similar agitation. The German minister
requested warships to respond to the disturbances, which had been aggra-

44. Powell to Hay, January 16, 1904, John B. Terres to John Hay, January 21, 1904, and
Powell to Hay, March 15 and May 11, 1904, all in CD; Stephen Bonsal, *The American
Mediterranean* (New York, 1913), 68–70; *New York Herald*, March 18, 1908, p. 4; R. Nortz
to Powell, May 5, 1904, in Powell to Hay, March 11, 1904, CD.

45. Frédéric Marcelin, *Bric-à-brac* (Paris, 1910), 60–61, 64–68, 159–60.

46. Nortz to Powell, March 10 and March 5, 1904, and Powell to Hay, May 19, 1904, all
in CD; Vansittart to Foreign Secretary, March 11, 1904, FO 35, Vol. 180.

vated by the high rate of exchange, inflation, and food shortages. In these cases, hostility to foreigners was expressed by the common people of the towns, those who bore the brunt of exploitative commercial practices. The German minister's reaction dramatized the direct political and economic control exercised over the mass of Haitian consumers by the metropoles.[47]

The second set of incidents involved hostility to foreigners on the diplomatic level. Antiforeign violence in the summer of 1904 culminated in the June 22 stoning of the French and German ministers and their wives by the palace guard. The envoys fled in their carriages and immediately cabled their governments when Haitian officials failed to reply to a note demanding an apology. Unbeknownst to the Europeans, they had intruded into a restricted alley that separated the palace from a prison. Their coachmen ignored the sentinels' warning to halt. The soldiers recognized the carriage and, not wanting to fire on the ministers, threw stones instead. Germany accepted the explanation, but France did not. Eight days after the incident, the French cruiser *Julien de la Gravière* arrived in port and anchored offshore directly in front of the National Palace. Nord Alexis quickly dispatched Secretary of State Murville Férère to invite the French and German ministers to the palace, where full apologies were offered.[48]

The periodic loss of face Haiti suffered seemed to strengthen its resolve to check foreign activity. Local authorities often served as the instrument of administrative action. In the remote northwestern city of Port-de-Paix, police confiscated imported merchandise. Throughout the summer, seemingly unrelated events in Port-de-Paix pointed to concerted, if covert, state activity. On August 20, burglars broke into the Catholic church, vandalized it, stole wine and wafers, and set it afire. The American consul supposed that voodoo was involved, and, indeed, "Gombo" (voodoo) rites took place outside the city two days later. Voodoo possessed the power to instill terror in those who were never completely at ease in Haiti, a fact well understood by Haitian authorities. Haitian resistance possessed a cultural as well as a political character. Within a week, the home of the German consular agent had gone up in smoke, and unknown persons had

47. Powell to Hay, May 11, 1904, in Dispatches from U.S. Ministers to Haiti; Powell to Hay, May 12, 1904, CD.

48. Powell to Hay, June 22 and June 23, 1904, CD; *Negro World*, November 8, 1924, p. 15; Vansittart to Foreign Secretary, July 3, 1904, FO 35, Vol. 180; Paul Desprez to Minister of Foreign Affairs, June 23, 1904, QDO, Vol. 12.

attempted to sabotage an elevated railroad belonging to the American-owned Compagnie Haïtienne.[49]

The cosmopolitan sector fought back. In December, 1904, it began to hoard Haitian currency in an effort to cause food shortages and cripple domestic trade.[50] Tensions continued to mount. The consolidation scandal peaked with the complete rupture of relations between Haiti and the Banque Nationale in 1905. The final break took place in the context of increasing hostility between the government and the foreign creditor community.

In 1904, Haiti had circulated so much unsecured paper that the value of the gourde had dwindled to nothing. Merchants had responded by jacking up prices, while workers' and civil servants' wages and salaries had remained unchanged. Marcelin responded to the crisis by proposing an interest rate reduction on the interior debt that would free enough additional revenue to float more new currency. The legislature passed his bill into law in June, 1905, despite the protests of creditors and foreign governments.[51]

The amount thus gained did not suffice to improve the economy. As the measure removed the possibility of approaching local sources for funds, Marcelin chose again to issue paper money. The previous year, American bankers had offered to pay off Haiti's debts if permitted to purchase and consolidate them, but this did not assure the finance minister. The Morgan group and other financiers expressed mild interest in Haiti from time to time, but they appeared too close and too powerful for comfort. "Our formidable neighbors have an appetite and a fine one," Marcelin warned. "The more they eat the hungrier they get."[52]

The Nord Alexis presidency survived the centenary but remained only a step ahead of its numerous adversaries. Its relations with foreign creditors, an area in which its vulnerabilities were exposed, continued to deteriorate. Officials of the French-owned Banque Nationale d'Haïti stopped honoring government drafts when Marcelin began issuing paper, but they failed to bring down the regime, which unexpectedly retaliated

49. Powell to Hay, June 18, 1904, CD; Carl Abegg to Powell, August 31, 1904, in Powell to Hay, September 4, 1904, CD.

50. Antoine, *Jean Price-Mars*, 47.

51. Rayford W. Logan, *Haiti and the Dominican Republic* (New York, 1968), 114; Chatelain, *La Banque Nationale*, 71.

52. Marcelin, *Bric-à-brac*, 174, 91; Finance Department report, Pt. 6, in *Le Matin*, October 27, 1908.

by withdrawing the bank's right to act as the government's treasury agent. The action was a calculated risk. Haitians traditionally struggled to survive the summer "dead season," the period between harvests when cash was short. It was a daring time to defy the bank, but the move proved immensely popular. Marcelin later attributed the longevity of Nord Alexis's presidency to this maneuver. The old general thus slew a symbolic dragon, and throughout the remainder of his term, the bank languished while Nord Alexis remained unassailable behind his large, loyal army and network of police activists.[53]

The Nord Alexis regime occasionally handled its domestic foes disingenuously and without recourse to brutality. The president of the Chamber of Deputies, arriving at the Legislative Palace one morning in March, 1903, found a horde of prostitutes and beggars from the public hospital on the premises. The sight of ragged, maimed, and unruly people upset the deputies and raised suspicions that the poor had been deliberately sent there as a veiled warning. The state's sophisticated understanding of the political culture, equally apprehended and manipulated by members of the ruling classes, and the rhetorical populism that governors could muster when needed made potential mobs dangerous instruments in the hands of the powerful. In the words of Deputy Benoit, "I know as well as you the difference between the people and the populace; the people, as the great poet said, represent Thought. When you see it, salute. But when you encounter the populace along your route, run quick, for the populace is a machine, it is insensible [inconsciente]." On another occasion, the deputies found intimidating policemen stationed in the meeting hall. When they asked the minister of the interior and police the reason for the unsolicited patrol, he replied that the officers were needed to control spectators and ensure respect for the Chamber.[54]

As time passed, the subtlety of the regime's efforts at control gave way to open and unmitigated repression. The intensification of conflict with the great powers over finance and commerce, the rivalry of the metropoles in Haiti, and a persistent if weak political opposition had led Nord Alexis to clamp an iron vise on the country by 1906. Ordinary civil liberties were suspended, and the customary military press-gang continued to operate. The regime kept political dissidents under surveillance and even hired a

53. Alain Turnier, Les Etats-Unis et le marché haïtien (Washington, D.C., 1955), 237; Chatelain, La Banque Nationale, 72–73; Marcelin, Le Général Nord Alexis, I, 237–40; Powell to Hay, March 9 and April 29, 1905, CD.

54. Le Moniteur, February 2, 1905, p. 106, March 25, 1905, pp. 178–79, November 19, 1904, p. 817.

New York detective agency to watch exiles in the United States and on St. Thomas.[55]

Nord Alexis's apparent invulnerability did not deter American intelligence operations in the country. Captain Charles Young, the U.S. military attaché, prepared a massive sourcebook for the War Department on "nearly every subject" pertaining to Haiti, complete with photographs. Navy ships made "almost incessant" visits to the Fort Liberté area.[56] The Americans were determined to assimilate the information they needed to maneuver to their advantage in the Black Republic. The effect of their activity was to strengthen the regime's resolve to maintain a repressive hold over the country. The Haitian government greeted the appearance of American ships in Haitian waters with great consternation. Léger complained to the State Department that Powell's requests to show the flag when no gunboats were needed had contributed to the defiant attitude evinced by some foreigners, most notably the Syrians. He characterized the American minister as an alarmist and claimed not to know when Powell was speaking for himself and when he was conveying the U.S. government's instructions. Léger played a minor role in effecting Powell's recall, shrewdly stepping up his attacks at times when the relatively inexperienced American was already under fire from the State Department.[57] Léger's precision timing owed something to his diligence in securing privileged information. Haiti retained informants in Washington. As early as 1898, Powell had complained to the State Department that the Haitian Foreign Office received his instructions as soon as he did. Increasingly unpopular and identified with the zealous pursuit of Syrian interests, Powell left Haiti late in 1905.[58]

Henry Watson Furniss, who had begun his foreign service career as consul general in Bahía, Brazil, succeeded Powell. Also a black American,

55. Furniss to Elihu Root, March 7, 1906, in Dispatches from U.S. Ministers to Haiti; E. C. Chayter, Report, June 18, 1906, Commander of USS *Marietta* to Commander Southerland, August 19, 1906, H. B. Schellings to W. F. Fulliam, August 17, 1906, all in NR; *Le Moniteur*, April 4, 1906, p. 182.

56. J. N. Léger to Adee, July 27, 1905, in Notes from the Haitian Legation.

57. Léger to Adee, April 5, 1905, CD; Léger to Adee, July 27, 1905, in Notes from the Haitian Legation; Léger to Secretary of State, March 30, 1905, Adee to Léger, April 3, 1905, Léger to Murville Férère, April 4, 18, and September 18, 1905, and Léger to Nord Alexis, December 19, 1905, all in Eugène Maximilien Collection, Schomburg Research Center, NYPL; New York *Times*, October 15, 1905, p. 1.

58. Powell to John Sherman, April 18, 1898, and Powell to William Day, May 18, 1898, CD.

Furniss was a Harvard-trained physician who owed his Haitian appointment to Booker T. Washington's political influence. Unlike some such appointees, however, Furniss, by temperament and education, seemed well fitted for so professionally challenging a station as Port-au-Prince. He had moreover met J. N. Léger in Washington, D.C., and had received the shrewd Haitian's stamp of approval. The Furniss appointment, as well as that of Young, signaled an intensified American interest in Haitian affairs.[59]

Haitian diplomacy during the early Nord Alexis years was a strenuous exercise in artful dodging and feinting. The undertone of menace that foreign residents felt owed something to the preconceptions they had brought with them to the country, but it also reflected a skillful and subtle orchestration on the Haitian government's part. Veiled but discernible hostility on the one hand, followed by effusive official professions of amity and cooperation on the other, left aliens bewildered. The considerable diplomatic correspondence regarding the propriety of sending gunboats to Haiti effectively illustrates this point. Ministers and consuls rarely agreed on the degree of danger to foreign interests in any given political crisis on the island. Uncertainty on this matter among the great powers demonstrated the envoys' lack of familiarity with their host society and their efforts to forestall each others' actions, but as important, it testified to the Haitian authorities' talent for dissimulation.

Nord Alexis's precautions did not lessen foreign military activity. Captain Young's reconnaissance had become blatant by the early spring of 1907. He had been asked to supply cartographic information of military value, and his letters to the army chief of staff General Leonard Wood, clandestinely secured by the Haitian government from Young's servant, contained detailed descriptions of geographic features, road systems, fortifications, and hospitals. To Léger, Young's activity meant that Washington had designs on Haiti's future. He pressured the American secretary of state, now Elihu Root, to have the captain recalled, but Young left only after he completed his mission.[60] Léger also attempted to plant a seed

59. *Who's Who, 1912–1913;* Dr. William R. Furniss, interview with author, May 12, 1980; R. W. Thompson to Emmett Scott, October 15, 1905, in Louis R. Harlan and Raymond W. Smock (eds.), *The Booker T. Washington Papers* (13 vols.; Urbana, 1972–84), VIII, 412; Léger to Nord Alexis, December 19 and December 11, 1905, in Eugène Maximilien Collection; Furniss to Root, July 6, 1906, in Dispatches from U.S. Ministers to Haiti; *Le Moniteur,* February 2, 1905, p. 106, and March 25, 1905, pp. 178–79.

60. Léger to Adee, July 27, 1905, in Notes from the Haitian Legation; Pierre Carteron to Minister of Foreign Affairs, April 20, 1908, QDO, Vol. 10; H. Pauléus Sannon, *Pour un*

of doubt in Root's mind about the utility of the acute Dr. Furniss. A master of innuendo, Léger implied that Furniss, like Powell before him, had become too peremptory. Perhaps his German wife, Léger insinuated, had unduly influenced him.[61]

The United States' persistent interest in Haiti seemed especially ominous to the Haitian government as the Nord Alexis administration drew to a close. The president wanted to control the January, 1908, legislative elections so that he could either be reelected or name his successor. Dissident deputies were jailed, and others fled to consulates and legations or sought exile. Haiti faced an election in which the only voters would be soldiers loyal to the incumbent.[62]

In September, 1907, a widely publicized court-martial of civilians took place in Port-au-Prince. The government prosecutor blamed the United States for Haiti's punitive attitude toward the political prisoners. In Furniss' words, the prosecutor told the military court that "it was necessary that all the prisoners should be found guilty and shot, even if the Government had to wade through blood to do so." The United States had to be shown, the attorney argued, that Haitians could maintain law and order themselves and thus avoid American intervention. Washington's policies were thus appropriated to justify a political repression that probably would have occurred even in the absence of the Roosevelt Corollary.[63]

The capital diplomatic corps called on the Haitian foreign affairs minister in a concerted body to ask him to intercede with Nord Alexis for clemency, but the appeal had no success. Officials in the U.S. State Department noted Haiti's seeming imperviousness to international opinion. "The butcher sentiment is too strong in Haiti to be overcome by foreign sentiment," the third assistant secretary, Alvey Adee, commented. "Foreign appeals for leniency only make [the Haitians] more determined to complete the killing." He saw Haiti as an autocratic state that "follows the policies of Toussaint Louverture and always will." Although an allusion to Dessalines would have been more apt, the point was clearly made. The

---

gouvernement stable (Port-au-Prince, 1930), 1–2; New York *Herald*, August 11, 1908, Sec. 7, p. 3, and August 12, 1908, Sec. 5, p. 3; Oliver Wardrop to Lord Lansdowne, June 26, 1903, FO 35, Vol. 179; Powell to Hay, June 19, 1903, CD; Léger to Nord Alexis, March 14, 1907, and April 5, 1907, in Eugène Maximilien Collection.

61. Léger to the Haitian Secretary of State, March 25, 1907, in Eugène Maximilien Collection; Furniss to Root, August 29, 1907, NF, 2126/12; Dr. William Furniss, interview with author, May 12, 1980.

62. Furniss to Root, August 29, 1907, NF, 2126/12.

63. Furniss to Root, September 26, 1907, NF, 2126/17–18.

Americans did not believe the Haitian government susceptible to ordinary pressures.[64]

At his post in Washington, Léger realized that the Americans had developed a harder line. He called Nord Alexis's attention to William Howard Taft's recent election as president. "I must tell you frankly," the Haitian minister wrote, "that I do not believe he is ready to let his country's neighboring republics continue the bloody game of civil war. What he does in Cuba and Panama clearly indicates his role in the future."[65] Indeed, the growing number of courts-martial, death sentences, detention, and censorship, all contrary to the Haitian constitution, made intervention seem increasingly likely. Locked into the vicious logic of defending its right to rule by reference to its capacity for violence, the administration snatched at the straws of rumor, fear, and deception. An inflammatory article in *Le Matin* accused the foreign community of planting a bomb, though no one had heard the explosion or seen any damage. H. Pauléus Sannon, the Haitian foreign minister, hedged and finessed on all diplomatic inquiries about this report. Furniss ultimately concluded that no bomb had gone off. *Le Matin* was correct, of course, in a deeper sense, as the crisis reached explosive levels.[66]

Haitian contacts with foreign envoys were now handled by the relatively inexperienced and unknown Sannon. Murville Férère had resigned in May, 1906, after differing with the administration over the handling of the French claims commission and for personal reasons. The Foreign Ministry was now powerless before the executive will.[67]

Many prominent persons fully supported the administration, and, according to Georges Corvington, the resulting "social peace" led to the proliferation of cultural and social organizations. Corvington sees the early years of the Nord Alexis regime as a *belle époque* of dazzling fêtes and society balls.[68] Contrasted against this gaiety loomed the somber specter of renewed civil war.

The privileged few remained impervious to the institutions of terror,

64. Furniss to Root, September 18, 1907, NF, 2126/15; Robert Bacon to Furniss, October 10, 1907, NF, 2126/16; Furniss to Secretary of State, October 18, 1907, NF, 2126/21; Adee to Bacon, October 19, 1907, and October 28, 1907, and Root to Furniss, November 2, 1907, all in NF, 2126/20.

65. Léger to President of Haiti, November 4, 1908, in Marcelin, *Le Général Nord Alexis*, I, 13.

66. Furniss to Root, October 25, 1907, NF, 2126/29–38.

67. Furniss to Root, May 16, 1906, CD; Vansittart to Lord Grey, May 24, 1906, FO 371, Vol. 81.

68. Corvington, *Port-au-Prince*, IV, 129–60.

which were largely reserved for those who had little or nothing and for those among the rich who questioned the political order. As 1908, the last year of Nord Alexis's presidency, began amid festive New Year's Day celebrations in Port-au-Prince's wealthy homes, members of the administration had already begun to think of how they could best preserve their gains. They realized that organized resistance to the president could be precluded through a parliamentary coup.

Rumors that Nord Alexis had made a deal with the legislative candidates circulated in Port-au-Prince. The elderly president expected to be elected to a life term through the alteration or abolition of the constitution. As the candidates were traditionally creatures of the president, had no contact with their constituencies, and sometimes did not know what district they represented, the idea was not farfetched. Nominated by the executive, they were elected by soldiers who dutifully voted under their commanding officers' aegis. Indeed, the administration successfully placed its candidates in the January, 1908, elections. Only soldiers chose the new lawmakers, whose number included fifteen relatives and godchildren of Nord Alexis.[69]

Clearly, constitutional methods would not suffice to depose the regime. Knowing this, the Firminists mounted a new insurgency in January, 1908. They counted on a complacent foreign community, by now thoroughly disenchanted with the president, and the growing opposition caused by economic distress and political repression to provide the favorable climate they needed. Firminists planned an attack on St. Marc and Gonaïves and awaited a shipment of arms from New York. Unbeknownst to the rebels, however, the U.S. government had already seized the cargo. The chief of the U.S. Secret Service, John E. Wilkie, reflected the phobia of revolution apparently already well developed in the American intelligence community. The goal of the Firminist revolution, according to Wilkie and as reported by the New York *Herald,* was the spread of insurgency from Española to Cuba. The government in Washington could not permit such criminal contagion to infect a state under its tutelage. The surprise confiscation of the Firminists' arms did not keep the rebels from taking St. Marc and Gonaïves, but without weapons these key cities could not be held.[70]

Nord Alexis accordingly planned to bombard St. Marc and Gonaïves in

69. Carteron to Minister of Foreign Affairs, January 6 and January 14, 1908, QDO, Vol. 1; Furniss to Root, January 15, 1908, NF, 2126/64.

70. New York *Herald,* January 24, 1908, p. 8; Léger to Nord Alexis, January 29, 1908, in Eugène Maximilien Collection; Carteron to Minister of Foreign Affairs, February 11 and

mid-January without giving official notice. Commander G. R. Marvell of the USS *Eagle*, an oceanographic vessel, was summoned hastily to St. Marc by the U.S. consul, Charles Miot. When he learned the Haitian government's intentions, the commander insisted that the bombardment be postponed until women and children had been evacuated. The Haitian minister of war and Haitian Admiral Lebon eventually agreed to delay the action until Marvell had consulted the American minister and had delivered a message to Nord Alexis from the admiral and the Haitian minister. Nord Alexis refused to suspend the order to bombard the town but gave assurances through Lebon that the St. Marc consulates, being guarded by Firminists, would not be fired on. In Gonaïves, Marvell landed twelve men and ordnance to protect foreign property in the absence of organized authority. French, German, British, and American officials vowed that Haiti would be held responsible for any damages.[71]

The Firminist insurgency collapsed immediately. Firmin again left the country, and his supporters took refuge in consulates and legations. European envoys granted the ritual asylum. Asylum at consulates rather than legations remained an uncommon practice outside Haiti, and its potential for abuse was enormous.[72]

France, under heavy official attack from the Haitian government for its granting of asylum, defended the policy on humanitarian grounds. In a land of assassination, poisoning, torture, and incarceration, Minister Pierre Carteron argued, asylum provided the only brake on tyranny and the only guarantee of human rights. On the other hand, he acknowledged that sanctuary might encourage Haitian dissidents to propel themselves into revolutionary activity, as they could count on an escape hatch. Just as significantly, the practice enhanced the influence of the diplomatic community, and even social climbing played a role. Acquaintance with an envoy could save a life.[73]

November 3, 1908 (QDO, Vol. 7), and November 22, 1908 (QDO, Vol. 1); Stabler, Memorandum, January 6, 1908, NF, 2126/42.5.

71. G. R. Marvell to Secretary of the Navy, January 18, 1908, NF, 2126/61–62, and February 5, 1908, NF 2126/129–30; Furniss to Root, January 17, 1908, NF, 2126/66–68; Pauléus Sannon to Carteron, January 18, 1908, QDO, Vol. 1.

72. "Note pour le conseil des ministres," February 21, 1908 (Vol. 7), with Carteron to Minister of Foreign Affairs, February 24, 1908, QDO, and Vols. 7–8, *passim*. On foreign involvement, A. P. Murray to Secretary of State for Foreign Affairs, February 14, 1908, and Arthur Rowley, Report on Haiti, February 9, 1908, FO 371, Vol. 466; Stimson to Root, January 27, 1908, NF, 2126/130; New York *Herald*, March 9, 1908, p. 3, and March 12, 1908, p. 3.

73. Carteron to Minister of Foreign Affairs, May 29, 1908, QDO, Vol. 8.

The United States did not share the European view of sanctuary. Officials in Washington saw it as perpetuating rather than neutralizing political instability in Haiti. Like Nord Alexis, the Americans entertained suspicions about the role of foreigners in Haitian insurgencies and would tolerate no political activity on the part of its representatives on the island. The United States opposed the right of asylum on the grounds that it encouraged irresponsible government by shielding dissidents from the consequences of dangerous political acts and interfered with the stability of existing regimes. Adee held that limiting the right of asylum would serve notice on other Latin states to correct their abuse of this convention. The State Department dismissed Charles Miot, the Haitian-born French citizen who acted as U.S. consul at St. Marc, believing him responsible for alleged revolutionary activities that his son, of the same name, committed. No sympathetic expression could be made to the rebels, nor could political refugees be harbored in American consulates. When the 1908 Firminist insurgency failed, the State Department ordered Furniss to congratulate the Haitian government on its victory.[74]

Widespread dissatisfaction greeted this action in Haiti. Furniss made a humanitarian appeal to the secretary of state. He reported that when fugitives sheltered in the St. Marc consulate had been expelled pursuant to Washington's instructions, government squads had gunned them down in the street within twenty minutes. Yet the State Department held its ground, insisting that the St. Marc situation was extraordinary because of the supposed activism of the consul there. The United States would not protect fugitives from due process, though it would henceforth shelter them from "lawless slaughter." Furniss tried to make U.S. officials understand that there was no due process in Haiti in the common American appreciation of the term. Commander Marvell of the *Eagle* seconded Furniss in a communication to the secretary of the navy. "The feeling among the foreigners in Port-au-Prince is very intense over the action of the American Government in the St. Mark affair," he reported, "and I have been reliably informed that the officials of the Haitian government itself do not like the stand taken."[75]

Haitians opposed the American position because all political careerists

74. *Ibid.*; Livingston to Secretary of State, December 3, 1908, NF, 2126/137; Stabler, Memorandum, January 16, 1908, NF, 2126/42.5; Adee to Bacon, February 21, 1908, and Bacon to Adee, February 20, 1908, NF 2126/123; Root to Furniss, January 22, 1908 (NF, 2126/53), January 20, 1908 (NF, 2126/50), January 31, 1908 (NF, 2126/75); Root to U.S. Consul in Gonaïves, January 28, 1908, NF, 2126/63.
75. Marvell to Secretary of the Navy, February 5, 1908, NF, 2126/129–31.

needed to be able to receive asylum. Europeans objected to that option because they realized that revolutionary succession, not due process, created Haitian governments. Pauléus Sannon, then foreign minister and shortly to seek sanctuary himself, criticized the United States for waiting until a time of civil unrest when the consulates were full to denounce asylum instead of declaring its policy during peacetime.[76]

The State Department also limited the embarkation of political fugitives. Traditionally, the losers of a revolutionary contest went into exile on another Caribbean island until executive clemency or a change in administration made it safe to return. Furniss was instructed to inform the diplomatic community that the United States would not sanction the landing of Haitians in Cuba, then under American "responsible administration."[77]

Despite—or because of—American intransigence, events conspired to involve the United States more deeply in the Haitian conflict. After the dismissal of Miot, a Danish businessman was appointed consul. The consular archives, the American flag, and the coat of arms remained in Miot's house because the Dane had not yet received permission from the Haitian government to remove them. The authorities, acting under the assumption that Miot's house was no longer the American consulate, raided it and removed the fugitives Miot was sheltering. As the Haitians had not acknowledged any change of location of the consulate, and the consular documents, flag, and shield remained in place, they had technically violated its integrity as foreign property. Yet the United States refused to follow up this possibility, arguing that during the period between the dismissal of Miot and the raid, there effectively had been no American consulate at St. Marc. The archives could well have been in storage, the State Department contended, and the paraphernalia had been used without authority. The U.S. government ordered the St. Marc consulate closed.[78]

After the St. Marc debacle, attention turned to the plight of the refugees in the Port-de-Paix and Gonaïves consulates of the United States. Only a presidential pardon could spare their lives. The New York *Herald*, through its local correspondent, offered to mediate in the asylum matter.

76. Furniss to Root, February 1, 1908, NF, 2126/124; Carteron to Minister of Foreign Affairs, February 6, 1908, QDO, Vol. 2.

77. Bacon to Furniss, February 7, 1908, NF, 2126/81; Philip C. Jessup, *Elihu Root* (New York, 1938), I, 288, 306.

78. Furniss to Root, February 15, 1908 (NF, 2126/146), February 20, 1908 (NF 2126/147), March 6, 1908 (NF 2126/171–75).

Haitian officials agreed to this. The United States, France, Spain, Portugal, and Sweden had extended sanctuary to political fugitives and were involved in unsuccessful parleys with the Haitian government on the question. Haitian officials made use of the *Herald* journalist to embarrass the envoys, for at the *Herald*'s request, it permitted the last Firminist refugees to safely leave the country. The *Herald* was rewarded by its own sensationalist publicity, and the metropoles by the conclusion of a worrisome affair. The United States resolved that never again would its consulates in Haiti be used for asylum. Despite some trepidation, the Haitian government formally abolished the practice in May, 1908. This action displeased the European states, which took the prohibition as an encroachment on their sovereign powers.[79]

The Firminist uprising and the asylum issue did little to repair the frayed fabric of Haiti's relations with the foreign community. Some businessmen and diplomats made known their support for a change of administration in Port-au-Prince but would not publicly endorse revolutionary insurgency. Only the United States maintained a relatively unruffled friendship with Haiti, and it appeared to be Nord Alexis's mainstay. Jean Jules Jusserand, the French ambassador in Washington, would not challenge the United States over its support for the regime. The good will of the Americans, he stated, meant more to France than did the Firminists' welfare. Furthermore, as officials in Washington seemed to believe that a revolution in Haiti would be followed by one in the Dominican Republic, France should avoid any association with Caribbean unrest.[80]

Although they had come down decisively against the reform forces, metropoles and their representatives continued to find the Nord Alexis regime difficult to live with. Threats of massacre and poisonings and general suspicion and fear clouded their relations with their hosts. They had chosen to abet a reactionary government, but it proved to be one that

79. Furniss to Root, March 10, 1908, NF, 2126/178–79, and March 19, 1908, NF, 2126/208; Root to Furniss, April 11, 1908, NF, 2126/221; Carteron to Minister of Foreign Affairs, February 11, 1908, QDO, Vol. 7, and February 19, 1908, QDO, Vol. 2; Victor Montasse to Carteron, June 20, 1908, QDO, Vol. 2; Carteron to Minister of Foreign Affairs, April 20, 1908, QDO, Vol. 10; New York *Herald*, March 10, 1908, p. 3; Furniss to Root, May 22, 1908, NF, 2126/221; Carteron to consular agents, May 21, 1908, QDO, Vol. 8.

80. Murray to Foreign Office, February 19, 1908, and Louis Mallet to Admiralty, March 26, 1908, FO 371, Vol. 466; New York *Herald*, February 19, 1908, p. 4; Adee to Bacon, February 19, 1908, NF, 2126/130; Victor Metcalf, Memorandum, March 26, 1908, NF, 2126/184–85; J. Jusserand to Ministry, February 21, 1908, QDO, Vol. 7.

refused to promote the imperialist enterprise. If there were no ambitious social reforms, there would be no increase in foreign penetration either. Nord Alexis used draconian methods to maintain the status quo. Part of the program necessitated keeping expatriates at bay. The consequent tension led foreigners to contemplate countermeasures. The idea of stationing a permanent ship off Española enjoyed currency in diplomatic circles, but the United States characteristically tried to discourage it. Prompted by persistent European fears, however, the U.S. Navy investigated the Haitian political climate in March, 1908.[81]

Although duly warned to take European opinions with a grain of salt, Captain Templin Morris Potts of the USS *Des Moines* cabled that the Haitian situation was indeed grave. Potts had spoken to leading foreigners and perused Furniss' dispatches. He believed that Nord Alexis was demented, and requested authority to cooperate with European naval officers in case of an attack on foreign subjects. Furniss had not reported any imminent crisis; however, Carteron, the French minister, later suggested that his American colleague had been pressured to minimize the peril. If foreign lives were not in danger, he argued, Furniss and the New York *Herald* correspondent would not have barricaded themselves in the U.S. legation with rifles, revolvers, and sabers at their sides. The United States simply wanted to keep the European powers from acting in Haiti, Carteron concluded.[82]

France and Germany found the American position especially frustrating. The United States opposed European interference, would not participate in a joint naval operation, and declined to intervene unilaterally. To the Europeans, the U.S. attitude enabled the Haitian government to abuse aliens. The Continental powers nevertheless remained uncomfortable with the prospect of Haiti under American control. The United States' influence in the Black Republic had already grown considerably. "It has been impossible for anyone to overlook the numerous Americans who have overrun every corner of the island" in recent years, British Consul Alexander Murray reported. The Yankees were "nominally passing as business men, timber merchants, etc but quite ignorant of business and

81. Furniss to Secretary of State, March 18, 1908, NF, 2126/180; Secretary of the Navy to Secretary of State, March 26, 1908, NF, 2126/184–85; Carteron to Minister of Foreign Affairs, March 20, 1908, QDO, Vol. 2, and November 18, 1908, QDO, Vol. 3.

82. Secretary of the Navy to Secretary of State, March 26, 1908, NF, 2126/184–85; Captain Potts to Secretary of the Navy, March 26, 1908, NR; Furniss to Secretary of State, March 23, 1903, and Bacon to Furniss, March 23, 1903, NF, 2126/170; Adee to Bacon and Bacon to Adee, March 30, 1905, NF, 2126/267; Carteron to Minister of Foreign Affairs, March 23 and April 20, 1908. QDO, Vol. 10; *Le Nouvelliste*, April 15, 1908, pp. 2–3.

not even knowing the different sorts of trees." They antagonized Haitians because of their racism, and Europeans resented the exclusionary commercial line they drew wherever they established protectorates in the Caribbean. In Puerto Rico, Cuba, and the Dominican Republic, the Americans had erected discriminatory barriers against European traders.[83]

Despite Murray's sentiments, the United States found increasing support in London, which did not want to alienate the American government over the small British interest in the island republic. Many British subjects in Haiti were blacks and coloreds. Often they had migrated to Haitian cities and towns without benefit of legal documents and, as they could not prove their British citizenship, were British only by ascription. A naturalization treaty signed with Haiti in 1906 allowed Britain to largely abandon the English-speaking West Indian population in Haiti and separate itself from the policies advocated by France and Germany.[84] Britain would not grant asylum to Haitians, believing that the absence of ministerial relations with Haiti prevented it from sheltering fugitives. At the request of the Haitian minister in London, the secretary of state for the colonies ordered British West Indian governors to prevent possible filibustering attempts on Haiti by exiles. Murray, who did not share the Foreign Office perspective, thought the United States' faith in its minister misplaced. Furniss, eager to spare Haiti foreign occupation, "studies . . . the interests of his race rather than those" of his country. Although Murray endorsed the Continental view of the Haitian crisis, the Anglo-American position, determined in Washington on the ministerial level, prevailed. Haiti simply was not important enough to Britain to risk alienating the United States.[85]

Disagreement continued as to how endangered foreigners were, but the sufferings of Haitians were indisputably real. On March 15 the administration executed the nation's most renowned poet, Massillon Coicou. France and Germany, though adversaries in Europe, now conferred over their strained relations with Haiti. As the only major advocates of a permanent patrol in Haitian waters, they had earned the re-

---

83. Furniss to Root, April 2, 1908, NF, 2126/235; Murray to Secretary of State for Foreign Affairs, April 30, 1908, FO 371, Vol. 467.
84. Grey to Murray, April 6, 1908, FO 371, Vol. 467; Carteron to Minister of Foreign Affairs, Enclosure, March 18, 1908, QDO, Vol. 11; James Bryce to Grey, March 28 and April 1, 1908, FO 371, Vol. 467; Warren G. Kneer, *Great Britain and the Caribbean, 1901–1913: A Study in Anglo-American Relations* (East Lansing, 1975), 119–23; Grey to Sénèque Viard, May 6, 1908, FO 371, Vol. 468.
85. Murray to Secretary of State for Foreign Affairs, May 14, 1908, FO 371, Vol. 467.

gime's hostility. J. N. Léger, commenting in the New York *Herald* on the renewed European calls for warships, let it be known that Haiti would fire on any foreign vessel that shelled its ports.[86]

By mid-March, dozens of persons had been arrested. The number included some wealthy Port-au-Princiens; the head of the powerful German firm Reinbold and Company; and Firmin's brother-in-law, who was executed. Anti-German sentiment, fostered by the regime in anticipation of the German government's protest, began to spread. Elite members of the palace guard, suspected of conspiracy, were arrested and then released. They escaped into legations after discovering that they too were to be shot. Carteron attempted to intercede on behalf of these French-trained officers. The Haitian government considered them deserters rather than political refugees but promised that they would receive fair trials. Carteron did not believe this guarantee.[87]

The disappearances and detention of prominent people, antiforeign sentiment, and fears that Nord Alexis would set aside the constitution deepened expatriates' anxiety. Tales of secret executions surfaced late in April, 1908. Long-term foreign residents sensed that the generally tolerant Haitian attitude toward them was undergoing transition. In the past, aliens' lives and property had been respected, as Haitians had realized that their sovereignty rested on such guarantees. Nord Alexis now encouraged the populace to attribute the country's poverty to strangers' machinations. J. N. Lèger, who realized more keenly than did the president the consequences of a direct confrontation, thought it possible to mitigate tensions through a deliberate effort at rapprochement among the elites. The suggestion came too late. The upper classes increasingly turned on the regime as the maelstrom of prison, torture, and assassination began to draw them in.[88]

The atmosphere was not improved by the failure of the spring rains. Starving peasants from the famine-struck countryside around Jacmel streamed into Port-au-Prince to beg in May and June, 1908. Food riots

86. Robert Cornevin, *Le Théâtre haïtien des origines à nos jours* (Ottawa, 1973), 11, 113; J. Michael Dash, *Literature and Ideology in Haiti, 1915–1961* (London, 1981), 21–22; Furniss to Root, April 2, 1908, NF, 2126/235; New York *Herald*, March 17, 1908, p. 4.

87. New York *Herald*, March 17, 1908, p. 4; Potts to Secretary of the Navy, March 26, 1908, NR; Furniss to Root, March 17, 1908 (NF, 2126/198–99), March 18, 1908 (NF, 2126/200), March 29 and March 30, 1908 (NF, 2126/210); Carteron to Minister of Foreign Affairs, April 27, 1908, QDO, Vol. 8.

88. Potts to Secretary of the Navy, April 27, 1908, NR; Léger to Nord Alexis, April 9, 1908, in Eugène Maximilien Collection.

erupted near Jacmel, and soldiers opened fire on the hungry. Peasants rolled up their dead, including children, in mats and buried them in shallow graves by the roadside. The relief shipment of food sent by the government to the southern provincial city had not been adequate. In Port-au-Prince, fire broke out at noon on a hot July day in the lower part of town and destroyed one-fifth to one-third of the city. Strong easterly winds carried sparks, which ignited house after house until the blaze reached the sea. A ten-block quarter south of the National Palace burned to the ground. The area included the Episcopal church, the Wesleyan chapel, the prison, the arsenal, and a powder magazine. Loss of life was not great, but the conflagration left thirty thousand homeless. The homes of the poor contained little of material value, but the fire demolished a number of shops, which had employed groups of three to fifteen workers. In the general despair that gripped the country, wrote Carteron, people looked for a hero who would "clean the Augean stables." No signs of vigorous leadership appeared, and foreigners speculated on the blessings to Haiti of a benign imperialism.[89]

Madame Nord Alexis, the famous Cécé of Creole song and story, died on October 11. She was a daughter of a former president and a niece of King Henri Christophe. Her marriage to Nord Alexis had reinforced a powerful alliance of wealthy northern families. Her demise, in Murray's words, "removed an important factor from Haitian politics." Nord Alexis subsequently made some staff changes, which included transferring the position of commander-in-chief of the army to himself and thereby diminishing the power of an ambitious rival, Cyriaque Celestin.[90]

Celestin was not the aged president's only problem. The government's inadequate response to the misery in the South was related to Nord Alexis's efforts throughout his presidential career to suppress southern dissidence. That dissidence found its champion in Antoine Simon, the *délégué* of the South and military head of a coalition that wanted to place a southerner in the National Palace. Nord Alexis's mid-November dismissal

89. New York *Herald,* June 8, 1908, p. 11, and June 16, 1908, p. 11; Murray to Secretary of State, June 30, 1908, FO 371, Vol. 468; Carteron to Minister of Foreign Affairs, August 1 and June 13, 1908, QDO, Vol. 2; Murray to Secretary of State for Foreign Affairs, July 8, 1908, and Captain G. Borrett to the Rear Admiral, 4th Cruiser Squadron, August 1, 1908, FO 471, Vol. 468.

90. *Le Moniteur,* October 14–17, 1908, pp. 629–30; Murray to Secretary of State, October 31, 1908, FO 371, Vol. 468.

of Simon from his post gave that general carte blanche to continue his operations.[91]

During the month of November, the government army, perhaps as a result of Celestin's demotion, responded sluggishly to Simon's attempts to seize executive power and failed to halt his advance on the capital, which he successfully captured on December 1. In customary fashion, the diplomatic community conducted Nord Alexis and his party to the French ship, *Duguay Trouin*, that would convey them to Kingston. The diplomats' presence hardly intimidated the angry crowds that accosted the former president. In the wake of Nord Alexis's departure, mobs looted twelve foreign stores and pillaged Frédéric Marcelin's properties, causing $150,000 damage.[92]

Nord Alexis lived on for eighteen months in Jamaica, where a British reporter interviewed him in 1909. His "shrunken and emaciated figure, with gray hair and long bony fingers, betokened advanced age," but his traits "show a man who in his prime must have possessed great physical strength and character beyond the ordinary." Nord Alexis died in Kingston on May 1, 1910.[93]

Ironically, neither the old-guard conservative, as represented by Nord Alexis, nor the reformer, as embodied in Firmin, succeeded in improving Haiti's international status. Firmin returned to Haiti in December, 1908, only to find that General Antoine Simon had already seized executive power through the traditional military means. Nord Alexis's successor was also a general but a man who lacked the desire to preserve the autochthonous independence that the crusty northerner had so cherished.

The war against reform had ended, and the warriors had been discarded. Even at its most intense, Firminism had never broken with the ritualized past and its processions of *chefs du pouvoir executif*. It addressed itself fraternally to the urban petty bourgeoisie but approached the peasants as master. A peasant soldier of 1902, bitterly aware of this, told a French consular agent why he had defected from the Firminist ranks. "If the revolution succeeds, is it me or my relatives who will get good jobs in the civil service or the customs bureau? Not a chance. They'll

---

91. Edgar N. Numa, *Antoine Simon et la "Fatalité Historique"* (N.p., n.d.), 23, 25, 14.

92. Carteron to Minister of Foreign Affairs, December 3, 1908, QDO, Vol. 3; New York *Herald*, December 4, 1908, p. 1.

93. George Barton, "Haiti's Refugee Despot in Jamaica," *Harper's Weekly*, January 2, 1909, p. 16; Murray to Secretary of State, June 1, 1908, FO 371, Vol. 914.

go to these kids with shined shoes who stay quietly at home while we're out getting ourselves killed!"[94] As an indigenous movement for change, Firminism maintained its potency until the U.S. invasion. As an incompletely conceptualized bourgeois movement, however, it failed to transcend the dynamics of traditionalist politics and was defeated by stubborn cosmopolitan resistance.

94. Quoted in Roger Gaillard, "Firmin et les Etats-Unis à travers un document inédit," Pt. 2, *Conjonction* (December, 1975), 132n65.

Anténor Firmin, Haitian statesman, scholar, and reformer

Reprinted from *M. Roosevelt, Président des Etats-Unis et la République d'Haïti*

Haitian Chamber of Deputies
Courtesy of the Archives of the Episcopal Church

A rural Haitian family, near the turn of the century
Courtesy of the Archives of the Episcopal Church

The northwestern town of Port-de-Paix, 1897
Courtesy of the Archives of the Episcopal Church

Outside the import-export house of J. L. Villanueva, Port-de-Paix
Reprinted from *Blue Book of Haiti*

Inside a Syrian merchant's shop

Reprinted from Blue Book of Haiti

Henry W. Furniss, U.S. Minister to Haiti, 1905–1913

Courtesy of Dr. and Mrs. William E. Furniss

American Consulate and Legation, 1912
Courtesy of the Archives of the Episcopal Church

A Haitian soldier, *ca.* 1915
Courtesy of the Archives of the Episcopal Church

A Port-au-Prince general store, 1919
Reprinted from *Blue Book of Haiti*

Women coffee sorters from the Vital plant in Jacmel
Reprinted from *Blue Book of Haiti*

The Madsen brothers, Haitian-Danish traders in Jacmel
Reprinted from *Blue Book of Haiti*

V

Worlds of Money

Tambour prèté pas fait bon danse.

A borrowed drum doesn't make a good dance.

—Haitian proverb

FOR GENERATIONS, merchant capitalism linked Haiti with the outside world. The mercantile system and the sociopolitical structure it created dominated Haitian economy and society into the contemporary period, but loans from the merchant community did not satisfy the state's pressing need for funds during an era of rapidly growing population and declining agricultural prices. Only the robust modern metropolitan banks could meet the requirement for long-term credits.

An expanding European banking industry at the turn of the century reflected the credit needs of large and growing corporations. The banks also lent to foreign governments, including those of less developed countries, that required money for internal improvements and currency reform. Cartels, by spreading the risks, could more profitably deal with marginal states, especially if customs controls or similar guarantees could be secured. Haitian officials traveled to metropolitan centers to capture investors. The state preferred to make its obligations multilateral; but because it refused to cede control of customs receipts it made little headway in attempts to borrow.

Commercial competition remained the most important form of rivalry among the great powers in Haiti, but diplomats and policy makers saw finance as an extension of the international contest. The financiers themselves were not always as ardently patriotic as governments might have wished. Profits often lay in multilateral cooperation rather than in competition.

In the United States, the Taft administration viewed the extension of credit to Haiti as promoting political stability and American influence. It wanted American capital represented in any major loan agreement. Policy

140

makers did not see finance as improving trade. The United States already dominated Haitian commerce, and in this pre–World War I era, its financiers opposed tied loans, which still derived from commercial treaties rather than from private loan contracts. The United States moreover did not identify itself as closely with Wall Street as France and Germany did with their respective exchanges. The financial wing of metropolitan penetration of Haiti thus unfolded gradually. Its importance remained primarily political.

Haitian nationals still participated in trade, but conspicuously few engaged in banking. Banks in Haiti operated in a primitive manner. Provincial merchants paid to have cash shipped to them from Port-au-Prince in order to pay customs duties. Officials then deposited the money in a local branch of the National Bank. Since the branch offices were mere depositories, the same money was loaded on the next steamer and sent back to the capital. "An antiquated and ridiculous system," a U.S. Navy officer termed it.[1] The Banque Nationale d'Haïti, the official treasury service and fiscal agent, made short-term loans to the government and paid its daily operating expenses. This privately owned institution lent no funds for the purpose of national development. Like individual merchant-bankers, it speculated on the rate of exchange. The chief officers, many of them drawn from the local foreign business community, dabbled in insular politics. The Banque Nationale took a commission on all paper issues effected by Haitian administrations despite charter prohibitions against this practice and levied a 2 percent commission on private checks. Most of the bank's profits were expatriated, for the institution had been organized principally to pay high dividends to its stockholders in France. Before 1905 the bank took these dividends from current government revenues.[2]

Just as French, German, and American merchants had their own interests to defend, financiers also arranged themselves along national lines at first, and the loan policies of the respective powers differed signifi-

1. République d'Haïti, *Statistique générale de la République d'Haïti* (Port-au-Prince, 1908), 54, 57; National Business League of America, *Practical Suggestions for the Development of American Export Trade* . . . (Chicago, 1908), 61–66; U.S. Department of Commerce, Bureau of Foreign and Domestic Commerce, *Trade Directory of Central America and the West Indies, 1915*, (Washington, D.C., 1915), 199–217; Commander of the 5th Naval District, Report, October 31–November 6, 1915, DF, 838.00/1369.

2. Leslie F. Manigat, "La substitution de la prépondérance américaine à la prépondérance française en Haïti au début du XXe siècle: la conjoncture de 1910–1911," *Revue d'histoire moderne et contemporaine*, XIV (1967), 339, 340.

cantly. From 1875 to 1914, France, for example, boasted the lowest interest rates in the world. Credit from France enjoyed great favor because the lenders were not particular about the quality of the enterprises they supported. French investors based their decisions on the solvency of the borrower and made their ostensible liberalism the basis for advancing national objectives. Herbert Feis described French finance capitalism as follows: "in the diversity of its connections and transactions, its willingness to deal with all comers, its zest for strangeness, the Paris market surpassed London and Berlin. . . . The world of investing was a mixed, transnational, Parisian one bringing together the figures of finance, public affairs, and journalism with the borrowing representative of the races of the continent, of the Latin American states, of the whole circle of the Mediterranean coast."[3]

French banks controlled overseas banks in underdeveloped countries through majority shareholding. The Banque de l'Union Parisienne was the chief power behind the Banque Nationale d'Haïti, holding 50 percent of its stock. French savings banks also profited from overseas investments. The Crédit Lyonnais did a large business in the high-interest-bearing securities of Latin American governments.[4]

France became a prominent lender during the 1875–1914 period because its anemic home industry could not absorb its surplus capital, derived from hundreds of thousands of small investors. The French avoided underwriting foreign industrial projects, having been stung by these before. Investors preferred the fixed-return, high-yield investments that loans to autocratic regimes in less developed countries generated. The political allegiance of such borrowers was a bonus attraction. According to Feis, "French foreign lending was not dominated by careful, objective measurement of economic opportunity. Guided and often controlled by government and the opinions of the financial institutions, it was swayed by antipathies and sympathies, traditional, emotional, political. These bound it to the countries of the Latins and Slavs. To retrace the history of French foreign lending would be, as a French writer has said, almost equivalent to writing the history of French political sympathies, rapprochements, vague dreams of influence, alliances in arms."[5]

    3. Herbert Feis, *Europe, the World's Banker* (New Haven, 1930), 33, 38; L. Abrams and D. J. Miller, "Who Were the French Colonialists? A Reassessment of the *Parti Colonial,* 1890–1914," *Historical Journal,* XIX (1976), 685–725.
    4. Feis, *Europe, the World's Banker,* 40, 42; Manigat, "Substitution," 342.
    5. Feis, *Europe, the World's Banker,* 50; Abrams and Miller, "Who Were the French Colonialists?" 718–19.

French policy rested on a close cooperation between government and bankers. The state often took the initiative in preventing loans to hostile powers; it made admission to bond listing on the Paris exchange contingent on political pledges, used its power to facilitate loans to allies, and appealed to financiers' patriotic sentiments in achieving these objectives. Banks reciprocated by reserving places on their directorates for retired diplomatic and Finance Ministry officials. Such government personnel found it to their own advantage to look out for the welfare of the banks.[6]

These characteristics had several implications for Haiti, which could benefit from the low interest rates and the French disinclination to insist on strict accountability regarding the application of moneys as long as the loans were repaid. French loans to Haiti were not tied, but officials in Paris demanded a properly Francophilic attitude from the government in Port-au-Prince. In 1910, Louis-Edouard Pouget, the Haitian finance minister, refused to approve a joint Franco-German loan proposal. Pouget's failure to cooperate cost him his portfolio and sent him on a search for asylum. He did not find it in the French legation. France jealously guarded Haiti as its own financial preserve, though certain Haitian officials made strenuous efforts to break away. France suppressed these strivings for independence by ensuring that Haiti had a bad credit rating. Despite its good record, the republic found itself perpetually blacklisted on all but the French exchange. Hibbert described this problem in a parable narrated by one of his characters in *Séna*. At a diplomatic ball, according to the story, a French officer invited the Chinese minister's pretty daughter to waltz. After the dance ended, the officer's companions asked him how he had enjoyed it. He complained that the girl had two left feet, but they were surprised to see him waltz with her again and again. Finally, out of curiosity, one of the other officers asked the girl to dance. He found that she waltzed divinely and was not even wearing a corset.[7]

German finance capitalism differed markedly from the French. It traveled abroad to areas in which German commerce wished to expand and experienced its greatest movement in 1905–1906. Unlike France, Germany had a mammoth industrial complex, which absorbed most of its investment capital. German citizens opposed foreign loans when capital

6. Feis, *Europe, the World's Banker*, 134, 158–59.

7. *Ibid.*, 126–27; Pierre Carteron to Director Conty, April 29, 1908, QDO, Vol. 1; Carteron to Minister of Foreign Affairs, QDO, Vol. 3; Henry W. Furniss to Elihu Root, January 1, 1908, NF, 2126/39; Louis Pouget to Secretary of State, December 17, 1910, DF, 838.51/188; Fernand Hibbert, *Scènes de la vie haïtienne: Séna* (Port-au-Prince, 1905), 42–43.

was needed for projects at home. Before 1914, half the Reich's overseas investments lay in fixed-income securities, and most of the variable-return investments were in the hands of the largest banks, which tended to retain them and assume any attendant risks.[8]

Four leading German banks split up a considerable part of the under-developed world among themselves. In Haiti, German capital was represented by smaller banks, such as the Berliner Handelsgesellschaft, which maintained a small interest in Haiti before World War I and did not rank among these four. Private multinational banks, such as Speyer, also had Haitian investments. The Dresdner Bank wanted to purchase the Banque Nationale and offer the government in Port-au-Prince a massive loan, but the French would not abandon this lucrative operation.[9]

In addition to these metropolitan agencies, resident foreign bankers operated in the Black Republic. Before 1910, only one of these was American, and the financial stake of powers other than France and Germany remained small. Many bankers combined money lending and speculation with commerce. The British consul characterized the merchant-bankers as "the most terrible shylocks I have ever met" and considered "the corruption in business circles" in Port-au-Prince "something past description."[10]

Haiti's tempestuous relations with bankers had been a serious handicap in the struggle for development. The state's earliest obligations to alien financiers resulted from the Boyer government's agreement in 1825 to indemnify the French planters who had been expropriated and expelled during the revolution and the war for independence. France insisted on 150 million francs in exchange for diplomatic recognition but halved this figure later. The Haitians had to meet payments on the indemnity and new installments on 30 million francs borrowed from French bankers in 1838 to finance the settlement. Despite civil wars and coups d'état in the nineteenth century, the obligations were upheld.[11]

In 1875 the foreign debt dropped to its lowest point in fifty years, but the Michel Domingue government contracted two new French loans at

8. Feis, *Europe, the World's Banker*, 61, 62, 66, 71, 77–78; Raymond Poidevin and Jacques Bariéty, *Les relations franco-allemandes, 1815–1975* (Paris, 1977), 159.

9. Manigat, "Substitution," 341–42, 342n1.

10. Joseph Chatelain, *La Banque Nationale, son histoire, ses problèmes* (Port-au-Prince, 1954), 46; A. G. Vansittart to Arthur Larcom, July 18, 1905, FO 35, Vol. 182.

11. Gérard Pierre-Charles, *L'Economie haïtienne et sa voie de développement* (Paris, 1967), 134–36; Mats Lundahl, *Peasants and Poverty: A Study of Haïti* (London, 1979), 366–67.

onerous discounts. Fifty million francs, borrowed in France in 1896, consolidated the debt incurred since 1875. Between 1875 and 1910, Haiti borrowed 166 million francs, half of which returned to the lenders under one pretext or another. Haitian public officials joined French financiers in enriching themselves at public expense. Attempts at monetary stabilization derailed when the coinage used to retire paper was smuggled out of the country and sold as bullion abroad. Chronic currency problems led to continued reliance on short-term loans from merchant capitalists. The Banque Nationale, chartered in 1880 to serve the republic, openly blocked Haitian efforts at fiscal and monetary reform.[12]

The permanent financial crisis in Haiti did not permit elaboration and development of infrastructural and public institutions. It contributed to the perpetuation of a system wherein the military remained the most efficient agent of social control. The dearth of capital made revolutionary insurgency both a desirable means to power and an instrument of foreign manipulation. Haiti was not alone in facing this dilemma; it was common to the independent republics of the Caribbean and Central America. The United States, in its pursuit of regional dominance, expressed an awareness of the chronic financial exigency in the area and its implications early in the twentieth century in the policies of President William Howard Taft.

Elected in 1909, Taft developed a distinctive leadership style, constituency, and approach to foreign policy. Whereas Roosevelt had sought to use American naval strength to guarantee the stability of the smaller Latin American republics and preclude European intervention in their affairs, Taft chose the United States' financial power as the primary instrument to achieve these objectives. The Taft administration reasoned that lending these republics the funds to run secure and competent governments ought to alleviate the problems that arose when European creditors closed in on delinquent accounts. If American capital could replace European in this area, the threat of Continental intervention would end and the safety of the Panama Canal's approaches would be assured.[13]

---

12. Pierre-Charles, *L'Economie haïtienne* 136; Benoit Joachim, *Les racines du sous-développement en Haïti* (Port-au-Prince, 1979), 181–86, 187; Lundahl, *Peasants and Poverty*, 272; Louis R. E. Gation, *Aspects de l'économie et des finances d'Haïti* (Port-au-Prince, 1944), 181.

13. Paolo E. Coletta, *The Presidency of William Howard Taft* (Lawrence, Kans., 1973), 183–86; Dana G. Munro, *Intervention and Dollar Diplomacy in the Caribbean, 1900–1921* (Princeton, 1964), 160–62.

Taft's adoption of this policy necessarily meant enlarging the foreign policy community, just as he had reorganized the State Department in 1909. If Washington wanted American bankers to lend money to poor nations, it had to accord the bankers a stronger voice in policy formulation. The Taft administration took the initiative in inviting bankers' participation. In so doing, it reacted to the cooperation between banks and governments increasingly under way in Europe and particularly to the operation of that joint effort as it affected the underdeveloped world. American finance capital, in its infancy, had begin to penetrate Latin America, Europe, and Asia. Once in these new areas, however, it found itself excluded from European cartels. A Johnny-come-lately to international banking, the United States had to barge in, as it attempted to do in China between 1909 and 1913.[14]

The Taft administration viewed the banking community as an agent of American foreign policy, but the banks had no such illusions. They demonstrated their pragmatism in the way they responded to the Haitian loan and bank reorganization project of 1909–1910. That project also revealed the limitations of nationalist thought in the Taft policies and illustrated the ultimate failure of those policies to deal successfully in nationalist terms with a phenomenon that quickly outdistanced the State Department's objectives.

Most observers understood that the Banque Nationale d'Haïti did not meet the country's needs for a treasury service, for investment capital, and for consumers' banking services. Its major purpose was to collect the debt owed France for loans contracted in the nineteenth century. During the administration of Florvil Hyppolite (1889–1902), the Haitian debt was consolidated, but evidence of irregularities and fraud in the issue of new bonds led to an investigation by the succeeding Nord Alexis administration. President Nord Alexis made political capital of the so-called consolidation scandal, which involved numerous Haitians and foreigners, including officials of the Banque Nationale d'Haïti.[15]

From 1903 to the end of the Nord Alexis regime in 1908, a power struggle between the executive branch of government and bank officials led to numerous confrontations over jurisdictional issues. Matters came to a head in 1905. After a dispute over a law that reduced the interest paid by the state to internal creditors, the administration cancelled the Banque

14. Robert H. Wiebe, *The Search for Order, 1877–1920* (New York, 1967), 231–32, 242–43, 245–48; Warren I. Cohen, *America's Response to China: An Interpretive History of Sino-American Relations* (New York, 1971), 77–84.

15. Manigat, "Substitution," 339; Gation, *Aspects de l'économie*, 200–203.

Nationale's charter. Under the leadership of Frédéric Marcelin, appointed finance minister on April 10, 1905, the Haitian government solved its money problem by simply issuing an inconvertible nickle currency. The policy invited a disastrous inflation but bought time for both Haiti and the Nord Alexis administration.[16]

Nord Alexis's successor, General Antoine Simon, at first showed few signs of abandoning the uncompromising stance the government had adopted toward the Banque Nationale. Less than three weeks after his December 6, 1908, inauguration, the Banque Nationale d'Haïti tried to mollify Simon by advancing a loan. The fear that Haiti would successfully locate funds in the United States lay behind the bank's effort to be conciliatory. It also faced pressure to negotiate from the French Foreign Office, which wanted to ensure that Haiti's obligations were retained in Paris, and not assumed by New York bankers.[17]

The Banque Nationale was a French venture, but France had begun distancing itself from the bank by 1908. Liquidating the moribund institution would benefit its stockholders, and, in any case, the French government would no longer subsidize it. A new bank could begin with a clean slate. French bankers and their partisans in Haiti believed that a reorganized bank could effect desirable changes in Haitian fiscal and monetary policy. They advocated general budgetary retrenchment, reduction of customs duties, debt consolidation, freezing of the prime interest rate, and adoption of a hard-currency standard. The director of the Banque Nationale d'Haïti, French citizen Paul Santellier, strongly favored selling the national debt to foreign creditors. Once Haiti had stabilized economically, he argued, investors would warm to enterprises designed to foster improvements.[18]

The program of austerity and the expatriation of the debt that Santellier advocated was an inevitable consequence of following the classic economic principles of money management universally in force during the era. Even under the best of circumstances, Haiti would require more capital than local financiers could supply, and no progress could be made unless the endless flow of funds into sinecures, pensions, functionaries' perquisites, and outright corruption was checked. Santellier's proposals, if

16. Chatelain, *La Banque Nationale*, 73; Frédéric Marcelin, *Le Général Nord-Alexis, 1905–1908* (3 vols.; Paris, 1909), I, 237–40; Manigat, "Substitution," 340.

17. Paul Santellier to Siège Social de la Banque Nationale d'Haïti, December 22, 1908, QDO, Vol. 3; Carteron to Minister of Foreign Affairs, August 25, 1908, QDO, Vol. 14; Chatelain, *La Banque Nationale*, 74–75.

18. Santellier to Carteron, April 4, 1908, QDO, Vol. 19.

executed, would bind Haiti ever more closely to France. The banker insisted that this was all to the good. Haiti could only avoid North American domination by resort to France, "her natural protector," which wanted no territory and which was strongly linked to its former colony by ties of language and culture. To Santellier's position, Carteron added his own belief that the Banque Nationale constituted the rightful instrument of French economic authority in Haiti. France needed an independent Haiti to ensure that the United States did not completely engulf the anticipated Panama Canal route trade.[19]

For nearly thirty years, metropolitan French lenders had no American competition in the Black Republic. American bankers did not wait with bated breath to enter the Haitian money market when European interests approached Port-au-Prince in 1909 with a plan for a bank reorganization. They did not see Haiti as a particularly attractive option and, as in many countries during the Taft era, had to be coaxed into entering the arena by the State Department. The National City Bank of New York and Speyer and Company had lent money to the German-owned Chemin de Fer de la Plaine du Cul-de-Sac (P.C.S. Railroad), but neither the National City Bank nor Speyer had business connections with the Haitian state in 1909.[20]

Yankee financiers had just begun to be deeply interested in wide-ranging foreign investments, and federal laws limited their ability to develop cartels overseas. Under the presidency of Frank A. Vanderlip (1909–1919), the National City Bank led the drive for international expansion and realized this goal. Participation in Haitian finance provided the bank with one of its first opportunities to break into a previously all-European financial market. French hostility to American entry could no longer be sustained given the Haitian preference for multilateral dealings, the maturation of American finance, and problems with the balance of power in Europe. The German minister and the French chargé d'affaires agreed that the European nations ought to march hand in hand against American imperialism but realized that such resolve probably could not be sustained over the individual self-interest of the respective countries.[21]

19. *Ibid.*; Santellier to Carteron, April 18, 1908, QDO, Vol. 19.

20. Munro, *Intervention*, 251–52.

21. Robert Stanley Mayer, "The Influence of Frank A. Vanderlip and the National City Bank on American Commerce and Foreign Policy, 1910–1920" (Ph.D. dissertation, Rutgers University, 1968), 23, 42; Frank A. Vanderlip to James Stillman, June 3, 1910, in Frank A. Vanderlip Papers, Columbia University; E. Jore to Minister of Foreign Affairs, December 10, 1909, QDO, Vol. 22.

Subscribers to the Haitian Loan in 1909

Firms	Nationality	Gourdes lent
8	German	1,054,000
4	American	405,000
8	French	264,000
1	Russo-Polish	180,000
4	British	179,000
10	Haitian	166,000
2	Danish	110,000
6	Syrian	105,000
3	Italian	22,000
1	Dominican	15,000

SOURCE: Jore to Minister of Foreign Affairs, September 9, 1909, QDO, Vol. 21.

In 1909, *Le Matin*, a Haitian newspaper, published a list of leading firms in Haiti that had agreed to collectively lend 2.5 million gourdes to the Haitian government. E. Jore, the French consul, curious as to the citizenship of the lenders, compiled a table based on the newspaper account and sent it to the minister of foreign affairs in Paris. Its most valuable feature, he wrote, was that it represented "almost exactly the proportion in which foreign capital is presently engaged in Haiti." He noted the preponderance of German capital and the lively struggle for influence between the United States and Germany, with France in third place.[22]

Jore had recognized the growing influence of the United States in Haitian finance. In 1910, Frank A. Vanderlip, president of the National City Bank, led a group of American bankers in investigating the feasibility of participation in a Haitian loan. They had corresponded with J. N. Léger during the previous Haitian administration and researched the outstanding difficulties between the Haitian government and the Banque Nationale. The bankers learned with satisfaction that Haiti planned to send three representatives to treat with officials at the Banque Nationale's Paris headquarters and to resolve conflicts between the Haitian government and French financiers about how the Banque Nationale should be man-

22. Jore to Minister of Foreign Affairs, September 9, 1909, QDO, Vol. 21.

aged. The Haitian loan would be worthwhile only if it was listed on the Paris exchange. The bankers from the United States required the full cooperation of the French for a successful venture.[23]

In April, 1910, the Haitian delegation arrived in New York City. Armed with the power to bind their government, the representatives had as their first obligation the salvaging of the Banque Nationale. That prospect failing, the delegation had the authority to annul the existing bank contract and make another arrangement with an American or European institution. The National City Bank wanted a customs control convention attached to any loan it might make, but dropped the stipulation when the Haitians balked at the idea, which was unpopular in Washington and Port-au-Prince alike.[24]

Europeans also expressed renewed interest in Haiti. On home leave in the summer of 1910, the German minister broached the subject of a joint Franco-German loan to a group of bankers. Anticipating American displeasure at being excluded from the consortium, the French and German financiers invited two New York firms with close German connections, Hallgarten and Company and Ladenburg Thalmann and Company, to advance a quarter of the capital in the proposed deal. Metropolitan German banks would put up another 25 percent, with French financiers supplying the rest.[25]

This invitation and the 1909 loan to the P.C.S. Railroad by the National City Bank and Speyer and Company showed the bankers' private diplomacy at work. The railroad could have been financed in Germany. Despite the militancy of the Reich regarding financial supremacy in Haiti, however, German financiers had no particular desire to antagonize the Americans. They, above all, recognized the transnational character of money and had long since transcended Taft's nationalistic position on finance capitalism as well as their own government's saber rattling on the subject. These banks did not confine their operations or their loyalties to any one state, and nationality functioned more as a convenience for them than as a matter of principle. By 1909, German merchants and bankers in Haiti had sidestepped American opposition to their presence by acquiring American citizenship. Interestingly, the German government accorded

23. Samuel McRoberts to Vanderlip, April 9, 1910, in Frank A. Vanderlip Papers.
24. *Ibid.*
25. Munro, *Intervention*, 247; U.S. Department of State, Division of Latin American Affairs, Memorandum, n.d., DF, 838.51/–; Edgar Speyer to Lord Hardinge, September 27, 1910, FO 371, Vol. 915; A. P. Murray to Secretary of State for Foreign Affairs, October 1, 1910, FO 371, Vol. 914.

naturalized German Americans official citizenship status. These dual nationals thus profited from important connections with financiers in German cities as well as in New York. The German merchant-banking house
Keitel and Company, the most powerful firm in Haiti, and Joseph Free-
man, who simultaneously represented Speyer and the National City
Bank, promoted a separate, German-chartered bank proposal. They heavily courted the Simon administration, which seemed to encourage their
activities. The German and American interests, the Haitians apparently
thought, would counterbalance one another.[26]

French and German bankers cooperated closely in Haiti, in spite of cool
relations between their respective homelands. This was not only an affair
of banks. France and Germany also cooperated to a lesser degree in Cuba
and Mexico. They teamed up against the United States or Haiti in perfect
harmony when the occasion warranted. The U.S. State Department nevertheless continued to think of banks in national terms. It refused to
consider Hallgarten and Ladenburg Thalmann as American and instead
viewed them as subsidiaries of German firms operating in the United
States. True American participation in the Haitian loan project could not,
therefore, be based on the involvement of these companies. The State
Department refused to approve the bid.[27]

The prospect of American participation in the Franco-German consortium did not please some Haitians. American lenders might impose difficult conditions on fiscal administration, and the geographical proximity of
the two countries could tempt them to interfere in Haiti's internal affairs.
Europeans who had no wish to share the projected enterprise fed these
suspicions, and all parties tried to win Haitian support for their own pet
reorganization plans through widespread bribery.[28]

Public corruption during Simon's regime revealed much about what
foreigners felt was at stake and can be used to measure its importance.
While Nord Alexis's opponents had complained about the "palace clique"
and about mercenary members of his family during his six-year presi-

26. Jore to Minister of Foreign Affairs, October 2, 12, and November 12, 1909,
and Pierre Lefevre-Pontalis to Minister of Foreign Affairs, October 16, 1909, all in QDO,
Vol. 22.

27. Raymond Poidevin, *Les Relations économiques et financières entre la France et
l'Allemagne de 1898 à 1914* (Paris, 1969), 584, 585; Munro, *Intervention*, 249; Huntington
Wilson, Memorandum, January 6, 1911, and State Department to American Legation, Port-
au-Prince, September 24, 1910, DF, 838.51/−.

28. Murray to Secretary of State, October 1, 1910, FO 371, Vol. 914, and September 15,
1910, FO 371, Vol. 915; Furniss to Secretary of State, August 29, 1910, DF, 838.51/94, and
September 2, 1910, DF, 838.51/97.

dency, his successor, General Antoine Simon, came to power on a promise of national reconciliation and on healthy endowments from merchant-bankers. Simon pardoned the exiles, tolerated the Syrians, and reopened talks with the Banque Nationale d'Haïti. His actions reflected the realization that the country had moved into a prolonged crisis and that the use of foreign loans to reconstruct the national economy was neither shameful nor unsound. The resident foreign community concurred, for it had been uncomfortably restricted during the Nord Alexis years and saw an opportunity to regain its old position with Simon as chief of state. Simon believed in loans and in the direct introduction of foreign capital. Once in the National Palace, he found that his policies dovetailed with those of the new American president, who promoted banking and investment in underdeveloped countries.[29]

To the Americans, exclusion from a loan consortium created the alarming possibility that Europeans would demand a customs receivership or take other drastic steps to secure guarantees for their investments. In the summer of 1910, Furniss cautioned President Simon against customs control arrangements and any German banking propositions supported by the government in Berlin. The American minister tried to tie Simon's current good relations with the United States to the anti-German posture he wished the Haitians to assume. He wrote to Washington officials that the Reich was "jealous" of the warmth Simon showed to American entrepreneurs. Furniss expected the Germans to begin courting the president's rivals. If these competitors succeeded, Furniss maintained, "German aggression" would supplant "American influence" in Haiti.[30]

The Germans did not constitute the monolithic presence often ascribed to them. Certain German merchant-bankers resident in Haiti opposed the plans emanating from Hamburg and Berlin. As bondholders, they protested Zimmerer's role in promoting a Franco-German cartel because they feared being sacrificed to Continental interests. The French minister, rather than the German financial community, endorsed the German proposal. Carteron flatly opposed participation by resident merchant-bankers in the consortium. Not only were most of these businessmen crooked, he believed; they were not French. Whichever bank contract the Haitians adopted, France, as the marketplace for such transactions, would benefit.

29. Edgar N. Numa, *Antoine Simon et la «Fatalité Historique»* (N.p., n.d.), 29–30.
30. Furniss to Secretary of State, July 30, 1910, DF, 838.51/81, and April 30, 1910, DF, 838.00/–.

The prospect of an active German financial presence in Haiti disturbed only the Americans. Murray, watching from the sidelines, saw the bank issue as a contest of superpowers. A Haitian he knew characterized it as the American eagle and the German wolf quarreling over the carcass of a lamb or, as Murray snidely put it, "a black sheep."[31]

Two rival banking groups formed during the course of 1910. Speyer worked with the National City Bank against Ladenburg Thalmann and Hallgarten, which were supported by Zimmerer. Eager to appear conciliatory, the Germans proposed multilateral control of Haitian finance through a tripartite international commission. The State Department rejected this, as multilateral control would give the Americans only a minority voice in the management of Haitian affairs. The National City Bank also opposed the idea; it favored American control, which would make it the dominant corporate interest in Haiti.[32]

Haitian authorities initially had two lender groups to consider. The Franco-German group planned a bank that would resume the treasury service that Nord Alexis had taken from the old bank in 1905, collect the customs revenues, pay the government's creditors, and set aside a fund to retire the present paper currency. Of the proposed 65 million francs, Haiti would receive only 72 percent after various commissions and charges. American policy makers claimed that the terms were too onerous for Haiti to assume. They also deemed certain features of the contract monopolistic and maintained that there was inadequate provision for the interests of foreign claimants and American bondholders. Collection of the country's revenues by a European corporation might also pave the way for future foreign intervention.[33]

The Speyer–National City Bank consortium, endorsed by the American minister to Haiti, Henry W. Furniss, had no detailed plan like that presented by the Europeans, and did not aggressively plead its case in Port-au-Prince. According to National City Bank officer Samuel McRoberts, his institution's circumspection was based on the view that a lender must be granted very favorable terms to make a Haitian loan attractive. Listing Haitian bonds on the Paris exchange was furthermore essential: this required that "the goodwill of the French market" be preserved. The American bankers thus coolly sidestepped State Depart-

---

31. Carteron to Minister of Foreign Affairs, April 28, 1908, QDO, Vol. 19; Murray to Secretary of State, October 27, 1910, FO 371, Vol. 915.

32. Division of Latin American Affairs, Memorandum, n.d., DF 838.51/–.

33. Wilson, Memorandum, January 6, 1911, DF, 838.51/–.

ment admonitions to move faster in Haiti and sought instead to purchase the Banque Nationale from its French owners. Uninterested in nationalist rivalry with the Europeans, the American group opted to enter the Haitian capital market at a moment and in a style of its own choosing. It failed to reach a satisfactory agreement with the Banque Nationale corporation and, by mid-April, 1910, at the same time that the Haitian delegation arrived, had decided to reach an accommodation with the French and German bankers.[34]

The United States assumed an entirely different attitude. It objected strenuously to the European plan and enlisted the aid of Britain in registering protests. The European bank reorganization and loan program nevertheless went for approval in the autumn of 1910. The Simon administration had already endorsed it. Observers noted how carefully its path was smoothed with gifts to legislators, who had become more amenable once the unpopular customs control provision had been deleted. The State Department ordered Furniss to exert all possible pressure to have the proposals voted down.[35] The Europeans gave him a good fight, and a tone of urgency developed in the diplomatic correspondence of these months. Telegrams flew back and forth as Furniss related tales of purchased votes, intimidated deputies, and Haitians' lack of confidence in the United States' caveats. Working with Britain, which also sought to block any German initiatives on the island, the United States made strong protests. The Germans encouraged the Haitians to think the United States was merely blustering, and offered to protect them against any retaliatory action the Americans might take.[36] The Europeans struggled fiercely to secure a foreign bank without American domination and, for the time being, won.

On October 26 the legislature voted the program through and dissolved the Banque Nationale d'Haïti, which ceded its charter. As part of the compromise, the government in Port-au-Prince renounced the sums awarded it by the special tribunals that had judged the consolidation

34. Samuel McRoberts to Vanderlip, April 9, 1910, in Frank A. Vanderlip Papers; anonymous letter to Jore, October 16, 1909, QDO, Vol. 22.

35. Murray to Secretary of State, October 1, 1910, FO 371, Vol. 914; Furniss to Secretary of State, August 29, 1910, DF, 838.51/54, and September 2, 1910, DF, 838.51/97.

36. Furniss to Secretary of State, October 1, 1910 (DF, 838.51/117), October 5, 1910 (DF, 838.51/114), October 7, 1910 (DF, 838.51/115); Pouget to Secretary of State, December 17, 1910, DF, 838.51/188; Murray to Foreign Office, September 15, 1910, FO 371, Vol. 915; Mitchell Innes to Lord Grey, November 28, 1910, FO 371, Vol. 915; Lemuel Livingston to Furniss, September 15, 1910, Post Records, Letters from Consuls to Ministers, Record Group 84, NA.

frauds. A new bank was created, the Banque Nationale de la République d'Haïti (BNRH), which kept the old bank's headquarters.[37]

After the Chambers had approved the contract, which included only French and German-American multinational private banks, the French invited the American metropolitan banks to participate. United States cooperation could only strengthen the security of any Continental investments. American interests acquired 20 percent of the consortium, and the State Department dropped its objections to the plan. The U.S. government accepted National City Bank's argument that the absence of a clause requiring a customs receivership ought to neutralize its opposition. Tortuously maintaining that the ratification of the plan by the Haitian legislature—even though it had ratified a different plan—nullified their criticisms of the project's exploitative character, the Americans exposed the frailty of their motives.[38]

The unprecedented opportunity to achieve greater control in Haiti, and to neutralize the European advantage that had gradually built up over the years, determined the change in policy. The United States' traditionally jealous concern over extrahemispheric intrusion into Latin American enterprises proved stronger than its doubts about the fairness of the bank concession. The final contract gave the Banque de l'Union Parisienne in France 75 percent control of the new bank. The American group, consisting of the National City Bank, the firms of Speyer, Ladenburg Thalmann, and Hallgarten, received 20 percent. The German Berliner Handelsgesellschaft held only the remaining 5 percent, but the multinational character of the German-American firms disguised German participation. The BNRH resumed its predecessor's role as the national treasury. It was to redeem the paper currency and act as the sole government depository. The bank gave priority to servicing the foreign debt and returning any surplus to the government. That debt now included a new $13 million (65-million-franc) loan, of which Haiti received only $9.4 million after discount. Soon after the Americans joined the consortium, Murat Claude, identified by both French and American ministers as one of many top officials who were friendly to their respective national interests, became finance minister in a general cabinet shuffle.[39]

37. Chatelain, *La Banque Nationale*, 75, 81–82; Innes to Grey, November 28, 1910, FO 371, Vol. 915.

38. Innes to Grey, November 28 and December 2, 1910, FO 371, Vol. 915.

39. National City Bank to Secretary of State, January 11, 1911, DF, 838.51/204; McRoberts and Milton Ailes to Secretary of State, January 10, 1911, and Philander Knox to McRoberts *et al.*, January 11, 1911, FO 371, Vol. 1131; Munro, *Intervention*, 254; Furniss

President Simon did not confine his program for Haitian development to foreign loans. In 1909 his administration approved a plan for a vast infrastructural program in the North. It granted a concession to an American speculator, James P. McDonald, to build a national railroad from Port-au-Prince to Cape Haitian and establish a fifteen-mile area of banana plantations along each side of the right-of-way. In 1910 the National City Bank lent McDonald half a million dollars to start work.[40] McDonald, ostensibly an independent promoter, contracted with the Haitian government for a guaranteed 6 percent interest on bonds issued to underwrite the cost of construction. This amounted to annual payments of two thousand dollars a mile. Further payments would accompany the government's acceptance of sections of track as they were completed. In addition, McDonald negotiated a monopoly on the export of fruit from the banana plantations. A glance at a map of Haiti reveals the enormous scope of this enterprise. At its narrowest point, the distance from Port-au-Prince due east to the Dominican border, Haiti is only thirty miles wide. McDonald's plan, if fully realized, would have given him half the arable land in the country and turned the northern plains into great latifundia.[41]

France, which had no developers operating in Haiti, expressed little interest in the project. The Germans, on the other hand, vigorously opposed the concessions, which would have preempted possibilities for German capitalist expansion. They enlisted the help of the minister of public works to delay the proposal's progress through government channels.[42] Other opponents of the McDonald contracts alerted the northern peasantry of an impending land grab by whites. Simon's enemies made considerable capital of the situation. The government's "selling the country" to the Americans and the behavior of officials fattening on the new graft strengthened their cause. The Simon administration had already earned a certain notoriety for such "jobs" as purchasing decrepit yachts in New York for use as "gunboats," paying up to twenty times their value, with functionaries and vendors pocketing the difference. Other schemes had involved official expenditures for goods and services that never mate-

to State Department, December 20, 1910, DF, 838.002/1; Carteron to Minister of Foreign Affairs, December 21, 1908, QDO, Vol. 3.

40. Murray to Secretary of State, October 27, 1910, FO 371, Vol. 915; Furniss to State Department, December 20, 1910, DF, 838.002/1.

41. Roger Farnham, Testimony, in SI, 107.

42. Jore to Minister of Foreign Affairs, August 12 and September 12, 1909, QDO, Vol. 4; Furniss to Secretary of State, February 17, 1910, DF, 838.00/489.

rialized, padded expense accounts, and legislative bills that awarded gratuitous money to Simon. McDonald finally allegedly bribed his concessions through the Chambers.[43]

The Simon regime's flagrant corruption did not stand alone in creating a favorable atmosphere for increased metropolitan involvement in Haitian affairs. Subtle changes in the powers' perception of Haiti had occurred. Roosevelt had suppressed arms sales to the Caribbean republics, but Taft and his secretary of state, Philander Knox, pressed their diplomatic representatives in Latin America to peddle American hardware—arms, matériel, and warships. Furniss persuaded Simon to buy a thousand old Springfield rifles and American coal.[44] The U.S. government's behavior contradicted the objectives of Dollar Diplomacy. If the goal of that policy was to create peace and stability through financial solvency, it failed in Haiti, which did not need an expensive navy of small, worn-out vessels. The American role in the bank reorganization is a rejoinder to the argument that Washington could not have told the Haitians how to spend their money. The United States had no qualms about imposing its will on Haiti in pursuit of its own interests.

As metropolitan competition embraced sales of military surplus to the Haitian government, France entered the lists. Like the United States, it used diplomatic channels to interest the Simon administration in outdated ships and machine guns. As the little island country was no match for a large, determined aggressor, the arms only served to suppress native dissidence.[45]

The Germans could not afford to sell arms to the government in Port-au-Prince in the tense climate that characterized the Reich's relations with the United States. They did, however, understand the implications of the McDonald contracts for their own future in Haiti and continued to agitate against them even after their successful passage through the legislature. Some Haitians, especially northerners whose communities would be affected by the railroad-plantation network, joined forces with the Ger-

43. Furniss to Secretary of State, June 14, 1912 (DF, 838.6156M14), October 27, 1910 (DF, 838.304/1), May 30, 1910 (DF, 838.6102), September 17, 1910 (DF, 838.001), April 24, 1911 (DF, 838.602); Munro, *Intervention*, 256; Murray to Secretary of State, April 30, 1910, FO 371, Vol. 914.

44. Furniss to Secretary of State, August 6, 1910, DF, 838.24, and February 12, 1910, DF, 838.34/–.

45. Minister of War to Minister of Foreign Affairs, February 24, 1911, and Nemours Auguste to Raymond Poincaré, July 10, 1912, QDO, Vol. 9; Lucien Maurouard to Minister of Foreign Affairs, December 29, 1910, QDO, Vol. 4.

mans in protest. The American consul in Cape Haitian believed that most of the northern antagonism to the McDonald contracts was politically motivated rather than derived from an honest concern for public welfare. Firminists and followers of General Cincinnatus Leconte opposed rural development, the consul wrote, because full employment would deprive the *caco* generals of willing soldiers and limit the possibilities for those wishing to "profit from the existing misery."[46]

Simon's partisans argued that his commitment to developing the country was demonstrated by the ease with which foreigners gained access to Haiti during his administration. The question seemed to turn on Simon's sincerity. Were the many concessions, loans, and contracts mere boodle, or were they inspired by a genuine desire to initiate improvements? His foes criticized his traditionalism, his lack of education, his unschooled following, his devotion to the African gods in an era when such faiths enjoyed no respectability at all in metropolitan countries, and his daughter's apparent influence in public affairs.[47]

The parasitic army constituted another reproach to the regime. Certainly Simon was not the first Haitian president to rely on armed force, nor the only one associated with press-gang recruitment, authoritarianism, and abuse of power. The resident diplomatic community deplored the Haitian military. "The better classes have nothing to do with the army," Furniss wrote. It "is the scourge of the nation . . . the evil eating out its very vitals and no stable government, no progress can be expected until its influence is curtailed."[48] The policy Furniss pursued in Haiti at the State Department's behest, however, enhanced the worst military characteristics of the Haitian government, as he and other diplomats drummed up trade for hawkers of outmoded guns and other secondhand weapons.

The metropoles alone did not create the Simon government, but that regime handily corresponded to a particular phase in their foreign policies. Taft's and Simon's presidencies began at about the same time. Taft emphasized the role he believed finance capital should play in international relations just when it became possible to discuss the revival of foreign banking in Haiti. France and Germany, aware of the new American activism in finance, initially wanted to exclude the United States from

46. Livingston to Assistant Secretary of State, June 26, 1912, in Post Records, Letters from Consuls, RG 84.
47. A revisionist view of Simon's daughter Celestina is found in Henry Austin, "Port-au-Prince or Port-au-President," *New England Magazine*, XLIV (1911), 625.
48. Furniss to Secretary of State, October 28, 1910, DF, 838.51/164.

banking in Haiti. They won the battle but, recognizing the Pyrrhic nature of the victory, ceded the war and admitted American partnership. In so doing, they acknowledged the American claim to political supremacy in the hemisphere and, in the words of the Haitian diplomat Pauléus Sannon, accepted a "financial Monroe Doctrine."[49]

The underside of international finance involved more than a little waste and theft. Speculative firms organized railroad projects in underdeveloped countries for the purpose of floating bonds. Payoffs to officials permitted the approval of loans that denuded national treasuries and worked to the disadvantage of all Latin Americans.[50] The order, civilization, and prosperity that the host countries supposedly enjoyed as a result of these ministrations never emerged. Commentators chalked it up to these nations' imperviousness to change. In Haiti, the cupidity of the Simon clique quickly became legendary, but few acknowledged the culpability of the metropolitan spoilers who dangled the temptations before these men.

McDonald's work on the National Railroad began in 1910. A group of rough-and-ready engineers arrived from the United States. Foulmouthed and combative, they squabbled with Haitian soldiers and taught their unskilled local helpers to curse in English. They shocked the Cape Haitian bourgeoisie by appearing at the gentlemen's club in shirt-sleeves. This first exposure to Americans could not have reassured northerners about foreign intentions. "The ignorant country people . . . really believed that these contracts authorized the Americans to take over," wrote U.S. Consul Livingston at Cape Haitian, "not only a vast extent of government lands, but also their little acre and cabin." The peasants personally feared McDonald, whose name "became a house-hold word and almost every unknown white man above the average in physical proportions was supposed to be that personage."[51]

The "little acre and cabin" were not as secure as Livingston wanted to think. Few peasants had clear title to the land they farmed, and much of it either belonged to the government or could be usurped by powerful private persons. Simon maintained that the public domain being developed by McDonald was mere scrub, semi-arid desert from which only a few scattered squatters would be evicted. The number of persons living on the land in question is not known, but it is certain that in the absence of

49. H. Pauléus Sannon, *Pour un gouvernement stable* (Port-au-Prince, 1930), 2–3.

50. Andre Gunder Frank, *Capitalism and Underdevelopment in Latin America* (New York, 1969), 290–94.

51. Livingston to Assistant Secretary of State, May 15, 1912, DF, 711.38/14.

specific guarantees and titles, the concessions threatened the peasants' livelihood and gave them no recourse if evicted except the possibility of working as wage laborers for the Americans.[52]

McDonald's supporters evoked a future age in which improved communications would break down the cultural barriers between the *habitant* and his urban neighbor. All attempts at national development in the twentieth century have involved measures of sacrifice, some on a terrific scale. In Haiti in 1910, however, the persons demanding the sacrifice would not be making it themselves. Simon and most of his officials hailed from the South. The northern peasant would bear the brunt of national development. In a country of keen regional consciousness, this fact did not pass unnoted.[53]

The Haitian need for investment capital was genuine. The reorganized bank contributed nothing toward developing the country, however, and rural Haitians continued to fall back on their own resources. Soon after the Firminist war of 1902, they began a seasonal migration to Cuba and the Dominican Republic to cut cane. Expanded production in those countries, better wages, and freedom from conscription contributed to the movement. Emigration increased during the decade beginning in 1910, and functionaries earned large sums selling passports to laborers at exorbitant prices. Many of those wishing to go to the Dominican Republic avoided the bureaucracy by slipping across the border at some unguarded point.[54]

Haitian laborers served as agricultural reserves in the Caribbean, joining the ranks of such West Indian workers as the Jamaicans who went to Panama to build the Canal during the same era. Metropolitan capital had not yet sufficiently penetrated Haiti to change the patterns of land tenure and create a landless, wage-earning agricultural class, but it brought the

52. Antoine Pierre-Paul, "La Banque agricole," *Revue de la Société haïtienne d'histoire et de géographie*, XXII (July, 1951), 30; Candelon Rigaud, *Promenades dans les campagnes d'Haïti* (Paris, 1928), 119; Paul Moral, *Le Paysan haïtien* (Paris, 1961), 50, 60.

53. J. C. Dorsainvil, *Manuel d'histoire d'Haïti* (Port-au-Prince, 1925), 286–87.

54. Lélio Laville, *La Traite des Nègres au XXe Siècle ou les Dessous de l'Emigration haïtienne à Cuba* (Port-au-Prince, 1933), 1–2; *Le Matin*, November 6, 1907, p. 1; R. L. Leroy to President of Haiti, August 30, 1911, and President Zamor to Minister of the Interior, October 25, 1911, in Kurt Fisher Collection, Schomburg Research Center, NYPL; Livingston to Furniss, August 24, 1910, in Post Records, Letters from Consuls, RG 84; Moral, *Le Paysan haïtien*, 60.

labor it needed to territories where such a pattern did exist. In the process, it depressed agricultural wages in those areas.[55]

Labor exports began to play an important role in supplying capital to the Haitian economy at a time when the demand for foreign imports grew without a corresponding rise in agricultural production. Industrial manufactures increasingly shared the Haitian market with items of staple consumption. Automobiles were introduced during the Simon era. Houses prefabricated in Chicago enjoyed great popularity in towns so often threatened by fire. But the United States did not monopolize the new freedom of access to Haiti. This worried the State Department, particularly after hearing news of French and German proposals for coaling stations at all open ports.

The French proposal outlined a coastal service connecting the Haitian seaports and feeding into a French Bordeaux-bound line, which also called at Dominican and Puerto Rican ports. A representative of the Compagnie Générale Transatlantique submitted a draft proposal to the legislature. A second proposal, drawn up by a Hamburg America Line official, presented a similar plan but arranged the routing as part of the German transport system. France and Germany might work together in the Caribbean in banking, but the Anglo-French Entente Cordiale made maritime cooperation impossible. The Germans took the matter of Caribbean naval stations very seriously. Wedged in an increasingly tight corner, Germany felt it had to match France's initiatives in Haiti.[56]

Coaling depots at each port were hardly necessary unless Haiti planned to supply European warships, an endeavor the United States strongly disapproved. In event of war, the Europeans would have good military positions in the hemisphere. The State Department did not object to a commercial coaling facility available to all nations as long as the Open Door was secured. Washington made the American ambassadors in Paris and Berlin aware of the French and German plans and had Furniss present to President Simon the United States' objections. Simon claimed ignorance of the proposed contracts, though his son, a deputy, backed the German version in the legislature a few weeks later. Simon swore, how-

55. Haitian Minister in Santo Domingo to Abel Léger, January 20, 1931, in Kurt Fisher Collection; Arismendí Díaz Santana, "The Role of Haitian Braceros in Dominican Sugar Production," *Latin American Perspectives*, III (Winter, 1976), 120–32.

56. Furniss to Secretary of State, June 3, 1910, DF, 838.802; Holger H. Herwig, *Politics of Frustration: The United States in German Naval Planning, 1889–1941* (Boston, 1976), 26–27, 30, 48, 103.

ever, to oppose such concessions and promised Furniss that the bill would die in the Senate. The American minister had misgivings about these assurances, but the contract was eventually amended out of existence.[57]

Although Simon satisfied the United States on the coaling station issue, American tolerance of the Haitian president was growing thin. Toward the end of his administration, Simon lost the remaining trust of the diplomatic community despite his professions of friendship. A courtly man whose pure white hair and beard contrasted strikingly with his black skin, Simon used his distinguished appearance to advantage. He associated easily with the common people, sharing their roots and playing the role of patriarch. His kindly but stately mien made him invaluable to foreign businessmen. On a visit to a French-operated cane plantation, for example, Simon exhorted the laborers to work hard and obediently for their foreign masters. Yet his powers could upset already nervous whites. The British consul related an incident in which Simon, attending the first communion for pupils at a convent school, ordered drums played in the schoolyard. "To the horror of the Sisters," Murray reported, the pupils and guests began to sing and dance a voodoo song of initiation.[58]

Simon had also begun to display authoritarian tendencies. Until the spring of 1909 the administration had tolerated a free press. The crackdown came in April, when the police arrested the editor of *L'Impartiale* and several other journalists for their editorials on the McDonald contracts. More arrests followed, particularly of Firminists. When a group of teachers from the formerly Firminist center of Gonaïves arrived in Port-au-Prince to complain that their salaries had been withheld, Simon received them politely. He told them that a teaching career demanded "a spirit of sacrifice." As the delegation departed, several members were seized and imprisoned.[59]

Expatriates also experienced the hard side of the avuncular Simon. British Consul Murray was stoned twice in the street and called a "rotten white dog." Rumors also circulated that a German had been stabbed and

57. Furniss to Secretary of State, June 3, 1910, Secretary of the Navy to Secretary of State, June 21, 1910, Alvey Adee to Thomas Dawson, in Furniss to Secretary of State, July 20, 1910, Furniss to Secretary of State, August 19, 1910, Dawson to H. Wilson, September 8, 1910, with Furniss to Secretary of State, August 20, 1910, Furniss to Secretary of State, October 14, 1910, all in DF, 838.802.

58. Murray to Secretary of State, April 30 and February 25, 1910, FO 371, Vol. 914; Furniss to Secretary of State, March 3, 1911, DF, 838.00/553; Admiral Caperton to Secretary of the Navy, Report, October 31–November 6, 1915, DF, 838.00/1369.

59. Maurouard to Minister of Foreign Affairs, April 29, 1910, QDO, Vol. 4; Murray to Secretary of State, April 30, 1910, FO 371, Vol. 914.

shot. Attacks on foreign residents were generally products of instigation. By the spring of 1910, rising opposition to Simon's policies necessitated militant action reminiscent of the Nord Alexis days. The administration sought to camouflage its "selling the country" by adopting a guise of covert opposition to foreign penetration, hoping that assaults on European businessmen and diplomats would vent the growing popular indignation and allow the traffic in concessions and other schemes to continue uninterrupted.[60]

European envoys evinced unhappiness with Simon well before Furniss expressed reservations. Furniss tried to cultivate a special relationship with the Haitian president. He doubted that other presidential contenders would so consistently favor American interests and saw the Germans as a continuing threat. "For this reason," Furniss wrote, "independent of the fact that General Simon is the head of the legal government and consequently has our support, he should be given all possible encouragement and aid."[61]

Furniss' support for Simon withered, however, in the face of the continuing persecution of elements of the elite. By March 1911, J. N. Léger, the Haitian most admired by Americans and most associated with their interests, including those of his legal client McDonald, was in hiding. Other prominent men had fled or were in prison.[62] This proved decisive in determining the American attitude toward Simon. The intimidation of persons regarded as links to the metropolitan community and its interests more deeply concerned Westerners than did the peasants and poor townsmen who suffered most from arbitrary arrests, torture, and summary executions. Only grave atrocities could stir up indignation over the treatment of the masses. Such indignation did occur as rumors of a massacre in Ouanaminthe, a town on the Dominican frontier, reached the coast.

Simon had never been popular in the North. The official press depicted his 1909 trip to the area as a glowing success, but stories about the president's encounters with northern hostility began to leak. His retinue had to pillage its way across the country because rural people refused to sell the rations it was prepared to purchase. The show of popular disaffection was intimately tied to northern anger over the McDonald contracts. It was expressed particularly in those areas where central authority was

60. Murray to Secretary of State, March 31, 1910, FO 371, Vol. 914.
61. Furniss to Secretary of State, April 30, 1910, DF, 838.00.
62. Furniss to Secretary of State, September 16, 1910 (DF, 838.602So1/6), February 14, 1911 (DF, 838.00/545), March 6, 1911 (DF, 838.00/552), June 5, 1912 (DF, 838.77/38), January 1, 1908 (NF, 2126/39).

weakest. Remote Ouanaminthe, far to the east, would not have been directly affected by McDonald's plans, but it traditionally supplied Haitian revolutions with *cacos*, Dominican mercenaries, arms, and pack animals smuggled in from across the border. Early in 1911 the warlords' customary challenge to incumbency united once more with popular dissatisfaction. In the North, war broke out on such a scale that the New York *Times* described it as "a virtual uprising of the people."[63]

Simon, challenged, personally headed a punitive expedition to Ouanaminthe. After suppressing the rebellion and allowing the army to loot the town, he ordered the execution of prisoners without trial. Among the condemned was a Franco-Haitian youth whose arms and legs were chopped off before he was finally put to death. Simon proclaimed the conquest of Ouanaminthe in *Le Moniteur*, the official newspaper.[64]

Simon never took direct responsibility for the slaughter, but critics widely blamed government troops. The social geography of the island made the interior inaccessible to foreigners. Trade with whites took place on the coast. An internal passport was required of urbanites who wished to travel in the hinterland. Only the occasional priest, concessionaire, fugitive, or exile ventured into the interior towns, which had few commercial outlets. Little news of such places reached the capital. Army posts represented their only contact with Port-au-Prince, and military use of force where a virtual news blackout existed could not be restrained.[65]

After leading his troops to an apparent victory over the northern rebels in February, 1911, Simon retired to the capital. His triumph proved illusory. In a stiff note delivered to Haiti through Sannon, now the Haitian minister in Washington, the United States formally protested the Ouanaminthe executions. A copy cabled to Furniss for delivery to the Port-au-Prince government underscored the American sentiment. The torture and executions in Ouanaminthe permanently soured Simon's relations with France as well, though the president tried to make amends

63. Murray to Secretary of State, November 1, 1910, FO 371, Vol. 914; *Le Moniteur*, 1909, *passim*, for laudatory accounts of Simon's provincial visits; New York *Times*, April 27, 1911, Sec. 3, p. 4.

64. *Le Moniteur*, February 15 and 18, 1911, with Furniss to Secretary of State, February 24, 1911, DF, 838.00/545; Murray to Secretary of State, March 31, 1911, FO 371, Vol. 1132; G. W. Lawes to Secretary of the Navy, March 7, 1911, with Furniss to Secretary of State, February 24, 1911, DF, 838.00/545.

65. Moral, *Le Paysan haïtien, passim*; Diana Callear, "The Stagnation of Peasant Agriculture in Haiti" (B.A. thesis, University of East Anglia, School of Development Studies, United Kingdom, 1977).

by offering a $45,000 indemnity.[66] Conflict with the legations, however, remained only one of Simon's problems. The North rose again in May. Rebels burned property belonging to the McDonald railroad group, which was openly identified with the Simon administration.[67] Revolution could not be prevented, for Simon's policies had provoked profound regional antagonisms. The North resented the McDonald contracts, the southern placemen filling northern jobs, and the grafters in Port-au-Prince. Simon appealed for American assistance in July, citing the need to protect the railroad engineers. American ships hovered in the vicinity but did not help Simon. Washington was convinced that the regime did not merit salvage. Simon had opened the country to foreign enterprise to an unprecedented degree, but the unprincipled character of such enterprise was dangerous. Although the Open Door remained ajar in Haiti, American policy makers, realizing the possibilities associated with the McDonald concessions, knew that Europeans could obtain similar largesse. In this instance, the Germans abandoned Simon for a candidate less friendly to American interests. Yet the only Americans who assisted Simon were McDonald personnel. Concerned for their jobs and their own safety, they gave the government the dynamite it needed to destroy the rebel village of Capotille. If anything convinced northerners of the mercenary character of Simon's rule, it was his collaboration with the hated railroad.[68]

The National City Bank of New York, one of the BNRH's principal shareholders, demonstrated no loyalty to Simon's regime. It sent a representative to see the president when his government was on its last legs. The delegate proposed that the administration give up its control of the Port-au-Prince municipal elections in order to appease powerful urban interests. Simon equivocated.[69]

By the summer of 1911 the great powers had decisively abandoned Simon. If he was to be saved, only his own efforts could do it. In order to prosecute a war against the North, Simon liberally dragooned unwilling southern conscripts. When he subsequently lost the allegiance of his

66. New York *Times*, February 22, 1911, p. 4; Murray to Secretary of State, March 31, 1911, FO 371, Vol. 1132.

67. Commander of USS *Chester* to Secretary of the Navy, July 27, 1911, DF, 838.640.

68. Furniss to Secretary of State, July 16, 1911, DF, 838.573; Commander of USS *Chester* to Secretary of the Navy, July 27, 1911, DF, 838.640; D. S. Benony, *Pour l'histoire; les événements de février, mai, juillet 1911* (Port-au-Prince, 1911), xi.

69. Furniss to Secretary of State, July 25, 1911, DF, 838.00/596.

native region in pursuit of the unpopular war, the end had arrived.[70] Late in July the diplomatic corps convened at the American legation. The envoys resolved to go en masse to the National Palace and urge Simon to resign. This concerted action was a major demonstration of metropolitan disaffection. The diplomats' concern that the northern army would invade Port-au-Prince should it encounter resistance prompted their action. While others made entreaties to Simon, the German and Dominican ministers and the acting British consul met with the rebels in an attempt to prevent looting in the capital city. The USS *Chester*, which had been in the waters off Cape Haitian, ostensibly to protect the American railroad investment, now anchored outside Port-au-Prince. The German *Bremen* arrived in port on the same day and refused to salute the Haitian colors.[71] Under the circumstances, Simon had no choice but to acquiesce. He asked for time to conclude his affairs.

During the night of August 2, rioting erupted in the city. The custom house and the homes of several Italian and Syrian businessmen were pillaged. Mobs completely stripped private mansions belonging to the Simon family. They carried away doors, windows, and flooring as well as fine furnishings. The *Bremen* landed marines to protect German private and public properties, including the premises of F. Herrmann and Company. Although assisted by the private troops of General Edmond Polynice and armed Herrmann employees, the German seamen and their commander were fired on and in turn shot and killed twenty Haitians. The HMS *Melpomene*, also on the scene, busied itself intercepting the messages to U.S. ships being radioed by Furniss. Both British and American navies thus kept abreast of events in town until the eventual restoration of order.[72] The rioting did not provide the sole focus of their interest. German movements were undoubtedly central to both the communications of Furniss and the *Melpomene*'s espionage.

Once again the cosmopolitan bourgeoisie set up the customary committees of safety. The successful northern rebellion augured another northern president. The moneyed interests at the capital wanted to ensure that the beneficiary would not be Anténor Firmin. Unpaid, ill, and exiled at St. Thomas, Firmin had no military support. In the North, his remain-

70. Dorsainvil, *Manuel d'histoire*, 351–53.

71. E. Garston to Secretary of State for Foreign Affairs, August 4, 1911, and Captain C. F. Henderson to Secretary of the Admiralty, August 18, 1911, FO 371, Vol. 1133; Furniss to Secretary of State, July 16, 1911, DF, 838.00/573.

72. Garston to Secretary of State, August 4, 1911, and Henderson to Secretary of the Admiralty, August 18, 1911, FO 371, Vol. 1133.

ing adherents warred with Cincinnatus Leconte, who, by opposing the railroad contracts, had captured the political allegiance of the peasantry. Neither Leconte nor the Firminists opposed foreign capital penetration in principle. Leconte's opportune and resolute identification with the anti-McDonald movement, however, gave him a decided edge in the North against Firmin's weak, divided, and penniless party.[73]

Firmin, who had not yet abandoned the hope of attaining power, did not proceed immediately to Haiti. He left St. Thomas shortly before Simon's fall, bound for Puerto Rico and the Dominican Republic, where he contacted American officials. Firmin declared that he would accept a modified customs receivership if he were president and expressed concern that the current rebels had no principled agenda for change. Such persons were at the mercy of unscrupulous brokers who emptied the national treasury and the customhouses while pulling the strings of uneducated puppet presidents. American officials would not grant Firmin an audience, even though he was willing to take steps that would end the ritual warfare surrounding presidential succession in Haiti. The State Department showed no interest, and neither did former president Theodore Roosevelt, whom Firmin asked to intercede with Taft on his behalf.[74] While Firmin was trying in vain to get the Americans' attention, Leconte arrived in Cape Haitian and began consolidating his forces for the march to the capital.

Leconte had the advantage of being in the right place at the right time, but the Firminists in Port-au-Prince put up a good fight for their absent leader. Narrowly averting armed warfare, they seized control of the committee of safety.[75] The diplomatic corps openly opposed them, however, and they had no control over General Polynice's army. Leconte's troops entered the city on the same day that Firmin's steamer arrived in port. The Lecontists, dressed in rags and carrying rifles, headed directly for the National Palace. Firmin was not allowed to disembark and, now broken, returned to St. Thomas, where he died five weeks later. Firmin's scholarly elevation had estranged him from the grimy world of Haitian politics, and his long absence from the country had attenuated his strength. "Firmin

73. General Davis to H. Wilson, December 27, 1910, DF, 838.00/513; Livingston to Furniss, January 8, 1911, in Post Records, Letters from Consuls, RG 84.

74. E. S. Edwards to Secretary of War, July 28, 1911, and Anténor Firmin to Theodore Roosevelt, July 24 and July 25, 1911, all in Theodore Roosevelt Papers, LC.

75. Furniss to Secretary of State, August 3, 1911, DF, 838.00/614; New York *Times*, August 6, 1911, Sec. 3, p. 4; Garston to Secretary of State, August 14, 1911, and Henderson to Secretary of the Admiralty, August 18, 1911, FO 371, Vol. 1133.

stands much higher in the general estimation than any other man in Haiti," the New York *Times* wrote, "but he does not know how to play the game." Cincinnatus Leconte could not match Firmin's intellectual abilities, but he had mastered the elements of power.[76]

Leconte presented Haiti with a *fait accompli*. This northern power broker enjoyed little popularity outside the insurgent zone. He had been involved in the consolidation scandal and as Nord Alexis's minister of the interior had ordered executions. The United States' chief concern involved Leconte's apparently warm relations with the Germans, in whose legation he had sought asylum after the first unsuccessful rising at Ouanaminthe. The belief that German merchants had financed his campaign caused further anxiety. Officials in Washington termed the German intervention in the August 2 rioting unwarranted. Had real trouble erupted, U.S. policy makers contended, the small number of German marines could not have kept order. Washington made recognition of Leconte's government contingent upon his disavowal of German influence, his appointment of pro-American ministers, his promise to protect American property, and his offer of compensation for damages caused by the fighting.[77]

In contrast to the untutored Simon, Leconte had studied in Europe and had occupied civilian posts. Dignified and correct in bearing, he wore, according to a British traveler, "shiny black broadcloth and the enormously long and narrow French boots . . . affected by all the Haitian men of fashion." Leconte carefully selected his cabinet and included at least one man who was seen as friendly by each of the states with which Haiti had relations. J. N. Léger and Edmond Lespinasse held the foreign affairs and finance portfolios, respectively.[78]

Early indications that Leconte planned to win the acceptance, if not the respect, of the metropolitan powers did not soften the increasingly demanding attitude of the BNRH. It wanted more control over customs

76. Henderson to Secretary of the Admiralty, August 18, 1911, FO 371, Vol. 1133; B. Danache, *Choses vues: Récits et souvenirs* (Port-au-Prince, 1939), 25. Compare Rodolphe Charmant, *La Vie incroyable d'Alcius* (Port-au-Prince, 1946; rpr. Port-au-Prince, 1981), 215, 250, for a more critical assessment. New York *Times*, August 27, 1911, Sec. 3, p. 4.

77. Knox to Furniss, August 18, 1911, DF, 838.00/660; Munro, *Intervention*, 257; Furniss to Secretary of State, August 19, 1911, DF, 838.00/661, and August 19, 1911, DF, 838.00/675.

78. Winifred Lewellin James, *Under the Mulberry Tree* (New York, 1913), 182–83; Garston to Secretary of State, August 18, 1911, FO 371, Vol. 1133.

revenues and refused to lend badly needed funds unless Leconte granted it the right to name customs officials and make regulations.[79] The U.S. State Department inadvertently pulled the rug from under the National City Bank's part in the maneuver, however, by authorizing an early recognition of the administration. The loan problem remained unsolved. Leconte finally turned to local bankers, and the American financiers temporarily lost an opportunity.[80]

When the Haitian government wanted to borrow again in September, 1911, the American minister managed to dissuade Leconte from securing funds from local merchant-bankers at usurious rates. But Furniss could not solve the problem of the BNRH's hostility to the government, "which causes the Legation not only considerable annoyance, but great embarrassment in its endeavor to increase American influence in Haiti."[81] Bulldozing the Haitians could only work against the implantation of American influence, all other things being equal. Other things were not equal, however, and the American banking interests seemed intent on preventing them from ever becoming so.

The bank now had a dual directorate of European and American financiers.[82] In the summer of 1911, American administrative control was increased significantly when Roger L. Farnham, a National City Bank vice-president, became vice-president of the BNRH. Farnham had begun his career at the turn of the century as a publicist for William Nelson Cromwell's Panama Railroad. A former New York journalist, Farnham rose in the hierarchy of the National City Bank through his Panama connections and maintained a long-standing friendship with Cromwell, whose law firm, Sullivan and Cromwell, he retained for years. Like his white-haired mentor, Farnham proved expert at Byzantine manipulations of public authorities and played a leading role in financial machinations in Haiti. During the years 1910–1915, Farnham, who is often portrayed by historians as the *deus ex machina* single-handedly plotting the American intervention of 1915, worked for the National City Bank. His activities in Haiti cannot be separated from the interests of that institution.[83]

79. Furniss to Secretary of State, August 4, 1911, DF, 838.51/259, and August 18, 1911, DF, 838.51/266. Compare Munro, *Intervention*, 257–58.

80. Gation, *Aspects de l'économie*, 211.

81. Furniss to Secretary of State, September 26, 1911, DF, 838.51/283.

82. Munro, *Intervention*, 255.

83. Dana G. Munro, interview with author, April 29, 1979. Farnham appears as a curiously lone actor in Hans Schmidt, *The United States Occupation of Haiti, 1915–1934* (New Brunswick, N. J., 1971), 48–50, 52, 53, 55; and Munro, *Intervention*, 255, 258, 332, 334.

The bankers' Haitian strategy involved keeping the legations in the dark about the negotiations taking place among the BNRH, the National City Bank, and Haitian officials on the subject of debt liquidation and refunding. At the same time, bankers fed certain information to the respective Foreign Offices. Their objective was to isolate the interested parties from one another and thus remain in control of the situation. Breaching the wall of secrecy required the legations to pay informants in the BNRH, but resort to such an expedient indicated how greatly communication with the bankers had already deteriorated.[84]

A November visit to Haiti by Farnham and associates highlighted the problem. Farnham's ostensible purpose was to readjust the McDonald contracts and discuss possible new credits for the Haitian government. The bankers made no offers but tried to force Haitian officials to make favorable concessions to the railroad as the price for initiating talks on a badly needed loan. Leconte's government resented the obligations inherited from Simon, and more trouble with foreign lenders could precipitate the kind of rupture that characterized the Nord Alexis regime.[85]

The National City Bank, a principal participant in the BNRH group, advocated a more active American policy in Haiti and was not above creating alarmist fears to bring this about. In a December, 1911, note to the State Department, the BNRH directors predicted a new insurrection of blacks against the supposedly mulatto government of Leconte. It based its appeal for customs control on that possibility. The bankers hoped to wear down Haitian resistance by creating obstacles to the extension of credit on ordinary terms. They also generated misleading impressions among American officials. In late December, shortly after the French ambassador in Washington had informed a State Department official, Thomas C. Dawson, of France's desire to participate in any customs receivership established in Haiti, Farnham telephoned Dawson and told him that Haiti had already agreed to accept American assistance in reorganizing its military and customs service.[86]

The National City Bank's report differed considerably from that of the American legation, which wired the State Department on December 22

84. Furniss to Secretary of State, August 18, 1911, DF, 838.51/266, and November 19, 1911, 838.51/291. The French legation in Port-au-Prince also lacked contact with the metropolitan banking consortium. Ministry of Foreign Affairs, "Etablissement d'un contrôle administratif en Haïti," January 22, 1911, QDO, Vol. 21.

85. Furniss to Secretary of State, November 7, 1911, DF, 838.51/290.

86. Ailes, Memorandum for Secretary of State, with William Doyle to H. Wilson, December 27, 1911, DF, 838.51/297.

that Haiti had entered negotiations with the Germans; if the American bankers refused to drop their insistence on customs control, a German loan would go through. Washington wisely refused to accept at face value Farnham's claim that Haiti would agree to a customs receivership: such control could be undertaken only if the Haitians requested it. The State Department also expressed mild concern at the bankers' prevarications. The duplicity of Farnham and his associates was so pronounced that to speak of them as "over-optimistic," as Dana G. Munro did, hardly does justice to a team of experienced, skillful liars.[87]

Leconte's administration also experienced tense relations with the National Railroad, whose unpopularity had put Leconte in power. Part of the newly forming peasant opposition to the president lay in his ultimate decision to honor the McDonald contracts. Aside from the guarantees demanded by the United States, rising opposition drove home the railroad's utility as a means of suppressing insurgencies. The corporate backers, however, were not in accord. Farnham, whose National City Bank shared ownership of the railroad, wanted McDonald to drop the banana plantation concessions in order to lessen peasant opposition. Because McDonald refused, Furniss reported, Farnham allegedly bribed deputies to oppose the McDonald contracts in the Haitian legislature.[88]

Farnham seemed to have a natural talent for wheeling and dealing. His ability to make alliances crossed traditional lines of national loyalty. He assiduously courted the German community in Haiti and tried to provoke foreign intervention. The State Department, McDonald, and others might find the German presence disconcerting, but this National City Bank representative did not. The National City Bank had done business with Germans in 1909 and would continue to do so.[89]

Although assailed by foes foreign and domestic, the Leconte government summoned sufficient energy to retard its enemies' progress and undertake limited reforms. Co-opting some Firminist ideas, Leconte tackled customs fraud and appointed an active and distinguished minister of education. The administration constructed barracks for the army, which was formerly quartered on public streets, instituted training in marksmanship, and attempted to develop a professional esprit de corps in the

---

87. Doyle to H. Wilson, December 27, 1911, DF, 838.51/297; Munro, *Intervention*, 258.

88. Furniss to Secretary of State, June 14, 1912, DF, 838.615M14.

89. *Ibid.*; James McDonald to Representative R. W. Austin, July 8, 1912, DF, 838.615M14/1.

presidential guard. Other improvements included the restoration of public buildings, street paving, and cleaning projects. The resurgence of the gourde, which gained against foreign currencies in 1912, indicated the sobriety of the regime. Changes in the judicial system and fair treatment of exiles also marked the new administration. Perhaps its single most striking characteristic was Leconte's insistence on reducing the level of acceptable corruption in government ranks. Eventually, diminished opportunities for extra income caused disaffection in the civil service.[90]

Foreigners greeted these changes with cynicism. The institutionalized attitude toward Haiti that had crystallized during the past fifty years of Haitian relations with the great powers led the latter to maintain a hard line on a country that they had come increasingly to see as unworthy of cultivation. The United States provides a clear example. Haiti faced a subtle prejudice in the State Department that its recent revolutionary upheavals only affirmed. The beginnings of honest government seemed evanescent phenomena to American officials. In early 1912, Secretary of State Philander Knox planned a goodwill tour of Central America and the Caribbean that included Haiti. Before the trip he was briefed as follows: "In Hayti, the less said the better. No government there is worth making any pledges to, for it cannot last long enough to make any effective pledges in return. The only durable dominating interests in Hayti are those of French and German speculative capitalists." Knox arrived in Port-au-Prince on April 3, 1912, and delivered a speech that contained a veiled warning to the Black Republic. The United States wanted to create "a highway for international commerce" in the Caribbean but could only do so in a stable political climate. A nation in conflict, Knox admonished, would not benefit from the opportunities that the Panama Canal made possible to the region.[91]

Knox's stay was brief. He admired the cleanliness and general appearance of Port-au-Prince, which had been tidied expressly for his visit, and attended a dull state dinner. After the banquet, toasts, and classical music, local drummers appeared. The Haitians became animated, but Knox did not enjoy the musicians. In his words, "the delicate entente with the Latins depended heavily on the flowing of champagne and other

90. Dorsainvil, *Manuel d'histoire*, 353, 354; Pierre Benoit, *Cent cinquante ans de commerce extérieure d'Haïti* (Port-au-Prince, 1954), 12, 22, 55; Georges Séjourné, *Une page d'histoire: La mort de C. Leconte* (Port-au-Prince, 1912), 13.

91. Adee to Knox, February 15, 1912, in Philander C. Knox Papers, LC; Knox, Address, April 3, 1912, *FR*, 1912, p. 545.

alcoholic preservatives."[92] Good will, then, meant no more than sparkling bubbles, whose fragility seemed to so resemble that of Haiti's leadership.

The dogged if unenthusiastic interest taken by American investors after 1910 and policy makers in Haiti convinced some observers that the business climate would improve. Syrian merchants also harbored optimism. Many Syrians who had left or been expelled by Nord Alexis had returned during the presidency of Simon, who had not objected to foreign enterprise of any kind. During the Simon administration Syrians had been almost the sole representatives of American commerce. Haitian consumption of U.S. goods had doubled between 1903 and 1911, which enhanced U.S. support for any foreign community in the Black Republic that would, as the Syrians were doing, promote that consumption, avoid involvement in Haitian politics, and stay clear of European intrigues.

Leconte had promised urban Haitians he would expel the newly enlarged Syrian population. His government continued to process claims filed by Syrians during the Nord Alexis years, and acted quickly enough to prevent the formation of an international claims commission, but it also revived the anti-Syrian law of 1903. Harassment typical of the 1903–1905 period resumed, but the situation had changed.[93] The Syrians now had a lobby in the United States. Trading activities had brought them into contact with important American firms, which willingly defended them. Syrian-Americans in New York publicized the plight of their business associates and acquaintances on the island. Syrians appealed to the National Association of Manufacturers, which counseled them on procedural matters and wrote to the State Department on their behalf. The Syrians based their petition on the claim that they traded almost exclusively with American firms and on the likelihood that their business difficulties would result in the diversion of the Haitian market to European suppliers. Midwestern meat-packers and New York dry goods jobbers would be the most directly affected. The Syrians obtained their strongest support from Swift and Company, Armour and Company, Pillsbury Mills, and the National Biscuit Company. Claflin, the largest American mail-order house of the period, and a number of other grain dealers and shippers also came to their

92. William Bayard Hale, "With the Knox Mission to Central America," *World's Work,* clipping in Philander C. Knox Papers.

93. New York *Times,* December 2, 1911, p. 4; Furniss to Secretary of State, July 5, 1912, *FR,* 1912, pp. 521–23; Séjourné, *Une page d'histoire,* 13.

aid; these firms had a small stake in Haiti, but it was increasing an-
nually.[94]

The Haitians meanwhile refined their case against the Syrian traders
by making a better brief for the legality of their antiforeign statutes. The
Haitian secretary of state cited the United States' exclusion of Chinese as a
precedent for his country's interpretation of national self-interest and
declared that granting licenses was a matter of executive privilege. The
Europeans, concerned for their own expatriate communities, held that
Chinese exclusion laws in the nations where they applied did not affect
those Chinese already living there. As there were no barriers against
Haitians trading in Europe, reciprocity demanded the same courtesy.
France in particular opposed the policy on the grounds that it restrained
trade and had resulted from executive fiat.[95]

The U.S. State Department conceded Haiti's right to bar Syrians. In
instructions to Furniss, it admitted that the United States excluded Chinese even when they were citizens of a nation whose subjects ordinarily
enjoyed free access to America. If the Haitians planned to enforce anti-
Syrian laws, they should give the Syrians enough time to conclude their
affairs. As these Middle Eastern traders had been tolerated for nearly
twenty years, there was no need to rush their departure now. Acting
Secretary of State Huntington Wilson ordered Furniss to demand equal
treatment for all Syrians no matter what their citizenship. These instructions were significant: of the 114 Syrians licensed to trade in Haiti in
1912, only 12 were American citizens.[96] Clearly, the United States meant
to sustain the Syrians as a group, regardless of their citizenship. This
support was not to be interpreted as a new American inclination to cooperate with Europeans in the Caribbean. The U.S. government did not want
to share responsibility for the Syrians' welfare with other powers, because
these Middle Easterners were valued only if they identified with American interests, as the British soon learned.

94. New York *Times*, December 21, 1911, p. 4; and December 22, 1911, p. 18; Furniss to
Secretary of State, December 19, 1911, DF, 838.111/41; Waterman and Meigs to Knox,
December 21, 1911, and George Zabriskie to Knox, December 22, 1911, DF, 838.11/36; Post
Records, Register of Official Letters Sent, RG 84, NA; Alain Turnier, *Les Etats-Unis et le
marché haïtien* (Washington, D.C., 1955), 1977.

95. Léger to Furniss, December 26, 1911, in Furniss to Secretary of State, January 16,
1912, FR, 1912; James Pyke to Secretary of State for Foreign Affairs, February 29, 1912, FO
371, Vol. 1832; Maurouard to Léger, January 3, 1912, in *Documents diplomatiques, affaires
diverses* (Port-au-Prince, 1913), 23–24.

96. H. Wilson to Furniss, January 20, 1912, FR, 1912; New York *Times*, December 21,
1911, p. 4.

On February 8, 1912, James Bryce, the British ambassador in Washington, informed Knox that Haiti had given the Syrians, including some British nationals, an ultimatum to liquidate their businesses by the end of May. As of the following day, their import permits would be suspended. The ambassador then requested that Furniss work jointly with the British chargé d'affaires in Port-au-Prince to force Haiti to repeal the decree, as producers in Manchester were adversely affected by it. Knox replied that he could do nothing in the absence of a treaty with Haiti specifying the rights of nationals in the respective countries. True to American tradition, he refused the British request for mutual action, for he wished to prevent European nations from championing the Syrians in the Caribbean. The British and the French were the most plausible European allies of the Syrians, but Germany, which had no nationals of Syrian origin, viewed them as commercial rivals. German traders would benefit if Haiti refused to grant licenses to Syrian merchants.[97] Knox wished to preclude any occasion for French and British activism in the region, and he also hoped to avoid creating a situation that would aid German commerce.

As for the Haitians, Knox felt that little could be said to them directly about the law, in view of similar American policies, but cautioned them to consider whether the disadvantages of pursuing an anti-Syrian program did not outweigh the benefits. Syrian firms owed money to American exporters who would suffer if the Syrians were expelled. The United States would also have to insist that all Syrians, no matter what their citizenship, be accorded equal treatment.[98]

Washington linked its support of the Syrians to its opposition to German expansion in Haiti. In a December, 1911, meeting with Leconte, Furniss insisted that the Syrian presence was innocuous. The Haitian president replied that the Levantine group exerted an unhealthy influence on the national economy. Citing the powerful German traders, Furniss challenged him to name those foreigners who did not.[99]

Furniss' allusions to German profiteering gave point to American re-

97. Pyke to Secretary of State, February 29, 1912, FO 371, Vol. 1382; James Bryce to Secretary of State, February 8, 1912, and H. Wilson to Bryce, February 16, 1912, *FR*, 1912, pp. 33–35; Warren G. Kneer, *Great Britain and the Caribbean, 1901–1913: A Study in Anglo-American Relations* (East Lansing, 1975), 105, 119–26, 210n31, 226n3; Furniss to Secretary of State, March 2, 1912, DF, 838.00/682.

98. Acting Secretary of State to Furniss, March 5, 1912, *FR*, 1912, pp. 536–37.

99. Furniss to Secretary of State, February 12, 1912, *FR*, 1912, pp. 532–33, and December 19, 1911, DF, 838.111/41; Lefevre-Pontalis to Minister of Foreign Affairs, October 16, 1909, QDO, Vol. 22.

sentment of the firm foothold that German commerce seemed to have in Haiti. The Germans had adroitly managed the tangled skein of European and American combinations against them, as well as the intricacies of Haitian law. Native Haitians fronted most of their retail establishments, and intermarriage allowed them to acquire and bequeath real property. The Germans mastered both French and Creole. They neutralized American hostility by bringing in German-American business partners. These naturalized American "semi-Germans" gave them access to U.S. capital markets. German enterprise was thus enabled to purchase a bankrupt American-owned street lighting company in Port-au-Prince and float bonds to support it with the aid of the National City Bank of New York. As increasing proscription threatened once again to drive the Syrians out of Haiti, German firms began purchasing Syrian inventories.[100]

Leconte's critics accused him of reviving the persecution of Syrians in order to pay off debts to German merchants and arms suppliers who had financed his successful insurgency. It is more likely, however, that small Haitian merchants would have benefited most from Syrian exclusion. The Germans competed only with the larger Syrian wholesale houses. Small Syrian shops posed no threat to their diversified interests. By 1912, most Haitian firms, however, were reduced to simple import activity and could no longer rival expatriate enterprises.[101]

Leconte issued an ultimatum for Syrians who were not protected by the law of 1903. Whatever their citizenship, they would have to leave the country by May 31. Furniss negotiated a delay for Syrian-Americans and those naturalized to European powers, but Syrians with Turkish papers were to be expelled. France, which held an informal protectorate over the Levant, protested. The United States refused to intercede for the Turkish nationals and consequently rejected a French request for joint action. Near the end of May, the French unilaterally sent a warship to Port-au-Prince with orders to stay until the Syrian question had been resolved. Despite the French naval presence, the Haitian government closed the

100. Furniss to Secretary of State, April 30, 1912 (DF, 838.42), February 10, 1912 (DF, 838.153C73/8), February 12, 1912 (DF, 838.111/61); Carteron to Minister of Foreign Affairs, August 12, 1909, and Jore to Minister of Foreign Affairs, October 12 and November 12, 1909, all in QDO, Vol. 22; Pyke to Secretary of State, June 30, 1912, FO 371, Vol. 1382.

101. Tribonien Saint-Juste, Statement in the *Daily Telegraph and Jamaica Guardian*, January 25, 1912, in Furniss to Secretary of State, March 2, 1912, DF, 838.00/682; Furniss to Secretary of State, December 10, 1911, DF, 838.111/41; Rev. L. Ton Evans, Statement, in SI, 159; Pyke to Secretary of State, March 30, 1912, FO 371, Vol. 1382; Séjourné, *Une page d'histoire*, 13.

stores of Turkish Syrians on June 1 without incident. Haiti had profited from the failure of the powers to coordinate their actions.[102]

Far away from the commercial conflicts of the capital, fighting broke out in 1912 on the Haitian-Dominican frontier. Peasants wishing to escape conscription and the petty tyranny of local commandants had squatted in the desolate no-man's-land between the two states. Fugitives and exiles from both nations had joined them there and made the regulation of the restless, violent border a recurrent problem for both countries. When the United States had established a customs receivership in the Dominican Republic in 1904, it had quickly suppressed the active smuggling taking place on the frontier. It also concerned itself with the new skirmishes. The State Department believed that the Haitian government had offered clandestine assistance to rebels in the Dominican revolution, which was raging in full force by January, 1912. Such aid would allow the Haitians to make quiet incursions on disputed border areas. Knox instructed Furniss to ask the Haitian government to refrain from such encroachments and sent observers, including Furniss himself, to report on the frontier crisis.[103]

The Haitian government continued to aid Dominican insurgents despite American objections, and the border became the locus of raids and an illicit arms trade. A Dominican presidential contender, Desiderio Arias, relied on Leconte's support, the State Department believed, because Arias had helped Leconte come to power. Despite this cooperation, the Haitian presence on the frontier remained weak. Furniss' difficult trip to the southeastern Pedernales in May, 1912, revealed how primitive life was in the remote hinterland where Leconte's reforms had not penetrated. Small, distant outposts, press-gang recruitment, and obsolete weapons characterized Haiti's covert efforts to extend its frontiers.[104]

Conditions in northern Haiti were also unsettled, as difficulties with the railroad had continued. A strike movement, attributed by Livingston, the U.S. consul in Cape Haitian, to political orchestration, was afoot

102. Acting Secretary of State to American Ambassador to Turkey, March 22, 1912, Furniss to Secretary of State, May 21, and June 1, 1912, State Department, Memorandum to French Embassy in Washington, May 29, 1912, all in FR, 1912, p. 538.

103. Edgar Furbush to Dawson, September 30, 1911, and Knox to Furniss, December 21, 1911, DF, 738.3915/84; Munro, *Intervention*, 260–61.

104. Commander of USS *Nashville* to Secretary of the Navy, March 8, 1912, with Department of the Navy to Secretary of State, March 21, 1912, DF, 838.00/684; H. Wilson to American Legation in Port-au-Prince, March 1, 1912, DF, 738.915/96; Furniss to Secretary of State, July 29, 1912, and enclosures, DF, 738.915/152.

among Haitian workers. The consul's report coincided with the completion of a major section of track. The Haitian government had to decide
whether to accept the work and make the necessary payments.[105]

Both border and railroad disputes were still unresolved when news
came to Washington of Leconte's sudden death on August 4, 1912.
Powder stored in a basement arsenal in the executive mansion had ignited.
The president, some relatives, and several hundred soldiers had died, and
the powerful explosion had leveled the building. Leconte's charred body
had been found dismembered, suggesting that he had been murdered
before the blast. Haitian authorities subsequently investigated, but they
failed to arrive at any firm conclusions. The American minister at first
accepted the tragedy as accidental because no successor immediately came
forward.[106]

He later confidentially expressed some doubts. James Pyke, the British
envoy, was less reticent. "In support of a theory of conspiracy," he
informed officials in London, "with the exception of one of the aides-de-
camp, no officer or person of any standing lost his life but the President."
Pyke noted that Leconte's bedroom, where the president had been at the
time of his death, had blown up before the powder magazine that destroyed the palace exploded. "There are also other indications—trivial in
themselves, but constituting in the aggregate a mass of circumstantial
evidence—of a plot."[107]

Leconte had had more than his share of enemies. He had come to power
on the backs of the *cacos* but had been at heart a cosmopolite. Professional
sinecurists, bankers of all nationalities, American exporters, peasant mercenaries, Antoine Simon, unreconstructed Firminists, and certain Dominican factions had been hostile. This time, presidential succession was
not automatic.

Haitians attributed the survival of their national independence to their
skill at juggling diverse, ambitious foreign powers. The debut of American financiers made the balancing act more difficult. Few believed that the
United States' presence portended a new day of greater peace, prosperity,
and stability. The proximity of the northern neighbor, its sponsorship of

105. Livingston to Assistant Secretary of State, June 26, 1912, in Post Records, Letters
from Consuls to Ministers, RG 84; Munro, *Intervention*, 258–59.

106. Séjourné, *Une page d'histoire*, 8; Dorsainvil, *Manuel d'histoire*, 355; Furniss to
Secretary of State, August 8, 1912, DF, 838.001/13.

107. Furniss to Secretary of State, September 17, 1912, DF, 838.001/14; Pyke to Secretary of State for Foreign Affairs, September 17, 1912, FO 371, Vol. 1382.

highly resented foreign traders, the machinations of the National City Bank of New York, and an import commerce of one-sided dependency did not augur well for such an eventuality.

The year 1910 was a turning point but not a radical departure from the past. Americans had slowly filtered into Haiti over the course of the previous decade. Many were traders and engineers on contract to public works projects and private concessions who had arrived long before U.S. bankers entered the loan consortium. The United States continued to be more significant as a trading partner than as an investor during the years before 1915.

Despite the American attempt to arrest multilateral influence in Haiti through the substitution of American for European capital, the events of the period indicated the enduring strength of French and German influence. Other traditional institutions, such as the army, the peasant mercenaries and their leaders, and political and civil service careerists, also proved impervious to reform. Interest in change never completely evaporated, but it was absorbed by mainstream, traditional politics. The presidents who succeeded Leconte all claimed to endorse the leading reform ideas of the period. Now that Firmin was dead, it was possible to speak enthusiastically of Firminism. No leader, including Leconte, transcended the ritualized politics of personalism and caudillismo. In this turbulent decade, meaningful change continued to elude Haitians as the Firminist movement disintegrated.

VI
Warlords and Revolution

Sè fè ki kupé fè.
Force responds to force.

—Haitian proverb

IT IS POSSIBLE to view the Leconte-Auguste-Oreste-Zamor succession as a single presidency. All these men based their strength on the support of the cosmopolitan elite and chose their officials from its ranks. All grounded their legitimacy in an avowed attachment to general principles of reform, such as army reduction and renewed commitment to public education, but were prepared to implement these sparingly and in urban areas only. Rural Haiti remained largely unimproved during these administrations. Only the quickening tempo of revolutionary insurgency altered the countryside, for these four presidents also shared ultimate failure as a result of their inability to accommodate dissident elements that were also contending for power.[1]

Tancrède Auguste, Leconte's immediate successor, presided over a government that endured nine months. Auguste, a planter and entrepreneur from Cape Haitian, had served as minister of the interior and police under Tirésias Simon Sam in 1896–1902 and was thus identified with an unpopular regime. In a spirit of reconciliation engendered by the shock of Leconte's death, Haitian factions nevertheless accepted his leadership. Like Leconte, Auguste was a powerful landowner and general who believed he could unite conflicting interests, and he swore to continue the Lecontist programs.[2]

1. Henry W. Furniss to Secretary of State, January 14, 1913, DF, 838.002/11; Madison Smith to Secretary of State, February 2, 1914, and enclosure, DF, 838.00/829; Alphonse Cillière to Minister of Foreign Affairs, July 1, 1913, QDO, Vol. 5.
2. William F. Powell to John Hay, May 24, 1902, CD; H. P. Davis, *Black Democracy* (2nd ed.; New York, 1929), 147; Furniss to Secretary of State, January 14, 1913, DF, 838.002/11.

Once installed in office, Auguste awarded portfolios to J. N. Léger and Edmond Lespinasse, who became foreign affairs minister and finance minister, respectively. (Léger had briefly quit public life during the Simon years to return to private practice. He counted James P. McDonald among his clients.) Auguste made Seymour Pradel minister of the interior in an attempt to appease those identified with the Firminist faction, and retained the northerner Tertullien Guilbaud as minister of education. Some discontent followed disclosure of these appointments: many resented the related Léger and Lespinasse families, which seemed to monopolize diplomatic posts. One of Léger's and Lespinasse's brothers-in-law, Solon Ménos, was minister at Washington, and still another headed the consulate in New York. Shortly before his death, however, Auguste reorganized the cabinet and dropped the widely disliked Lespinasse.[3]

Auguste inherited Leconte's foreign policy problems, and those that most engaged his short-lived government were the National Railroad and the McDonald concession.[4] The Auguste regime, which shared Leconte's appreciation of the railroad's utility as an instrument of state security, wished to maintain full control over it and to be assured of the quality of the work being done. The speculative character of the railroad contract from its inception militated against the last point. The National City Bank, realizing that the Haitian government's obduracy had not been mitigated by the change in presidents, asked the State Department to force officials in Port-au-Prince to accept the Cape Haitian–Grande Rivière section of track, a section marked by flawed workmanship. On August 10, 1912, apparently after having conferred with Roger Farnham, Secretary of State Knox instructed the U.S. minister, Henry Furniss, to persuade the Auguste administration to settle with the railroad company. This note marked the U.S. government's initial, and inauspicious, contact with the Auguste government.[5] The pressure Furniss was to apply would necessarily be informal and indirect, as the United States had not yet recognized Auguste.

The Haitian government's railroad commission filed a generally nega-

3. Furniss to Secretary of State, January 14, 1913 (DF, 838.002/11), June 5, 1912 (DF, 838.77/38), October 13, 1908 (NF, 2126/308); Catts Pressoir, Ernest Trouillot, and Henock Trouillot, *Historiographie d'Haïti* (Mexico City, 1953), 275, 239.

4. Furniss to Secretary of State, June 5, 1912, DF, 838.77/38; Winifred Lewellin James, *Under the Mulberry Tree* (New York, 1913), 167.

5. Philander Knox to Furniss, August 10, 1912, and Knox to Roger Farnham, August 10, 1912, DF, 838.77/42; James Pyke to Secretary of State for Foreign Affairs, August 30, 1912, FO 371, Vol. 1382.

tive report on the progress and caliber of railroad construction, and officials in Port-au-Prince subsequently refused to guarantee the National Railroad Company's bonds.[6] The manner in which the Port-au-Prince terminal was located and constructed provides an example of the conditions that aroused Haitian opposition. The station was located at La Saline, an impoverished quarter where migrants from the countryside arrived in the capital city. La Saline, then as now, comprised a swampy area that is impassable for vehicles during summer floods. Furniss and an American engineer inspected the station and sections of track on the Port-au-Prince–Arcahaie line. They noted the "wavy" appearance of the badly laid rails, easily discerned by the untrained eye. The engineer termed the work grossly substandard: the tracks were dangerous for trains traveling at a mere twenty miles an hour. No less a personage than John Allen, the American manager of the BNRH, confessed that the Haitians had been cheated.[7]

This admission did not alter American insistence that Haiti approve the railroad as built, but both public and private American officials wanted to maintain the illusion that the issues of diplomatic recognition by the United States and acceptance of the railroad construction by Haiti were not linked. They were, of course, and Washington withheld recognition until the matter was settled. The United States and Haiti entered full relations on September 24. Four days later the railroad work was accepted in its entirety and the bond issues guaranteed.[8]

The McDonald concession, which was originally conceived of as operating in tandem with the National Railroad, provided another source of disagreement. Through informants, Furniss supplied the State Department with a description of an interview between Farnham and Auguste in which Farnham depicted Washington as the villain in the Haitian government's conflict with the National Railroad Company. Farnham sounded the president out on the matter of fruit and sugar cultivation, assuring him that his own plantations would be taken care of. Auguste replied that his personal enterprise was small but that, in any case, he would not grant monopoly privileges. The president wanted agricultural export companies in Haiti that would not compete with native commerce unless they

6. Dana G. Munro, *Intervention and Dollar Diplomacy in the Caribbean, 1900–1921* (Princeton, 1964), 259.

7. Furniss to Secretary of State, May 13, 1913, DF, 838.77/76; Solon Ménos, Reply to the National Railroad Company memorandum, September 21, 1916, DF, 838.77/168.

8. Furniss to Secretary of State, August 13, 1912, DF, 838.77/42; Pyke to Secretary of State for Foreign Affairs, August 30, 1912, FO 371, Vol. 1382; Munro, *Intervention*, 259.

paid an additional tax equivalent to an export duty.[9] Like most Haitian politicians, he saw large concessions primarily as instruments to create revenue for the state.

In concluding his interview with Farnham, Auguste declared that had he been president in 1910, no bank or railroad contracts would have been approved. As he was faced with a *fait accompli,* however, he would be just, provided that the arbitration clauses in the contracts were respected. He would resign rather than permit disagreements to reach a crisis level that involved diplomatic intercession. Farnham, according to Furniss' information, was not happy with the president's firm responses.[10]

The new administration experienced other difficulties with the BNRH. It desired a more conciliatory financial institution that would more readily provide the investment capital and banking services the country needed. This attitude mirrored wider Haitian sentiment. "Every Haitian that I have heard talk of the matter is on the side of the Government," Furniss reported. At the clubs, the elite spoke strongly against the bank, "which is frequently styled as a 'bucket shop' making its dividends by speculation with the Government's funds."[11]

Furniss reiterated his criticisms of the BNRH in a February, 1913, dispatch to Washington, which pointed out the deleterious effects that the bank's exports of gold to Europe were having on the local money market. In an act of dubious propriety, the State Department communicated the contents of the dispatch to a National City Bank representative. A vice-president of the bank assured U.S. officials that the BNRH shipped the gold not to manipulate the exchange rate but merely to service the debt in accordance with the loan contract. Furniss, he declared, simply had "not taken pains to inform himself" of that fact.[12]

Finally, Auguste disagreed with Americans on another sensitive matter. He shared Nord Alexis's and Leconte's view of the Syrians and tried to drive out those who had returned during the lenient Simon administration. The Auguste government did not pass specific legislation against the Syrians, for fear of incurring American disapproval. Instead, the climate would be made so uncomfortable for Syrians that they would leave voluntarily. Many Syrians who had become Haitian citizens and had even done

9. Furniss to Secretary of State, November 26, 1913, DF, 838.77/69.

10. *Ibid.*

11. C. Dautant, *La Banque Nationale qu'il faudrait* (Port-au-Prince, 1912), 18; Furniss to Secretary of State, November 16, 1912, DF, 838.516/7.

12. William Jennings Bryan to Furniss, March 12, 1913, DF, 838.516/9; Milton Ailes to State Department, March 7, 1913, DF, 838.516/10.

a tour of military service found themselves being forced out. As they were Haitian nationals, no foreign power could protect them. *Le Nouvelliste* noted with pleasure that when Port-au-Prince housewives came down to the commercial Bord-de-Mer district to do their 1913 New Year's shopping, they found most of the stores managed by Haitians. *Le Nouvelliste* hoped that Haitian commerce was on its way to being fully restored. The journal seemed oblivious to the distinction between ownership and management. The presence of Haitians behind counters disguised the continuing control of foreign entrepreneurs.[13]

By any measure, Haiti was losing ground. The bank and the railroad did not meet the nation's dire need for genuine development because they had been organized only to generate income for overseas investors. The United States had achieved a new eminence in Haiti by 1913. A decade earlier, Washington had supported a bevy of obscure small traders. Now it promoted the rapidly diffusing interests of a Stateside bank whose fortunes were increasingly tied to American foreign policy objectives.

President Auguste did not live long enough to resolve these dilemmas. His health was failing, and in May, 1913, he became extremely ill after a tour of the North. Auguste died suddenly in Port-au-Prince on May 2. The president is said to have suffered from a combination of ailments, and the belief that he was poisoned still circulates. While Auguste lay dying, Haitian officials took the opportunity to reject all the completed sections of the National Railroad. No chief of state could be held responsible for the move, and resolution of the issue was postponed until the accession of the next executive.[14]

On May 4, the very afternoon of Auguste's funeral, the legislative corps met to choose a successor. Ambitious generals had already massed loyal troops around the city, and gunfire erupted in the cathedral during the funeral rites. A decision had to be made quickly. Sporadic shooting interrupted the parliamentary deliberations, but the lawmakers, allegedly aided by alternating applications of carrot and stick, emerged by early evening with a successor: Michel Oreste. As a duly elected civilian, a member of the Port-au-Prince political establishment, and a man who had

13. Furniss to Secretary of State, March 25, 1913, *FR*, 1913, pp. 577–78, and April 10, 1913, *FR*, 1913, pp. 579–80; *Le Nouvelliste*, January 15, 1913, p. 3.

14. Furniss to Secretary of State, April 29, 1913, DF, 838.001/Au4; John Russell, Memorandum, in Russell to Secretary of State, February 27, 1926, DF, 838.51/1872; Farnham, Memorandum, n.d., DF, 838.77/77.

favored the BNRH and Syrian interests while in the Senate, Oreste counted on the general approval of the great powers.[15]

Oreste, a native of the coffee-exporting coastal city of Jacmel, practiced law in Port-au-Prince. A senator during the Nord Alexis years, he had defended those accused in the consolidation scandal. Oreste had returned to the Senate in 1912. He began his presidential administration with the hope that he could continue his predecessors' programs but failed ultimately to reconcile the factions. His own pessimism was perhaps best expressed by his decision to take his seven-year presidential salary in a lump-sum advance. The president first incurred the displeasure of a sector with which he had been publicly associated. Expatriates opposed his efforts to enforce a 1903 law that imposed a 10 percent tax on corporations and partnerships. The law exempted sole proprietorships and professional occupations, categories in which most Haitian entrepreneurs were to be found. If Oreste meant to force foreign businessmen to pay a larger share of governmental expenses, he could expect no support from them.[16]

The 1910 BNRH contract had called for a program of currency reform, and the government had deposited ten million francs in the bank for that purpose. The fund provided for the retirement of the paper money in use and the substitution of a hard currency less susceptible to seasonal and speculative fluctuations. The state and the BNRH continually disagreed on how the program should be carried out. The bank wanted complete, immediate retirement, but the government insisted that such an undertaking could be disastrous for the economy. A sudden withdrawal of paper and the subsequent coinage of money in Paris, as BNRH officials suggested, could also prove expensive. A gradual retirement would bring in American money to replace gourdes without any official effort. During the Auguste administration, the legislature had approved a bill that enabled the president to delay the redemption process if he felt it necessary. The ensuing quarrel with the bank over monetary reform then took on an expressly political character.[17]

15. Furniss to Secretary of State, May 10, 1913, DF, 838.00/722; Russell, Memorandum, in Russell to Secretary of State, February 27, 1926, DF, 838.51/1872; Dantès Bellegarde, *Histoire du Peuple haïtien, 1492–1952* (Port-au-Prince, 1953), 239; Pyke to Lord Grey, Annual Report on the Republic of Hayti, 1913, FO 371, 2000.

16. *Le Nouvelliste*, May 19, 1913; Jacques C. Antoine, *Jean Price-Mars and Haiti* (Washington, D.C., 1981), 85; Furniss to Secretary of State, June 28, 1913, DF, 838.00/727; Louis R. E. Gation, *Aspects de l'économie et des finances d'Haïti* (Port-au-Prince, 1944), 7g–7h.

17. Furniss to Secretary of State, September 23, 1912, DF, 838.516/6.

The BNRH insisted on integral retirement and, during Oreste's presidency, refused to yield to the government the ten million dollars deposited for currency reform, despite guarantees that the funds would be used for that purpose. Port-au-Prince interpreted the refusal as a defiant act and an infringement on its sovereignty in matters of national interest. It did not regard the BNRH contract, which in any case said little specifically about implementing monetary reform, as beyond its ultimate jurisdiction.[18]

Over the years Haitian regimes made sporadic attempts to strengthen the currency. A law of August 26, 1913, created a gold gourde pegged to the dollar at an exchange rate of five to one. The law was the culmination of a period of gradually rising monetary value that had begun in 1911 and was marked by increased coffee production and an invigorated purchasing power in rural areas.[19] Suppliers were forced to raise the real price paid to peasants for agricultural commodities but balanced this against the higher price they charged for retail imports. Wholesale merchants were the major beneficiaries of the stronger gourde, which inconvenienced those participants in the cash economy whose salaries were traditionally paid in hard currencies and who were faced with higher prices for such locally prepared commodities as bread. The dual currency system accentuated class distinctions as the dollar-based economy remained the province of the well-to-do.[20]

No gold gourde was ever actually struck, but as an economic fact of life, the gourde's surging value carried the cost of production, as well as real wages, upward. Few merchants and commodity brokers saw this as healthy. They favored a depressed gourde that would lower costs and thus prevent "overpricing" of Haitian coffee abroad and Haitian labor at home. The Haitian economy, in their view, should continue to creep along as it had always done, with the poor absorbing the social price of stagnation.[21]

In 1913, Oreste faced not only economic problems but also the disin-

18. Joseph Chatelain, *La Banque Nationale, son histoire, ses problèmes* (Port-au-Prince, 1954), 93.

19. Pierre Benoit, *Cent cinquante ans de commerce extérieur d'Haïti* (Port-au-Prince, 1954), 22; Gation, *Aspects de l'Economie*, 212.

20. Furniss to Secretary of State, September 23, 1912, DF, 838.516/6; Gation, *Aspects de l'économie*, 263.

21. Gation, *Aspects de l'économie*, 71; Furniss to Secretary of State, June 28, 1913, DF, 838.00/727, and August 20, 1913, DF, 838.512; Pyke, Annual Report, 1913, FO 371, Vol. 2000.

tegration of the alliance that Auguste and Leconte had forged with the mercenary generals. Money spent judiciously in the countryside, they had hoped, would buy time for reform in the city.[22] Oreste also made payments to potential enemies, disguising the disbursements under the rubric "secret police" as a convenient way to avoid public scrutiny of the accounts. He failed, however, to satisfy the recipients. Nor could he fully pacify the poor but ambitious youth of the towns. These were new men— products of the population explosion that had followed the agricultural prosperity of the early 1890s. Restive, underemployed, and lacking outlets for their talents, they challenged the traditional notion that opportunity was the prerogative of the rich only. In an earlier day, some would have been Firminists. As for the upper classes, they reproached Oreste for having too many people deemed socially insignificant in his cabinet.[23]

Attempts at military reform, particularly budget reduction, and the establishment of a civilian police organization caused discontent among ranking army officers. Oreste wanted to break the *délégués*, the military governors of provinces, who, as often as not, proved to be rivals for any incumbent. It was not clear, however, if the president could genuinely afford to dismiss them. The resignation of the Zamor brothers, powerful militarists who had been the *délégués* of the departments of the North and the Artibonite, respectively, did not mean that they were out of the picture; rather, it indicated that Oreste could make no further claims to controlling a faction that would now seek the main chance. Nor was trouble confined to the North. Hostility to Oreste surfaced in his immediate milieu in the form of anonymous threatening notes he found pinned to his clothing and bed linen.[24]

Given his domestic difficulties, Oreste needed no trouble with the United States. A number of questions nevertheless remained unresolved between the two republics. The issues of monetary reform, the status of the railroad, and the role played by foreigners led U.S. Secretary of State William Jennings Bryan to send Assistant Secretary of State John Osborne to Haiti on a special mission in June, 1913. Osborne was instructed to deal with these matters and also to negotiate for the purchase of the Môle St. Nicolas. The Môle, a promontory on the northwest coast of the

22. Furniss to Secretary of State, July 17, 1913, DF, 838.00/728.

23. Luc Dorsinville, *La Chambre des Deputés Répresentait-elle la Nation?* (Port-au-Prince, 1930), 2–4.

24. Furniss to Secretary of State, June 28, 1913, DF, 838.00/727; Cillière to Minister of Foreign Affairs, December 16, 1913, and July 1, 1913, QDO, Vol. 5; Pyke to Secretary of State, June 30, 1913, FO 371, Vol. 1657.

island equipped with a large, deep, natural harbor, had been the focus of a Haitian-American dispute in 1891, when an attempt by the United States to obtain the port precipitated a foreign policy crisis.[25] Maintaining the independence of the two states of Española and their territorial integrity was a canon of Haitian statesmanship. Fears that the island would come under colonial domination had prompted Haiti's nineteenth-century interventions in Dominican affairs. Requests that insular land be alienated deeply disturbed Haiti.[26]

The 1913 demand for the Môle was intended, in Bryan's words, "to take it out of the market so that no other nation will attempt to secure a foothold there." The plan provided for American occupation of the harbor and a ten-mile hinterland. Residents could become U.S. citizens if they desired, and those who wished to remain Haitian would sell their property at an agreed-on price.[27]

Washington did not repeat earlier errors. Eschewing the crude navalism of 1891, which had antagonized both Haitian officials and the American minister, Osborne worked jointly with Furniss to achieve a compromise with the Haitians whereby the United States would withdraw its request in exchange for assurances that Haiti would not sell, lease, or rent the Môle St. Nicolas to other foreign powers or investors. The State Department's tactic may have been designed to impress upon Oreste the seriousness of such an action by alarming him. The United States also informally requested through Osborne that the president of Haiti confer with the American government on any cabinet changes he wanted to make. The views of the great powers would be taken into account in any case, but such an open demand for consultation signaled that with Woodrow Wilson's accession to the presidency the tolerance of traditional Haitian politics that had characterized Republican administrations was a thing of the past. Even before the advent of the spasmodic revolutionary wars of 1914–1915, the Americans had begun to arrogate authority to themselves in the Black Republic.[28]

---

25. Anténor Firmin, *Diplomates et diplomatie* (Cape Haitian, 1899); Frederick Douglass, *The Life and Times of Frederick Douglass* (1892; rpr. New York, 1962); Ludwell Lee Montague, *Haiti and the United States, 1714–1938* (Durham, N.C., 1940); Rayford W. Logan, *The Diplomatic Relations of the United States with Haiti, 1776–1891* (Chapel Hill, 1941).

26. Bryan to Woodrow Wilson, June 14, 1913, in Arthur S. Link (ed.), *The Papers of Woodrow Wilson* (55 vols.; Princeton, 1978) XXVII, 193.

27. *Ibid.*

28. Ferdinand Mayer to Lester Woolsey, August 7, 1913, DF, 838.002/73.

Osborne discussed the railroad and the BNRH with top private and public officials during his trip. Despite the State Department's high level of cooperation with the National City Bank of New York, which had substantial interests in the BNRH and the National Railroad Company, it continued to resist open identification of its aims with those of the banking corporation. The National City Bank, represented in Haiti by Roger Farnham, threatened to have the BNRH suspend payments to the government in Port-au-Prince if it was established that Haiti had intentionally stalled on approving the controversial track sections rejected when Auguste died.[29]

Farnham also suggested the creation of a mixed commission to review and adjudicate the railroad dispute. Officials in Washington remained lukewarm to these ideas because they entailed the possibility of European action at undesired levels. Should the BNRH suspend payments, Furniss pointed out, Haiti would simply resort to local merchant-bankers. As to the second proposal, the Wilson administration was no more receptive than were its predecessors to sharing decision making in Haiti with the French, Germans, and British.[30] Under Taft, the National City Bank had been encouraged to interest itself in Haiti. Once in the arena, it in turn began to push the State Department to commit itself more fully to intervening in Haitian affairs. That agency was not yet ready to take such a step, and Osborne's efforts in Haiti bore little fruit.

The American legation posed a problem for Farnham and the National City Bank because Furniss blocked their efforts to paint for the State Department their own portrait of conditions in Haiti. The bank's hostility to Furniss had first manifested itself when Taft was president, but during the Wilson administration, conditions ripened for the American minister's removal from office. The dismissal coincided with the nationwide displacement of black federal appointees in the United States. This allowed Wilson to appease southern supporters and to gratify his own racist instincts as well. Wilson had apparently made private, verbal promises to blacks during his candidacy, but these remained unfulfilled. In August, 1913, William Frank Powell, Furniss' predecessor in Haiti, now a Democrat and a journalist, accused Wilson of causing the ship of state to founder "upon the rocks of unredeemed pledges" to Afro-American voters.[31]

---

29. Furniss to Secretary of State, July 24, 1913, DF, 838.77/95.

30. *Ibid.*

31. Dana G. Munro, interview with author, April 29, 1979; Powell to Wilson, August 25, 1913, in Link (ed.), *Papers of Wilson*, XXVIII, 221–23; Kathleen L. Wolgemuth,

At first, neither Bryan nor Wilson intended to reserve the Haitian post for whites on a permanent basis. Certainly a few black "deserving Democrats" could be found. In June, 1913, Bryan recommended the temporary appointment of a white man as minister "until affairs there could be straightened out," and then the position would revert to blacks. The principal aim was to be rid of Furniss. "We need to make a change there immediately," Bryan informed Wilson.[32] Officials of the BNRH and the National Railroad had begun to deal directly with the Haitian government, bypassing Furniss completely. Supporters of American policies in Haiti during the subsequent military occupation make much of Haiti's desire to break with the tradition of receiving black diplomats from the United States, but little evidence from this period supports that view. Certain members of the upper class, notably Frédéric Marcelin, expressed antagonism to black Americans, but others, such as Clément Magloire, editor of Le Nouvelliste, did not.[33]

The Wilson administration appointed Madison Smith, a former Missouri congressman with no prior diplomatic experience, in Furniss' stead. Smith soon gained a reputation for intemperance and instability. An elderly man with traditional American prejudices, he disliked social intercourse with Haitians and possessed little of the sophistication characteristic of the milieu in which he was to function.[34]

The Osborne mission, the dismissal of Furniss, and the appointment of Smith did little to advance American objectives in Haiti. U.S. aims centered on keeping European influence in check. Despite the steps taken to secure the inalienability of the Môle, European powers still posed a commercial challenge to American hegemony. German traders in particular continued to gain commercial and political influence. Few Americans invested in Haiti. The improvements in merchandising that Powell had reported ten years earlier proved ephemeral. The U.S. government did not use tourism or cultural missions or even cruisers on friendly calls to

"Woodrow Wilson's Appointment Policy and the Negro," Journal of Southern History, XLIV (1959), 158–73.

32. Bryan to Wilson, June 19, 1913, in Woodrow Wilson Papers. LC.

33. Pyke, Annual Report, 1913, FO 371, Vol. 2000; Le Nouvelliste, June 25, 1913, p. 1; Le Matin, April 1, 1907; Bishop Hurst to Emmett Scott, n.d., in Papers of the National Association for the Advancement of Colored People, LC.

34. Stephen Leech to Grey, January 20, February 13, and January 28, 1914, all in FO 371, Vol. 2001; Pyke, Annual Report, 1913, FO 371, Vol. 2000; Cillière to Minister of Foreign Affairs, January 23, 1914, QDO, Vol. 5.

break the ice and thus proved indifferent to even simple programs that could have enhanced the standing of the United States in Haitian eyes.[35]

Anxiety about the role of foreign powers shaped a considerable part of Wilson's early Haitian policy. Officials on the scene believed that the United States could improve relations with Haiti through friendlier acts and constructive projects,[36] but Wilson preferred an approach that resembled later cold war policies. In his view, Britain and Germany were the chief threats to the Caribbean hegemony he wished to secure for the United States. His tactics thus stressed deterring the major powers rather than seeking a rapprochement with the independent republics in the region.

Ironically, the same reliance on finance capital that had characterized the Taft administration continued to be a key element in Wilsonian management of Latin American states. American concern with the Black Republic foreshadowed by only two years the sweeping changes in foreign banking created by the partnership between the major credit institutions and the Wilson administration. Wilson accompanied his advocacy of and assistance to American overseas banking with a shift in emphasis in Dollar Diplomacy. Taft's formulation had stressed the pacificatory effects of "stabilizing" Latin American governments through loans. For Wilson, loans extended American influence abroad by freeing Latin American countries from reliance on aggressive and usurious European creditors. A jealousy of the multilateral diplomacy practiced by many Latin American states underlay this view of the political uses of lending.

American support for financial penetration of Haiti by National City Bank did not represent a vastly new policy. It simply continued an old relationship that became increasingly unfavorable for the Haitians. American finance capital arrived late in the island republic. Staple exports from the United States preceded it by more than a century and permeated the economy to a much greater degree. American capital brought in its wake more consistent involvement by Washington but did not initiate the involvement. Finance capital found an unexpected ally in Wilson, whose political beliefs coincided with the bankers' mission.

Wilson combined a belief in representative democracy and due process with a repugnance toward revolution and any other extralegal approach to government. He maintained a fundamental distaste for societies in which

35. Moore, Memorandum, December 27, 1913, DF, 711.38/15.
36. *Ibid.*

such methods formed the major mode of political expression. Wilson moreover had to accommodate the banking sector's desire for overseas expansion. By 1913, financiers had come to believe that their own wealth and the general prosperity of the nation depended on the development of foreign capital and export markets. Agitation for banking reform had begun during the Taft administration as a consequence of the panic of 1907. The struggle was now carried forward as bankers and opponents of the "Money Trust" competed for control over any new banking structure. Wilson sympathized with investors' desires to move into international markets, and by supporting the Federal Reserve Act, he helped lay the foundation for the expansion of American banking abroad during and after World War I.[37]

Wilson's dislike of violent political change and his disinclination to recognize governments formed as a result neutralized any Pan-Americanist sympathies for Haiti. As global war threatened he and his counselors saw Haiti as a menace to hemispheric security. Wilson's response to the Haitian challenge involved him in a Dollar Diplomacy more highly developed than Taft's, though Wilson had publicly denounced Taft's policy as imperialist. Having decided to approach Haiti primarily through financial avenues, Wilson embarked on an intimate adventure with National City Bank. Once enemies at home, Wilson and the bank functioned as partners with common interests abroad.

Wilson based his objections to revolutionary change in Latin America on mechanistic assumptions about the nature of social change. He conceived of Latin American peoples as requiring a period of tutelage before they could gradually develop higher, more perfect forms of political and societal organization. Like Theodore Roosevelt, he believed in the possibility of universal progress, but he did not think that change should be abrupt or originate in extraconstitutional policies. The guarded attitude most American statesmen maintained toward the European presence in the hemisphere also marked Wilson's Latin American program. He was suspicious of German activity, especially in Mexico, and feared a general resurgence of British strength in Latin America once the Panama Canal was finished.[38]

37. Walter LaFeber, *Inevitable Revolutions* (2nd. ed.; New York, 1984), 49–54.

38. Arthur S. Link, *Wilson: The Struggle for Neutrality* (Princeton, 1960), 497–98; Richard D. Challener, *Admirals, Generals, and American Foreign Policy, 1898–1914* (Princeton, 1973), 399–400; Warren G. Kneer, *Great Britain and the Caribbean, 1901–1913: A Study in Anglo-American Relations* (East Lansing, 1975), 214–25; Arthur S. Link, *Wilson: The New Freedom* (Princeton, 1956), 304–14.

In the fall of 1913, Wilson addressed representatives from South American countries and others at the fifth annual convention of the Southern Commercial Congress, then meeting in Mobile, Alabama. In his Mobile address, the president couched his concern for hemispheric security in terms of Latin American freedom from foreign exploitation. He compared the Latin countries' plight with the good fortune of the United States. "You do not hear of concessions to foreign capitalists in the United States," Wilson commented. "They are not granted concessions. They are invited to make investments." He then noted how financiers dealt with the southern republics: "They [the Latin American republics] have harder bargains driven with them in the manner of loans than any other peoples in the world. Interest had been exacted of them, that was not exacted of anybody else, because the risk was said to be greater; and then securities were taken that destroyed the risk—an admirable arrangement for those who were forcing the terms!" Wilson declared the global priority of "human rights, national integrity, and opportunity as against material interests." North Americans could sympathize with the predicament of Latin Americans whose freedom was compromised from abroad, he claimed, because of similar attempts made against the United States in the weakness of its youth. These experiences made the United States disavow the use of classic imperialist aggression to extend its sway in the hemisphere. "I want to take this occasion to say that the United States will never again seek one additional foot of territory by conquest," Wilson announced.[39] He designed the Mobile address to appeal to Latin Americans on the basis of an identity of interests. Wilson's words harked back to the original tone of the Monroe Doctrine, but circumstances had completely changed since the enunciation of that policy. Wilson tried to interpret the American role as one of participation in a fraternal union bound by a common past of anticolonial struggle, but the reality was that the "material interests" against which he rhetorically arrayed himself were clearly dominant in his own diplomacy. Wilson might sound Bolívar's war cry against the European oppressor, but the onerous loan terms he cited in his speech could well have been those imposed on Haiti with his full approval. The Mexican Revolution provided the immediate context of Wilson's Mobile speech. One leading historian has extolled the president's commitment to the democratic goals of that revolution, but even here, Wilson's policies were aimed at containing revolutionary insurgency and protecting foreign property.[40]

39. Link (ed.), *Papers of Wilson*, XXVIII, 50, 451.
40. Link, *The New Freedom*, 350.

The fear of a revitalized Britain also played a role in Wilson's thinking. Roosevelt and Taft believed that they had neutralized the British. As part of John Milton Hay's Canal strategy, a truce had been worked out with Britain that left the United States dominating the Caribbean region and offering protection of British interests. Some observers, especially those associated with the military, doubted if Britain's retirement from the field would long outlast the completion of the Panama Canal. Nevertheless, with the British temporarily out of the way, Roosevelt and Taft could concentrate on German expansion in the area. By 1913, however, the British had raised their consulate to a legation and accredited their minister in Havana, Stephen Leech, to Port-au-Prince as well. The British were searching for oil reserves in the Americas and flexing their muscles in Mexico and Colombia. Wilson thought a general reassertion of Britain's power in the hemisphere and difficulties over the Canal quite possible.[41]

British influence in Haiti did not compare with Germany's. Here, the Reich loomed as the largest obstacle to the creation of American predominance. U.S. policy makers seemed more concerned about German potential and ambitions than about anything concrete that Germans had actually done. Domestic constraints limited the expansion of German finance capital in Latin America. The empire subsidized trade only for the purposes of stimulating greater commercial activity and maintained a cautious loan policy.[42] In the absence of a study assessing the value of the Germans' investments in the Caribbean region, the scope of their influence, the extent of their power, and the degree to which the kaiser's government committed itself to underwriting German commercial interests there, the significance of the German political threat remains a matter of conjecture.[43] One can only assume that Washington officials who stressed the necessity of curbing German expansionism acted out of a belief that the kaiser had the capacity and the desire to cause considerable trouble, rather than that he was actually doing so.[44]

As for German military aggression, American strategists anticipated the possibility that the German government might secure a naval base in

---

41. *Ibid.*, 330–31, 350; Kneer, *Great Britain and the Caribbean*, ix–xv; Challener, *Admirals, Generals*, 330.

42. Link, *The New Freedom*, 303.

43. Herbert Feis, *Europe, the World's Banker* (New Haven, 1930), 68.

44. Hans Schmidt, *The United States Occupation of Haiti, 1915–1934* (New Brunswick, N.J., 1971), 50; Lamar Cecil, *Albert Ballin: Business and Politics in Imperial Germany* (Princeton, 1967), 152–53; Holger H. Herwig, *The Politics of Frustration: The United States in German Naval Planning, 1889–1941* (Boston, 1976), 67–92, 72–76.

one of the independent states. Policy makers did not think that the German navy would actually attack the United States. Their evaluation rested on a belief that officials in Berlin sought only a mercantile center from which to operate in Latin America. Germany's readiness to treat the Monroe Doctrine with decidedly less circumspection than did other European powers nevertheless made military planners uneasy.[45]

The popular fear of German ambitions provided a convenient ex post facto rationalization of any summary action the United States might take in Haiti, where conditions after 1913, particularly the dazzlingly rapid succession of governments, caused further trepidation. Once the European powers were at war, the prospect of the Caribbean's becoming a battleground for imperial conflict aroused new anxieties. The U.S. government developed a hard line on Haiti during the Oreste administration, and by the summer of 1914, the State Department's view of the perpetual crisis in the Black Republic had congealed. Robert Lansing, the new State Department counselor, was the prime mover in developing this policy. Lansing elaborated a general Latin American position that illustrated a new concern with European activity in the hemisphere and echoed the traditional interest in preserving a peaceful climate that would preclude intervention.[46]

Lansing upheld the fundamental philosophy underlying the Monroe Doctrine but advocated moderation in its use. Each incident that impelled the United States to enter a dispute between a European and an American government had to be examined on its own merits. Lansing agreed with Theodore Roosevelt that in some instances the United States might permit Europeans to compel Latin Americans to meet certain obligations. The major criterion for distinguishing proper and improper demands rested on the element of permanence in a given situation.[47] The United States would not let a European power set up an ongoing colonial or neocolonial presence.

Lansing's reading of the Monroe Doctrine also upheld Roosevelt's interpretation in another particular. Monroe's original intention had been to safeguard the right of the Latin states to conduct revolutions and thus eliminate imperialism in the Americas. As Roosevelt saw the doc-

45. Challener, *Admirals, Generals*, 16–17; Herwig, *Politics of Frustration*, 67–92, esp. 72–76.

46. Challener, *Admirals, Generals*, 28, 29; Herwig, *Politics of Frustration*, 93–109.

47. Robert Lansing to Secretary of State, June 16, 1914, in U.S. Department of State, *The Lansing Papers, 1914–1920* (Washington, D.C., 1939), 461, 460.

trine, revolutions had come to facilitate imperialist ingress. They therefore had to be contained. Lansing went a step further in carefully distinguishing between the Pan-Americanism inherent in the original conception and the interests of the United States as he interpreted them. "The Monroe Doctrine is . . . a national policy of the United States," he declared. "It is not a Pan-American policy." The United States therefore opposed the alienation of any national territory in the hemisphere, even though the state in question might make the concession willingly. "The opposition to European control over American territory is not primarily to preserve the integrity of any American state—that may be a result but not a purpose of the Doctrine," Lansing wrote. "The essential idea is to prevent a condition which would menace the national interests of the United States." In Lansing's opinion, a European state that became the dominant power in an American republic had to feel the weight of the Monroe Doctrine. That hegemony had been peacefully achieved made no difference, he wrote, for the effect was the same as if actual conquest had occurred.[48]

In 1912 and 1913, Haiti remained outside the U.S. administration's focus. There had been no revolutions: accident had apparently determined the Auguste and Oreste presidencies. For a while, an ostensible continuity of policies papered over the differences between the two Haitian administrations. In January, 1914, the illusion of stability was shattered as fighting erupted in many parts of the country.[49] Two distinct factions emerged from the conflict.

One faction comprised the Zamor family, which had united a following through the customary extended family ties, patronage, and militarism. Two Zamor brothers, Charles and Oreste, were *délégués* of northern provinces who had established a highly autocratic rule marked by blatant nepotism and favoritism. Oreste Zamor would later become president of the republic, but both brothers were powerful forces in Haitian politics. President Leconte and his successors had acceded to this because they had had no choice. The Zamors commanded their own armies and maintained close relations with Dominican counterparts who could assist them in a military campaign. Michel Oreste tried clandestinely to undermine these warlords by manipulating the legislative elections of 1914. The attempt

48. *Ibid.*, 461, 464.
49. Smith to Secretary of State, January 7, 1914, DF, 838.00/743.

failed, and the Zamors' resignation from their posts as *délégués* precipitated new conflict.[50]

The second faction supported General Davilmar Théodore of Ennery. Théodore, also a northerner and a warlord, cooperated as readily as the Zamors with Dominican mercenaries. In mid-January he operated from Dajabón, a settlement across the border from the Haitian town of Ouanaminthe.[51] Faced with attack from the two strong rebel armies, Oreste was faltering by the end of the month. In a last-ditch effort to save the administration, the Haitian minister in Washington, Ulrich Duvivier, offered the United States control over the customhouses in exchange for military support of the incumbent. The offer was declined.

The BNRH directors also requested American involvement. Already disgruntled by Oreste's eleventh-hour decree that paper money would be retired at five gourdes to the dollar, the bank and its shareholders were distressed to learn that the Cape Haitian customhouses had been seized by rebels. The revolutionists refused to remit any of the customs receipts to the BNRH. The National City Bank, Hallgarten and Company, Ladenburg Thalmann and Company, and Speyer and Company fired off a joint telegram to Secretary of State Bryan, pleading for action to prevent default on the loan. Bryan accordingly ordered U.S. Consul Lemuel Livingston to persuade the insurgents to make the payments. Livingston was to impress upon them the portent of Wilson's Mobile address, demand that American and other foreigners' life and property be respected, and "insist on constitutional methods of reform." The massing of nearly a thousand American troops on U.S. Navy ships along the Haitian coast gave point to Bryan's instructions. The United States was not alone in reacting in this manner. Intent on protecting German investments, the *Vineta* left St. Thomas on January 24, steaming full speed for Port-au-Prince.[52]

On January 26, St. Marc fell to Zamorist rebels. The conquest of this city, traditionally the gateway to the capital for insurgents and thus the

50. Lemuel Livingston to Secretary of State, January 19, 1914, DF, 838.00/778; Joseph Jérémie, *Mémoires* (Port-au-Prince, 1950), 42; J. C. Dorsainvil, *Manuel d'histoire d'Haïti* (Port-au-Prince, 1925), 5–8; Cillière to Minister of Foreign Affairs, December 16, 1913, QDO, Vol. 5.

51. Livingston to Secretary of State, January 12, 1914, DF, 838.00/777.

52. Smith to Secretary of State, January 10, 1914, DF, 838.515/8, and January 24, 1914, DF, 838.51/319; Bryan to the American Legation in Port-au-Prince, January 25, 1914, DF, 838.51/319; New York *Times*, January 25, 1914, Sec. 2, p. 1.

last stronghold of incumbency, effectively ended the Oreste regime. Oreste boarded the *Vineta* two days later, leaving Haiti without a government.[53] One hundred fifty men from the USS *Montana* landed, and German marines also disembarked. The French ship *Créole*, cruising near Mexico, was put on alert, and the USS *South Carolina*, with nine hundred men aboard, made its way from Guantánamo Bay under the command of Captain John Russell, a former judge advocate general of the navy whose knowledge of international law was thought an asset in this situation.[54] The U.S. Navy fielded three ships to France's and Germany's one. This show of strength indicated the primacy that the Americans now assumed in Haitian waters.

The revolution against Oreste had not been especially bloody or bitter. The United States insisted that the Haitians go through the motions of a presidential election. It would tolerate no overt dictatorship, but the pressure of various private armies and the presence of more than a thousand foreign troops precluded the possibility of elections as Americans understood them. A neutral Haitian mercenary force camped in Croix de Missions and offered itself to the highest bidder. The presidency would go to the contender who could pay for this and similar outfits.[55]

In the absence of the good reporting formerly provided by Furniss, American intelligence in 1914 relied on reports sent to the State Department by its own special agents and Roger Farnham. Farnham and his representatives in Haiti acted as a shadow diplomatic and consular agency, often beating the regular team to the punch. His telegraphed report of a train robbery near Cape Haitian, for example, reached Washington two and a half hours before Livingston's.[56] Farnham's experience as a newsman served him well, but the value of his communications was compromised by their self-interested content. He relayed alarmist messages laden with interventionist recommendations and misrepresented the views of Haitian officials. Nothing in the State Department correspon-

53. Cillière to Minister of Foreign Affairs, February 7, 1914, QDO, Vol. 5; Farnham to Secretary of State, January 26, 1914, DF, 838.00/771.

54. New York *Times*, January 28, 1914, p. 1, and January 29, 1914, p. 3.

55. *Ibid.*, February 1, 1914, Sec. 2, p. 12; Smith to Secretary of State, February 15, 1914, DF, 838.00/808.

56. Livingston to Secretary of State, telegram, June 19, 1914, received 4:10 P.M., DF, 838.00/933; and Farnham to Secretary of State, telegram, June 19, 1914, received 1:40 P.M., 838.00/934.

dence indicates that American officials thought Farnham out of line.[57]

The closer the rebels came to the capital, the keener the contest for the presidency. When Théodore arrived in Gonaïves, he found the city had already declared its support for Oreste Zamor and that Zamorists were infiltrating his forces. The showdown came on February 2, when after a pitched battle Théodore retreated to the North and Zamor proceeded to Port-au-Prince with four thousand men. Six days later, the deputies placed in office by Oreste elected Zamor president. Zamor swore to uphold Lecontism and appointed officials who had been associated with the late chief. Léger held the foreign affairs portfolio once again. Lespinasse became finance minister. These choices suited the metropoles and in their eyes lent the proper tone to the new administration.[58]

The United States waited for more settled conditions to extend recognition. Washington officials wanted first to ascertain that Théodore had been swept from the field and that the Zamor government could endure. Taking the Zamors' eventual complete conquest of the country as sufficient indication that their rule rested on popular consent, Bryan ordered Smith to recognize the presidency of Oreste Zamor on March 1, 1914.[59]

The veteran foreign minister J. N. Léger had stalled on all outstanding issues pending recognition. Even after diplomatic relations had been normalized, Smith could not budge Léger on the questions of customs control, lighthouses for Panama Canal traffic, an arbitration protocol, and visas for Syrian-Americans wishing to return to Haiti.[60] This was all the more remarkable as the Zamor government had no financial resources. Bureaucrats had stolen what was left of the unpledged customs revenues. Army and civil service salaries consequently remained unpaid. The government could not put up any collateral, and the BNRH refused to extend credit, thus exacerbating the crisis. "They think they will be able, in our

---

57. See the following barrage of correspondence from Farnham to the Secretary of State in early 1914: January 26 (DF, 838.00/770), January 26 (DF, 838.00/77), February 2 (DF, 838.00/791), February 2 (DF, 838.00/792), January 31 (DF, 838.00/793), February 5 (DF, 838.00/809).

58. Bellegarde, *Histoire du Peuple haïtien*, 243; Smith to Secretary of State, February 7, 1914, *FR*, 1914, p. 337; New York *Times*, February 10, 1914, p. 3.

59. Bryan to Smith, February 9, 1914 (*FR*, 1914, p. 338), February 26, 1914 (*FR*, 1914, pp. 339–40), March 1, 1914 (*FR*, 1914, p. 341).

60. Smith to Secretary of State, February 28, 1914, *FR*, 1914, p. 340; Bryan to Smith, March 1 and March 2, 1914, *FR*, 1914, p. 341.

economic stress, to put the knife to our throat," *Le Nouvelliste* opined. Haiti would not accept foreign control of its revenues. "All sacrifices, but never that one!"[61]

Davilmar Théodore was the chief beneficiary of the Zamor government's financial predicament. Théodore had not abandoned his presidential hopes and awaited a propitious time to begin an insurgency. Former president Antoine Simon and certain expatriate traders supported his candidacy. Peacemaking attempts in May by Livingston and the bishop of Cape Haitian failed, as Théodore proved resolute in his determination to topple his adversary.[62]

In order to forestall Théodore, Zamor had to settle his debt to his military allies and find payroll funds. Foreign loans could not be obtained without yielding to metropolitan attempts to gain leverage, so Zamor went to the local merchant community and concluded three agreements totaling nearly three million dollars. Germans held most of the bonds, for which certain customs duties had been pledged.[63]

The increased German control of the public debt stimulated swift action in Washington, which approached the Zamors through its new minister in Haiti, Arthur Bailly Blanchard. Blanchard, a white Louisianan and a career diplomat, had spent many years at the U.S. embassy in Paris. Haiti did not interest him, but he remained a long time at a post that, as a result of the U.S. military occupation, became largely ceremonial. Blanchard proposed to the Haitians that the president of the United States name a general receiver for their customs receipts, a financial advisor to the Haitian government, and a staff for these officials. The U.S. government thought Haiti should apply all its revenues to servicing the public debt and allow the United States to prevent any interference with collection. The Americans ought furthermore to be consulted prior to any increase in the Haitian debt. Policy makers modeled these demands on the U.S. customs convention with the Dominican Republic.[64]

61. Cillière to Minister of Foreign Affairs, March 16, 1914, QDO, Vol. 26; Smith to Secretary of State, February 28, 1914, and Bryan to Smith, March 6, 1914, DF, 838.51/327; *Le Nouvelliste*, March 16, 1914.

62. Cillière to President of the Council, March 12, 1914, QDO, Vol. 5; U.S. Department of State, Division of Latin American Affairs, "Memorandum Regarding Political and Financial Conditions and Administration of Customs Houses in the Republic of Haiti, March 25, 1914," DF, 838.00/917; Bryan to John Terres, May 18, 1914, and Livingston to Secretary of State, May 26, 1914, *FR*, 1914, pp. 344–45.

63. Clipping enclosed in Penfield and Penfield to Bryan, May 26, 1914, DF, 838.111/187; H. P. Davis, *Black Democracy* (2nd ed.; New York, 1929), 149, 150.

64. Lucille Atcherson, "History of the Haitian Loan Negotiations," February 1923, DF,

In mid-March, Dr. Fritz Perl, the German minister to Haiti, declared that Germany must be included in any multilateral customs agreement.[65] The French also pressed for participation in a Haitian receivership. In a letter to U.S. Secretary of State Bryan, Jusserand recalled France's position when the United States forced Liberia to reorganize its finances in 1911–1912. His reference to Liberia indicated a waning interest in Haiti and an increasing inclination to relegate it to the status of an American dependency. In this instance, France's concern with the customs receivership reflected its desire to ensure that its interests would be protected.[66] The Germans, however, continued to oppose American intervention in principle. Collectively, the Europeans proposed a customs board with proportional representation, an idea the United States rejected because of the minority status such an arrangement would impose on it.[67]

The multinational firm Grace Brothers, chief underwriter of the McDonald consortium, favored a version of the European plan. Afraid that the cycle of revolution would cause Haiti to default on the railroad bonds, the company wrote to the Banque de l'Union Parisienne suggesting that Zamor be forced to accept a customs receivership in exchange for recognition by the United States, France, and Germany. Without funds, he would eventually have to come to terms. The company wanted American intervention but preferred that control of Haitian finances be international.[68]

The Zamor regime nevertheless continued to resist the receivership idea when approached by American officials. It was commonly thought that no administration could survive such a concession. Alphonse Cillière, the French minister, characterized such frequently voiced patriotic sentiment in Haiti as actually contrary to the interests of its ruling class. No

838.51/15001/2; Davis, *Black Democracy*, 150–51; Winby to Charles Evans Hughes, April 6, 1921, DF, 838.00/1838; Munro, *Intervention*, 339; Rachel West, *The Department of State on the Eve of the First World War* (Athens, Ga., 1978), 118.

65. Bellegarde, *Histoire du Peuple haïtien*, 244; Minister of Foreign Affairs to Minister in Haiti, December 26, 1914, and Guillaume de Bray, Note, February 25, 1914, QDO, Vol. 26.

66. J. Jusserand to Gaston Doumergue, March 12, 1914, and Jusserand to Bryan, March 12, 1914, QDO, Vol. 26; New York *Times*, May 14, 1914, p. 1.

67. New York *Times*, May 31, 1914, Sec. 3, p. 3; Bray, Note, February 25, 1914, and French Minister of Foreign Affairs to French Minister in Haiti, February 26, 1914, QDO, Vol. 26.

68. Grace Brothers and Co. to the Banque de l'Union Parisienne, n.d., 1914, QDO, Vol. 26.

matter what occurred, he was sure, BNRH shareholders would emerge unscathed. Popular indignation against the bank would simply aid American bankers at the expense of metropolitan French financiers.[69]

France's insistence that it be included in a customs regime wavered before the prospect of having its interest in Haiti served without effort on its part. Jusserand explored this possibility. An international agreement including Germany, he thought, might be just as irksome as a receivership executed by the Americans alone.[70] Relying on the United States to guard French interests in Haiti would free France to occupy itself with other matters.

In their effort to bring Zamor to his knees, the metropolitan governments practiced a crude gunboat diplomacy in Port-au-Prince in 1914. In May a French cruiser trained its guns on two Haitian ships in Haitian waters and demanded immediate payment of the interest on the bonded debt. The local crews jumped overboard and swam ashore, and the French began towing the two vessels toward St. Thomas. The craft were released when the government in Port-au-Prince sent a launch out after them, carrying the money the French had demanded.[71]

Britain also resorted to gunboat diplomacy, giving Haiti a twelve-hour ultimatum to produce $62,000 for a British subject whose sawmill had been destroyed during the Leconte insurgency. A court of arbitration upheld the claim, a decision given additional weight by the presence of HMS *Suffolk*. The Haitians capitulated. The legislature held Léger responsible for failing to assuage the British through diplomatic means. It demanded and secured his resignation.[72]

These humiliating episodes illustrate the limits of Haitian multilateralism when confronted by the great powers acting in concert. They did not constitute the sum of Zamor's financial and political problems. The need for money and the necessity of forestalling even greater metropolitan aggressiveness led him to hold talks with private concessionaires about the possibility of leasing or selling the Môle St. Nicolas. These discussions were clandestine, because widespread public knowledge of the regime's willingness to alienate a part of the national domain meant its rapid downfall, a demise in which the United States might well assist.

69. Cillière to Minister of Foreign Affairs, March 14, 1914, QDO, Vol. 26.

70. Jusserand to Ministry, n.d., received March 14, 1914, QDO, Vol. 26.

71. New York *Times*, May 14, 1914, p. 1.

72. *Ibid.*, May 17, 1914, p. 8, and June 24, 1914, p. 12; Grace Brothers and Co. to the Banque de l'Union Parisienne, n.d., 1914, QDO, Vol. 26.

However secret the meetings were, the Americans found out about them. The United States opposed any territorial alienation, even to a private American concern. As concessionaires could not be easily controlled, such an enterprise might drift into foreign hands. The State Department sent a special agent, Ross Hazeltine, to Haiti to improve the department's intelligence gathering.[73]

Davilmar Théodore meanwhile made political capital out of Zamor's willingness to entertain American suggestions regarding customs control. Fortunately for Zamor, he knew nothing of the Môle talks. Théodore mounted a spring offensive in the North, and in June, Zamor left Port-au-Prince at the head of an army to suppress the insurgency. As he campaigned during the summer of 1914, the U.S. Navy maintained readiness in Haitian waters. In August, Zamor suspended retirement of paper money and authorized use of the interest on the ten-million-franc retirement fund for current operating expenses. The BNRH refused to disburse the money.[74]

Dominican mercenaries, operating on a frontier Zamor could not control, sustained the northern insurrection. Théodore easily slipped back and forth across the border and exhausted Zamor financially through this cat-and-mouse game. Hazeltine reported that the Dominican authorities had as little control over the frontier as did the Haitians. Banditry, rebellion, looting, and arson spread through the zone east of Cape Haitian as *cacos* attacked plantations belonging to government officials and sympathizers. The insurgents' growing strength threatened the Cape's food supply.[75]

Believing that Zamor's back was to the wall, the BNRH did its utmost to promote an American customs receivership backed by military occupation. The bank's position toward the government remained wholly opportunistic. Zamor sidestepped its refusals to issue funds and its obstructive tactics by resorting again to an interior loan. In early June he borrowed

73. J. B. Stabler, Memorandum, May 14, 1914, DF, 838.00/1668; William Phillips to Secretary of State, May 23, 1914, DF, 838.00/1667.

74. Livingston to Secretary of State, May 26, 1914, DF, 838.00/930; Davis, *Black Democracy*, 151.

75. Cillière to President of the Council, March 19, 1914, QDO, Vol. 5; Bryan to the American Legation in Port-au-Prince, May 8, 1914, DF, 838.00/922; Terres to Secretary of State, May 9, 1914, DF, 838.00/922, and April 13, 1914, DF, 838.00/926; Ross Hazeltine to Secretary of State, June 10, 1914, DF, 838.00/939; Livingston to Secretary of State, July 12, 1914, DF, 838.00/948; Commander Eberle to Secretary of the Navy, July 2, 1914, DF, 838.00/953.

$312,500 from small merchants and predominantly German Port-au-Prince financiers.[76]

In July, Roger Farnham arrived at Cape Haitian aboard a U.S. Navy ship. Traveling as an executive of the National Railroad Company rather than as a National City Bank vice-president, he called on Zamor. Apparently unable to achieve his objectives with the president, he began parleys with the rebels in October. Charles Zamor, minister of the interior, thought Farnham was assisting the insurgents. More likely, Farnham had bets placed on all factions.[77]

As for Oreste Zamor, his problem with Farnham reflected his administration's difficulties with bankers in general. His greatest dilemma was not the threat posed by Théodore or other militarists but his government's inability to borrow. The only remaining collateral consisted of a stamp tax, which lenders would not accept.[78]

Zamor had succeeded in wresting Ouanaminthe from the rebels by September, but the victory did not last. Impotent in the face of the BNRH's intransigence and irresolute regarding foreign customs control and land sale or lease, Zamor had little choice but to resign. He did so on October 29 after less than eight months in power. An American journalist covering the fighting in Haiti in the summer of 1914 pointed to the curious calm in the zones he observed. The conflict seemed to him—and, he claimed, to Haitians—more an exercise than a matter of passion. He quoted a Haitian as saying that such wars were fought to win, not to kill. To many Haitians, inured to the ritual of revolutionary succession, Théodore and the Zamors represented factions in which they had no tangible stake. If few outside official circles took the contest seriously, however, that nonchalance did not long endure.[79]

76. Smith to Secretary of State, June 10, 1914, DF, 838.00/939; Davis, *Black Democracy*, 150.

77. Boaz Long, Memorandum, July 2, 1914, DF, 838.00; N. C. Twining to Secretary of the Navy, October 17, 1914, DF, 838.00/1013; Farnham to State Department, October 28, 1914, DF, 838.00/1631.

78. Hazeltine to Secretary of State, July 30, 1914, *FR*, 1914, pp. 351–52; Davis, *Black Democracy*, 151.

79. Bryan to A. Bailly Blanchard, October 7, 1914, *FR*, 1914, pp. 353–54; Livingston to Blanchard, September 5, 1914, DF, 838.00/984; Davis, *Black Democracy*, 150, 151; George Mygatt, "Stalking the President of Haiti," *Outlook*, CVII (1914), 971–77.

VII

"La Fatalité Historique"

Jou malheur lait caillé cassé tête ou.
On a bad day even clabber breaks your head.

—Haitian proverb

PRESIDENT DAVILMAR Théodore was the latest representation of the Haitian cycle of revolution and counterrevolution. The Wilson administration, consistently opposed to revolution as political process, attempted to arrest the pattern of recurrent insurgency in Haiti. The outbreak of World War I in 1914 intensified Washington's efforts to remove Haiti as a possible pawn in European combatants' calculations.

Washington planned to approach the new Théodore government with a proposal to negotiate a customs convention and hold national elections under American supervision.[1] Lansing stressed the importance of the elections, considering them as indispensable as a customs agreement. He sent Blanchard a memorandum outlining American policy. The United States "desires nothing for itself from Haiti," the statement read. The U.S. government did not seek any special benefits for American citizens. The State Department spelled out three major points in the note. It called for the complete cessation of fighting, the "immediate reconstitution of political authority," and the substitution of constitutional change for revolutionary succession. In addition, it suggested that three expedients would facilitate achievement of these objectives. Haitians or American advisors would choose a provisional government, whose president could not seek permanent office. Americans would observe subsequent elections, and if they were satisfied that the elections had been fair and lawful, the United States would support the resulting regime.[2]

Davilmar Théodore sidestepped this plan by being duly elected presi-

---

1. Robert Lansing to A. Bailly Blanchard, October 31, 1914, *FR*, 1914, p. 356.
2. Memorandum in Lansing to Blanchard, November 4, 1914, *FR*, 1914, p. 357.

dent of Haiti by the legislative corps on November 10. The State Department countered by making full recognition of his administration contingent on his agreeing to parleys concerning "questions of interest" to the United States. Until this was done, Théodore would only be the provisional president in American eyes.[3]

The Haitians proved adamant on the recognition question. They pointed out that Théodore had been legally elected, and they offered to send a group of commissioners to Washington for a conference, provided that the government was formally recognized. Bryan promised that recognition would be granted as soon as the commission arrived in Washington and signed a customs convention. Haiti was also to settle the bank and railroad matters, accord protection to foreign interests, and forswear any alienation of territory for the military or commercial use of a European government. The State Department initially demanded that Haitian commissioners come to Washington as a prerequisite to recognition, but its fundamental distrust of Théodore led it later to insist that the agreements be signed first.[4]

Recognizing the financial problems that Théodore had inherited, the United States offered to help him secure a loan from the BNRH, but the elderly general could not afford to meet the American demands. He had defeated the Zamors, but their partisans continued an armed resistance in the North, where they seized Ouanaminthe and its environs, as well as other important centers in the northern interior. One of Théodore's most powerful lieutenants, Vilbrun Guillaume Sam, a man the president feared rather than trusted, had recently demanded and quickly received an appointment as *délégué* of the North.[5]

Théodore realized the likelihood of a revolt followed by foreign intervention if he yielded to any American request the Haitian public thought subversive. To avoid taking a step so unpopular as to lead to its own collapse, his government made a counterproposal designed to forestall the United States' initiative. Written by the minister of the interior, Rosalvo Bobo, it contained a generous offer of mining concessions to Americans.[6]

3. William Jennings Bryan to Blanchard, November 12, 1914, *FR*, 1914, p. 359.

4. Blanchard to Secretary of State, November 28, 1914, Bryan to Blanchard, November 24, 1914, Lansing to Blanchard, November 21 and November 28, 1914, all in *FR*, 1914, pp. 360–61.

5. Roger Gaillard, *Les cent-jours de Rosalvo Bobo* (Port-au-Prince, 1973), 23; Lemuel Livingston to Secretary of State, December 19, 1914, DF, 838.00/1072.

6. Gaillard, *Rosalvo Bobo*, 24–27; Blanchard to Secretary of State, December 2, 1914, *FR*, 1914, p. 363, and December 12, 1914, *FR*, 1914, pp. 367–69.

So ardent was the popular opposition to this plan that the Senate called in the minister for foreign affairs, Joseph Justin, to testify about the regime's contacts with American representatives. As Blanchard narrated the event, "the Senate rose in a body, denounced the Minister for Foreign Affairs, and accused him of endeavoring to sell the country to the United States, and a concerted attempt was made to [deal] him severe blows. He was rescued through the efforts of Senators and Cabinet Members, and under their protection left the Senate amidst the wildest excitement. [The] Minister for Foreign Affairs has since presented his resignation."[7] No one rushed to take Justin's place, and in the absence of a correspondent, Blanchard found he could not negotiate freely with the Haitians. He had to resort to direct appeals to Théodore, a task made difficult by the president's reluctance to personally direct foreign policy. In an audience at the National Palace, the French minister, Pierre Girard, found the president "an old man, visibly tired, whose mind seemed elsewhere." Théodore sat mutely through the interview.[8] His exhaustion and his untenable situation led to an impasse. The State Department tried to unblock it by allowing Blanchard to withdraw the demand for customs control, at the price of recognition. Washington was not ready to force a receivership on Haiti but based recognition on Haitian willingness to directly address the issues of customs control; conflicts among the Haitian government, the BNRH, and the National Railroad; nonalienation of territory; and protection of foreign interests.[9]

The United States meanwhile rejected the Haitian counterproposal. Port-au-Prince continued to offer favors to American business interests despite the militant rhetoric it released for popular consumption at home. The State Department did not seek such favors, Bryan insisted. American business would find its way in Haiti of its own accord, he told Blanchard, once political conditions had stabilized. Haiti could expect only speculative and exploitative terms from investors until a more favorable business climate prevailed. In the meantime, he instructed Blanchard to remit precise information on all Americans who were interested in Haitian concessions so that the quality of each venture could be assessed on an individual basis.[10] This position harmonized with Wilson's Latin Ameri-

---

7. Blanchard to Secretary of State, December 4, 1914, *FR*, 1914, pp. 363–64.

8. Pierre Girard to Minister of Foreign Affairs, December 14, 1914, QDO, Vol. 27.

9. Blanchard to Secretary of State, December 7, 1914, *FR*, 1914, pp. 364–65; Bryan to Blanchard, December 12, 1914, *FR*, 1914, p. 367.

10. Bryan to Blanchard, December 19, 1914, *FR*, 1914, pp. 370–71.

can policy as enunciated in the Mobile address. Wilson disapproved of adventurism in Latin America, even when undertaken by Americans. The ephemerality of such investments and their vulnerability to foreign transfer made them undesirable in his eyes.[11]

The American offer to intercede on Haiti's behalf with the BNRH demonstrates the continuity of that institution's conflict with the Haitian government. Théodore, like others before him, failed to secure BNRH cooperation. Thus, two weeks after his inauguration, "Frè Da" (Brother Davilmar), as he was popularly called in Creole, proposed to the legislature a large independent issue of paper money.[12] The State Department instructed Blanchard to discreetly oppose the bill until the matter could be brought up with the Haitian commission in Washington. The American offer of assistance in securing a loan subsequently hinged on the cancellation of the currency issue. Faced with Haitian obstinacy, Bryan threatened to withdraw the offer. Finally, the secretary of state advised Blanchard that if the projected sixteen million gourdes were circulated, the United States would follow the BNRH in refusing to recognize them as legal tender.[13]

The Haitian argument for the gourde issue rested on the view that the BNRH had violated the original 1910 contract by refusing credit. As the contract contained arbitral clauses created to eliminate the need for diplomatic intervention, the American legation was not justified in advocating the BNRH's interests. If the BNRH could claim that it was forced to operate under duress as an excuse for suspending payments to the state, its refusal to reach a new understanding with Théodore similarly allowed the president to safeguard the survival of his administration by the only expedient left to him—seizing the state assets stored in the bank. As the controversy raged, the gourde slid in value from four to eight to a dollar.[14]

In the deteriorating situation, the regime had little choice but to abandon attempts at reconciliation with foreign interests. It issued commercial paper, called *bons* in French and scornfully referred to in Port-au-Prince as the *Bons Da*, a ribald Creole pun that played on the French word for

11. Arthur S. Link, *Wilson: The New Freedom* (Princeton, 1956), 320–21.

12. Blanchard to Secretary of State, November 24, 1914, *FR*, 1914, p. 361.

13. Bryan to Blanchard, November 27, 1914 (*FR*, 1914, p. 362), December 4, 1914 (*FR*, 1914, p. 364), December 7, 1914 (*FR*, 1914, p. 365).

14. Haitian Foreign Office to Blanchard, December 15, 1914, in Blanchard to Secretary of State, December 24, 1914, *FR*, 1914, pp. 373–75; Admiral Caperton, Statement, in SI, 289–93.

voucher and the Creole word for buttocks, and reflected the widespread lack of faith in the scrip. Yet the large numbers of unruly soldiers bivouacking in the streets of the capital underlined the urgent need for a popular trading medium. Men who had fought for Théodore now demanded their pay. Small merchants, reluctant to accept the *Bons Da* as currency but too afraid of the soldiers to refuse them, closed their shops. The closing of the larger German establishments soon followed, resulting in a spontaneous business strike that was essentially a vote of no confidence in the government.[15]

During this stalemate, the BNRH grew fearful of a possible surprise raid on its vaults by Haitian officials. A BNRH vice-president in New York, Henry H. Wehrhane, secretly wrote to Bryan to request that specified gold coins and ingots be brought to the United States aboard the next available navy vessel. Bryan agreed to the plan and helped the BNRH make the arrangements in mid-December. To ensure that the Haitians would be caught off guard, he instructed Blanchard to inform them that the United States would undertake no fiscal oversight of their country without their consent.[16]

The biggest worry for the BNRH and for Blanchard, charged with aiding in the expatriation of the money, was getting it from the vault to the waterfront undetected. "The state of mind of the population" required the use of marines, which Bryan freely sanctioned.[17] The final plan, as worked out by the BNRH, the American minister, and the commander of the USS *Machias,* was as follows: "The gold will be removed from the bank at one o'clock when all Haitians are either eating their lunch or taking their 'siesta' and the streets are practically deserted. Eight men armed with stout canes and concealed revolvers, will go to the bank and load the gold on a wagon and ride on the wagon with it from the bank to the wharf. Men with stout canes, with an officer in charge, will be strolling at intervals on the streets through which the wagon will pass."[18] On December 17, Blanchard conferred with the Haitian minister for finance and the minister for foreign affairs, now Joseph Louis Borno. He said nothing to them about the removal of the gold, though they agreed to

15. H. P. Davis, Memorandum, n.d., DR, 838.616/175.

16. Henry Wehrhane to Bryan, December 8, 1914, *FR*, 1914, p. 365; Bryan to Blanchard, December 12, 1914, *FR*, 1914, p. 367.

17. Blanchard to Secretary of State, December 14, 1914, and Bryan to Blanchard, December 15, 1914, *FR*, 1914, p. 369.

18. Commander of USS *Hancock* to the Navy Department, December 19, 1914, DF, 838.00/1075.

the United States' demands on all outstanding questions except that of customs control. At one o'clock that afternoon, pursuant to plan, American soldiers carried a half-million dollars in specie to the *Machias* "without a hitch."[19] The money was deposited in the National City Bank in New York City.

Haitians were shocked and angry when they discovered the action, which left an enduring legacy of bitterness in Haitian-American relations. Some expressed surprise at the collusion and duplicity of the U.S. government because of the liberal rhetorical stance the Wilson administration had adopted regarding Latin American finances. So infuriated was the Haitian public that the French manager of the BNRH felt obliged to go into hiding. Solon Ménos, the Haitian minister in Washington, demanded that Bryan disavow the "arbitrary and offensive intervention" committed by the U.S. Navy and the American legation. The BNRH itself had opposed gold outflows because of the European war, Ménos recalled. Had the institution believed that a dispute with Haiti was imminent, it could have resorted to arbitration. The United States' decision to use a warship rather than a friendly merchant steamer indicated neither amicable nor disinterested intent.[20]

In his New Year's Eve reply to Ménos, Bryan denied that the *Machias* maneuver was anything other than a "protective measure merely, in behalf of American interests which were gravely menaced." Revolutionists controlled Haiti, he claimed. The gold they might demand would be used to finance counterinsurgency. Its removal to a safe place had been necessitated by fears of precipitate action by officials. The navy vessel, Bryan added erroneously, was used only because of the lack of other transport. The BNRH would have been held responsible if the gold in question had been removed by Davilmarists or ordinary looters. Four hundred thousand dollars remained in the vaults in Port-au-Prince, Bryan contended. As revolutionary forces were now massing in the North, the expatriation of the gold only proved the bank officials' wisdom and foresight. The *Machias* incident, the secretary of state argued, did not affront Haitian sovereignty but rather supported it. On the same day, Bryan ordered Blanchard to brook no interference with the BNRH. The United States would not recognize a forced closure.[21]

19. *Ibid.*

20. H. P. Davis, Memorandum, n.d., DF, 838.616/175; Haitian Minister to Secretary of State, December 22, 1914, *FR*, 1914, pp. 371–72, and December 29, 1914, *FR*, 1914, pp. 377–78.

21. Secretary of State to Minister of Haiti, December 31, 1914, *FR*, 1914, pp. 380–81, 382.

The *Machias* incident represented close collaboration between the State Department and foreign banks to extend Dollar Diplomacy to Haiti and to protect the Europeans' customary avenue of financial exploitation. A desire to create an American customs regime in the Black Republic was not limited to these interests, however. The commercial sector, which had long acquiesced to the high risks associated with Haitian trade, also began in 1914 to lobby for a Haitian protectorate.

Lobbying by certain American business interests for decisive action played a role in the customs receivership agitation. Persons affiliated with the American Tobacco Company or personally connected with James Buchanan Duke negotiated with the Haitian government for a tobacco monopoly but made little headway because of the rapid succession of governments. The talks also involved a representative of the British Tobacco Rehandling Company, which appeared to be in partnership with the American firm. The Haitian tobacco business, Smith had reported months earlier, was controlled by independents who managed to withstand the competition of the larger, more efficient companies. The Tobacco Rehandling Company was now taking the lead in setting up small tobacconist shops in several Haitian cities.[22]

James Duke had quit the combine by August, 1914. In his place, new capital, believed to represent the Guarantee Trust Company of New York, emerged. The group wanted a monopoly of the import and export of tobacco, the right to bring in Cuban workers, and 75 percent of all profits from sales of Haitian tobacco.[23] The tobacco combine failed to make progress in its talks with the government in 1914 but continued to engross the trade, perhaps intending to present the Haitians with a *fait accompli*. When it projected a plan to monopolize the match and soap trades as well, however, it ran afoul of other long-established firms that had enjoyed this business. Fairbank and Babbitt Soap, Proctor and Gamble Distributing Company, and Armour and Company addressed letters of protest to the State Department about this matter early in 1915.[24]

Washington flatly opposed commercial monopolization in Haiti. Blanchard laid American objections before the new administration of

22. Dunkerson and Co. to Claude A. Thompson, April 28, 1914, DF, 838.61331/T55.

23. Ross Hazeltine to Secretary of State, August 5, 1914, DF, 838.61331/T55/4.

24. Luckett-Wake Tobacco Co. to Secretary of State, March 1, 1915, DF, 838.61331/T55/9; N. K. Fairbank to Secretary of State, March 30, 1915, DF, 838.61331/T55/16; Babbitt Soap Co. to Secretary of State, January 1, 1915, DF, 838.61331/T55/17; Armour and Co. to Secretary of State, March 31, 1915; Proctor and Gamble Distributing Co. to Bryan, April 8, 1915, DF, 838.61331/T55/22.

Vilbrun Guillaume Sam. Representatives of five independent American tobacco companies meanwhile called on the U.S. secretary of state to protest the danger that the tobacco combine represented to them. The United States could do little directly to prevent the engrossment of the Haitian tobacco trade by the larger firms. Since Haiti had abrogated the Haitian-American reciprocity treaty of 1864 during Nord Alexis's presidency, no legal agreement existed between the two countries that could bind Haiti to commercial behavior approved by the U.S. government.[25]

In mid-April, the Luckett-Wake Tobacco Company advocated American intervention in Haiti in a letter sent to Senator Ollie James, a Kentucky Democrat. This company, based in Louisville, then the chief tobacco trading center in the United States, had operated in Haiti for thirty years and opposed the cartel, which had not been able to surpass it in normal competition. Luckett-Wake saw in the scheme a precedent for the monopolization of all Haitian commerce and proposed joint action by the United States and Britain to establish a stable regime, prevent bankruptcy, and stem revolution. It recommended that recognition of Sam's government be contingent on an Open Door for British and American merchants. Luckett-Wake predicted that intervention would inevitably come. "It is a duty we cannot escape."[26]

The State Department took the correspondence on the tobacco combine seriously but failed to repudiate the arrangement.[27] The chief promoter of a Haitian cartel, E. S. Edwards, defended his enterprise by citing Haiti's hunger and unemployment, which, he claimed, underlay its frequent revolutions. Haitians lacked entrepreneurial experience and could not stabilize their economy without help. As members of "the African race," they would abandon revolution once they were fully employed. Edwards went on to outline a Haitian project that would encompass not only tobacco but soap, matches, sugar, and banking.[28]

Edwards' optimism was lost on the Division of Latin American Affairs, which, unlike certain other State Department offices, remained hostile to the plan. One observer took a dim view of the offers, informing the State

25. Office of the Solicitor to Office of the Trade Advisor, April 6, 1915, DF, 838.61331/T55/21.
26. Luckett-Wake Tobacco Co. to Senator Ollie James, April 16, 1915, DF, 838.61331/T55/26.
27. Robert Bacon to John T. Coughlin, May 15, 1915, DF, 838.61331/T55; Dunkerson and Co. to A. Bruce Bielaski, May 8, 1914, DF, 838.61331/T55/1.
28. E. S. Edwards to Secretary of State, May 18, 1915, DF, 838.61331/T55/29, and June 17, 1915, DF, 838.61331/T55/32.

Department that Haitians considered such concessionaires "bluffers." Certainly a monopoly on simple, common items of peasant consumption would not benefit the country. Josephus Daniels, secretary of the navy, later recalled that "the State Department was deaf to the entreaties" of American businessmen who early favored intervention.[29] Daniels' account was not wholly accurate, because the State Department did listen to these petitions. The Haitian political atmosphere nevertheless provided a far greater incentive for policy makers to make a decision than did concern for particular companies' interests.

As pressure from business mounted, the National City Bank and other shareholders in the National Railroad Company pressed harder for customs control. In January, 1915, the Haiti Company, managed by W. R. Grace and Company, informed subscribers that as the American government appeared ready to act, a reorganization of the firm's Haitian operations seemed in order and should be implemented before any intervention took place. It proposed to settle with McDonald, but in such a manner that he would not be in control.[30]

Farnham suggested to the State Department that an American holding company take over the BNRH. Supporting the rights of an American firm under those circumstances, however, meant that intervention in Haiti might necessarily involve cooperation with the French. Nor was the State Department willing to guarantee the interests of any corporation in advance. It preferred to keep its options open.[31] Officials in Washington nevertheless responded to certain pressures. These stemmed from business elements that wanted formal intervention; a sector of the Haitian bourgeoisie that believed the United States could mediate Haiti's troubled politics; the French and Germans, who were anxious to remain reasonably at par with one another and to be represented in any decision the United States might make; and President Wilson, who wanted to neutralize conflict in a nation whose problems he perceived as subverting hemsipheric security.

The world war lent urgency to businessmen's anxieties and compounded the economic and political problems the Haitians faced in 1914. The shortage of commercial shipping caused difficulties in marketing coffee

29. Charles C. Cowan to State Department, July 9, 1915, DF, 838.00/1208; Josephus Daniels, "The Problem of Haiti," *Saturday Evening Post,* July 12, 1930, p. 32.

30. Haiti Co., Memorandum, in Frank A. Vanderlip Papers, Columbia University.

31. State Department Counselor's Office, Memorandum on Paul Fuller's report, n.d., DF, 838.00/1197.

that left Haiti with little revenue and purchasing power. The large numbers of unpaid and disgruntled soldiers thronging the streets of Port-au-
Prince during the Théodore presidency were augmented by beggars and
other destitute people, who congregated in public places. By late 1914 the
quiescent attitude earlier observed by the American reporter for *Outlook*
had vanished. Continuous warfare took its toll on the people. "The situation here and in the surrounding country is really dangerous," Lemuel
Livingston reported from Cape Haitian. "The hatred and vengeance engendered by the recent revolutions . . . may lead to desperate acts here-
tofore unknown in Haiti."[32]

For the bourgeoisie, world war meant fewer pleasures. Fine clothing
now had to be made in Haiti. No entertainers arrived from France, so
theatergoers relied on local troupes and films. To make matters worse, the
archbishop of Port-au-Prince banned the tango. Many Frenchmen left for
the front, and certain Francophiles, feeling for France the ardor they could
not muster for Haiti, departed with them. The summer of 1915 brought
intestinal fever to the capital. An epidemic of chicken pox, a dangerous
ailment in a debilitated population, followed quickly.[33]

As expected, the *cacos* stepped up their northern campaign early in
1915. Their ranks included those who had broken with Théodore as well
as Zamorists who had never acknowledged the defeat of their candidate. A
tightly knit northern coalition sought the downfall of the incumbent. At
its head was Vilbrun Guillaume Sam, a son of former president Tirésias
Simon Sam who had served as minister of war and the navy in his father's
cabinet. The younger Sam received financial support from his father and
was also aided by a German-Haitian group in St. Marc.[34]

The constant insurgency in Haiti distressed Woodrow Wilson. "The
more I think about the situation the more I am convinced that it is our
duty to take immediate action there such as we took in San Domingo," he
wrote Bryan. "The United States cannot consent to stand by and permit
revolutionary conditions constantly to exist there."[35] Ignorant of
Wilson's predisposition and heedless of how rapidly changes in the world

32. Livingston to Secretary of State, December 19, 1914, DF, 838.00/1072.

33. Georges Corvington, *Port-au-Prince au Cours des Ans, La Métropole Haïtienne du XIXᵉ Siècle* (5 vols.; Port-au-Prince, 1976), IV, 288, 299–300, 310.

34. Livingston to Secretary of State, January 27, 1915, *FR*, 1915, pp. 462–63; William F. Powell to William Day, August 1, 1898, CD; Jacques C. Antoine, *Jean Price-Mars and Haiti* (Washington, D.C., 1981), 9, 29.

35. Woodrow Wilson to Bryan, January 13, 1915, DF, 838.00/1378.

balance of power were occurring, Vilbrun Sam's coalition of forces made rapid progress in its sweep of the North.

Prompted by a request from the consular corps in Cape Haitian, the U.S. Navy served as a guardian of foreigners' lives and property during Sam's insurgency. The flagship USS *Washington* sailed to the Cape on January 19, 1915. Rear Admiral William B. Caperton met with Livingston, who advised him to exact from Sam a promise to refrain from looting and burning on his way to the capital. Caperton, accompanied by his chief of staff and Livingston, then visited revolutionary headquarters, where Sam, clad in footman's livery, received them at the door. Once the company had settled in a reception room, Sam returned, this time differently dressed, and identified himself. The ploy had allowed him to size up Caperton before the interview began.[36]

Sam promised to accede to Caperton's wishes that pillaging and arson be avoided. The admiral then returned to Port-au-Prince, where Blanchard needed him to back up warnings to Théodore to refrain from raids on the BNRH vaults. Yet as Sam moved south his army found itself continually confronted by American vessels. At Gonaïves, it was the *Wheeling*, whose commander reminded Sam of his pledges to Caperton. At St. Marc, the *Des Moines* awaited the *cacos'* entry. When the insurgents finally arrived there, having first tried to avoid the Americans by advancing to Arcahaie instead, they found both the *Des Moines* and the *Wheeling* present in anticipation of a major confrontation between the two Haitian armies. As the three thousand rebels poured into St. Marc, Théodore's forces began a wild, panicky retreat. The American commanders, observing this, again extracted promises from Sam that there would be no looting or violence. St. Marc fell on February 18, and Théodore's chief counselor General Horelle Monplaisir, died there. The following day, the rebels advanced to within three miles of Port-au-Prince and laid siege to the city, cutting off its water and food supplies. Théodore resigned, a victim of the destabilization policies of the great powers, as Sam, in anticipation of his election, assumed "executive power."[37]

In Washington, the Wilson administration sought to assess Sam's strength, negotiate an understanding about customs control, and learn if the new Haitian president was amenable to a more intimate relationship

---

36. David F. Healy, *Gunboat Diplomacy in the Wilson Era: The U. S. Navy in Haiti, 1915–1916* (Madison, Wis., 1976), 22–23.

37. Blanchard to Secretary of State, February 25, 1915 (*FR*, 1915, p. 466), January 26, 1915 (*FR*, 1915, p. 462), February 19, 1915 (*FR*, 1915, p. 464).

with the United States. Accordingly, Secretary of State Bryan sent a commission, headed by John Franklin Fort, a former governor of New Jersey, and Charles Cogwell Smith, a New Hampshire lawyer, to treat with Haitian officialdom. Fort and Smith had enjoyed some success in a similar mission to the Dominican Republic. Bryan instructed Blanchard to act as the third member of the commission.[38]

Fort and Smith disembarked in Port-au-Prince on May 5, just in time for Sam's inauguration. Bryan had made recognition of the Sam government contingent on a satisfactory report from Fort and Smith. Ulrich Duvivier, the foreign minister, questioned the commissioners' credentials, however, and Sam refused to speak officially until formal recognition had been extended. Fort and Smith meanwhile found Port-au-Prince so unpleasant that they lived on board a ship in the harbor. The commission returned to Washington after ten fruitless days in Haiti.[39]

Once in control, Sam quickly consolidated his power. He appointed a fairly prestigious cabinet and took the additional precaution of jailing as many powerful Zamorists and Davilmarists as possible. He sought and obtained recognition from France, Germany, and Italy. Sam survived financially by taking the treasury service from the BNRH and making the commercial firm of Simmonds Frères a collection agent.[40]

Despite Sam's efforts, some Zamorists managed to escape. He detained Oreste Zamor but Charles Zamor found asylum in the French legation. Rosalvo Bobo, a Capois physician and Théodore's minister of the interior, fled to the Dominican Republic and, with the help of Desiderio Arias, the Dominican minister of war, began to mount yet another insurgency.[41]

The State Department viewed Bobo as undesirable, largely on the word of Livingston, who described him as a medical charlatan and a demagogue. This negative evaluation owed something to Bobo's cold and implacable anti-imperialism and his self-identification with the Firminist movement.[42] American antagonism to Bobo may have helped his chances.

38. Bryan to Blanchard, February 20, 1915, FR, 1915, p. 464.

39. John F. Fort to Wilson, July 30, 1915, DF, 838.00/1276.5; Blanchard to Bryan, March 9, 1915, and Fort to Bryan, March 12, 1915, FR, 1915, p. 468; Healy, *Gunboat Diplomacy*, 40–41; Dantès Bellegarde, *Histoire du Peuple Haïtien (1492–1952)* (Port-au-Prince, 1953), 249.

40. Blanchard to Secretary of State, March 25, 1915, FR, 1915, p. 469; Caperton, Statement, in SI, 299, 323; Bellegarde, *Histoire du Peuple Haïtien*, 246.

41. Minister Sullivan to Secretary of State, March 28, 1915, FR, 1915, pp. 469–70.

42. Livingston to Secretary of State, May 21, 1915, DF, 838.00/1183; Gaillard, *Rosalvo Bobo*, 18–19n, 23, 72, 76.

Haitians recalled that as Sam progressed to Port-au-Prince he seemed to be accompanied by the U.S. Navy. The commanders had emphasized their admonitory purpose but had then escorted the rebels to St. Marc and merely stood by while they trounced the Haitian army. Some saw the Americans opposing Théodore and supporting Sam, despite their talk about political order and due process. Only the United States' failure to recognize the new regime would neutralize such a suspicion. Under the circumstances, Bobo could easily portray himself as uncompromisingly patriotic and above the temptation to rise to power on the shoulders of a foreign government.[43]

The United States prevailed on the Dominicans to flush Bobo from his stronghold at Monte Cristi, but by April 25 he had secured the loyalty of certain Haitian army units stationed in the North. These marched to Cape Haitian, where, with other Bobo supporters, they looted the customhouse. Loyal troops sent to quell the mutiny confronted the rebels near the Cape on May 14, 1915. Government forces suffered heavy casualties and retreated, leaving arms and ammunition. The battle for Cape Haitian raged through June.[44]

The cycles of revolutionary warfare had altered northern life. Livingston described the grim new atmosphere, so unlike the holiday ambiance of past revolutions. No matter how stylized these successive seizures of power had been in the past, the social costs they were now incurring had become unacceptably high. Fires, bombardments, looting, assassinations—all prevented Haiti from building on its modest material base. Livingston reported that rebel discipline, strict at first, had broken down. In mid-June, insurgents publicly displayed the heads of two condemned prisoners. "Dr. Bobo and his civil followers are posing as a 'progressist' party," Livingston remarked "but this is the first time that such savagery has been committed at Cape Haitian during the seventeen years of my residence here."[45]

The business community was hostile to the Boboists and refused to lend them money. It could expect reprisals. As the rebels gathered strength, government officials took refuge in the French consulate. France, with the greatest economic stake of any foreign power in Cape Haitian, had not sent a cruiser there, because of wartime exigency. In

43. Sullivan to Secretary of State, June 16, 1915, DF, 838.00/1200; C. C. Willard to Joseph Shea, June 26, 1915, DF, 838.77/119.

44. Livingston to Secretary of State, June 16, 1915, DF, 838.00/1200; Willard to Shea, June 26, 1915, DF, 838.77/119.

45. Livingston to Secretary of State, June 16, 1915, DF, 838.00/1200.

February, 1915, Jusserand proposed that France and the United States collaborate on the financial reorganization of Haiti. Lansing, however, believed that the suggestion undermined the Monroe Doctrine. He told Jusserand that the Germans had already made such a request. The French did not press the matter, and Bryan assured them that the United States would impartially oversee the interests of all foreign nationals in the Black Republic.[46]

Impelled by the possibility that Bobo might be successful, the State Department decided to recognize the Sam government and offer it military support. Sam was approached through Paul Fuller, a special agent who arrived in the spring of 1915, charged with tackling the problem of ongoing revolution before large European navies became available to deal with the Haitian question in their own way. Sam sorely needed military assistance but refused to accept it without control over the deployment of American troops. He could hardly sanction the entry of an army of occupation. Washington would not give a Haitian executive power over its armed forces, of course, so Fuller's mission, like that of the other special agents, came to naught.[47]

Once back in Washington, Fuller denied that Haiti's intransigence stemmed from ignorance of American sentiments. Fuller believed the situation "intolerable" even to Haitians and cited an "almost universal desire" for American help. He had not been instructed to demand customs control or ask that the republic's sovereignty be in any way formally infringed, but he found Haitians nervous on the subject of fiscal autonomy and territorial integrity. "No Haitian politician wanted to be on record as selling their country to the Americans," but only a full-scale occupation could alter local conditions.[48]

By the middle of June, 1915, Sam had regained control of Cape Haitian. Leading rebels sought refuge in the French consulate, and the Haitian government threatened to storm it and remove them. The French consul, a newcomer to Haitian revolutions, asked Girard, the French minister, to send for a warship. On June 18, sailors of the cruiser *Des-*

46. Secretary of State to Wilson, February 25, 1915, in U.S. Department of State, *The Lansing Papers, 1914–1920* (Washington, D.C., 1939), 465–66.
47. According to Alvey Adee, a formal letter of recognition was prepared but not sent. Adee to Paul Fuller, December 29, 1915, DF, 838.00/G94/1. There is, however, a copy of the letter in the Kurt Fisher Collection, Schomburg Research Center, NYPL. Link, *The Struggle for Neutrality*, 531–32. Fuller to Secretary of State, June 14, DF, 838.00/1197; Antoine, *Jean Price-Mars and Haiti*, 88.
48. Fuller to Secretary of State, June 14, 1915, DF, 838.00/1197.

cartes landed at the Cape to guard the local branch of the BNRH, the French consulate, and Catholic Church properties.[49]

In response, the USS *Washington* returned to Cape Haitian to "relieve" the French. On the evening of July 1, the captain of the *Descartes* called on Caperton aboard the *Washington*. The French commander reiterated his country's acceptance of American supremacy in Haiti and disavowed any intent of challenging it. Haitian protests, the presence of the Germans, with whom France was at war, and the obvious concern of the United States had made action necessary, the Frenchman said. He acceded to Caperton's view that the *Descartes'* presence compromised Haitian neutrality, but he could not sail without orders from his own government. These were unlikely to come unless the French Foreign Office was convinced that French interests were secure.[50]

Security for French interests could be assured if both sides in the civil war agreed to keep out of Cape Haitian. Requests for such guarantees were forwarded to General Probus Blot of the government forces and to Bobo's headquarters in Petite-Anse. The restriction created difficulties for the rebels, whose resources were limited. Bobo's following had expected to make use of goods commandeered in Cape Haitian. As of mid-July the rebels had failed to hold any principal town, though battles and skirmishes continued in the northern plains.[51]

Just when it seemed that the government was gradually quelling the insurrection, trouble erupted in the capital. Sam was using two hundred Zamorist and Davilmarist hostages, in jail in Port-au-Prince, as insurance against revolution. Hundreds of other dissidents were in legations and consulates. A small group of rebel commandos, who, unbeknownst to the absent consul, were using the Portuguese consulate as a base of operations, attacked the National Palace in the early hours of July 27. President Sam and his family ran next door to the French legation. Employing a courier, Sam ordered the commandant of the jail where the political prisoners were housed to do what that official thought proper with regard to the inmates.[52]

49. Livingston to Secretary of State, June 19, 1915, *FR*, 1915, p. 472; Robert B. Davis to Secretary of State, June 23, 1915, *FR*, 1915, p. 473; Girard to Minister of Foreign Relations, June 16, 1915, QDO, Vol. 6.

50. Caperton to Secretary of the Navy, July 3, 1915, *FR*, 1915, p. 474; Healy, *Gunboat Diplomacy*, 43–44.

51. Gaillard, *Rosalvo Bobo*, 76–77; Healy, *Gunboat Diplomacy*, 47–48, 52.

52. Robert B. Davis to Secretary of State, telegrams, 9 A.M. and noon, July 27, 1915, *FR*, 1915, p. 474; Gaillard, *Rosalvo Bobo*, 83–87.

What followed has often been retold by eyewitnesses and historians. The jailer had the prisoners, including former president Oreste Zamor, brutally executed. After the massacre, 167 persons, representing some of the most influential Haitian families, lay dead. When the victorious insurgents went to liberate the prison, they discovered the mangled corpses. The commandant had fled to the Dominican consulate.[53]

A tragedy of retribution followed the massacre. General Polynice, whose three sons had perished in the prison, shot and killed the commandant inside the Dominican consulate while restless crowds circled the French legation, where Sam was hiding. The American chargé d'affaires, Robert Beale Davis, cabled for naval support and rushed to assist the beleaguered Girard and his family. The British Minister joined them. Tensions appeared to have lessened by midmorning, so the diplomats dispersed. Convinced that the danger had abated, the French minister opened the big louvered doors of the tropical villa to air it. Suddenly men leaped over the locked wrought-iron front gate and entered the house. A crowd of nearly eighty found Sam hiding in a bathroom and dragged him out. In the presence of his family, the president was clubbed and stabbed to death by members of the Port-au-Prince gentry. They then delivered Sam to the mob outside the gate. The crowd dismembered him, carrying away pieces of his body. Aboard the USS *Washington*, now in sight of the harbor, Admiral Caperton dimly saw an object being dragged along the ground.[54]

Davis and the united diplomatic corps asked Caperton to land troops immediately. Angry and hysterical people filled the streets. No legation was safe: two had already been violated. Sam's death had been a massive convulsion of the Haitian body politic and a reaction against more than a half-century of decay. All classes participated in the murder, and all classes struck out against the rottenness of the old order. Now that this visible, and mortal, symbol of the past had been destroyed, would new and better institutions arise?

Haitian political life had degenerated quickly between 1910 and 1915. The expatriation of resources and capital by the foreign and foreign-oriented enclaves intensified this deterioration. Exploitation had been proceeding for some time, but now crises followed one another in ever more rapid

---

53. Gaillard, *Rosalvo Bobo*, 87–89; Robert B. Davis to Secretary of State, telegram, 6 P.M., July 27, 1915, *FR*, 1915, pp. 474–75.
54. Caperton, Statement, in SI, 306.

succession. These were crises dictated by the structure of Haitian politics, but the structure was rapidly becoming dysfunctional as recurrent warfare sapped the nation's vital energies. By 1914, more astute members of the upper classes had begun to realize that they were killing their golden goose. An era of diminishing returns could be dimly perceived on the horizon. Advocacy by Haitians and foreigners alike of customs receiverships and protectorates reflected the belief that only direct control could assure the perpetuation of the exploitative system. Such agencies as the BNRH and the U.S. State Department thus became increasingly strident in their attempts to destabilize Haitian regimes.

Capitulation in the form of a customs regime, territorial concessions, or other visible manifestations of submission meant surrender on the part of the leadership. Elite elements, who served as a bridge between the impoverished majority and the great powers, were locked into an impossible situation. If they abdicated responsibility or defied metropolitan demands, they forfeited their broker's role. They had failed in the delicate balancing act required of them.

Other contradictions were posed by revolutionary succession and the *caco* system. These traditions illustrated the intense conflict in Haitian society and its inability to equitably distribute the country's modest resources. After Leconte's death, the urban, metropolitan-oriented leaders elected Auguste in an effort to appease the landed proprietors. Auguste and his successor, Michel Oreste, could not preserve Leconte's consensus. The chieftains of the North, whose wealth rested on peasant soldiers and laborers, soon resumed their bids for power. They had as a resource the mass base that the legislators, professionals, and intellectuals of Port-au-Prince lacked, but they too ultimately relied on foreign support.

Despite northern warlords' ability to make good use of populism, personalism, and *compèrage*, they shared with cosmopolitan groups the perception of the laborers and peasants as a faceless, exploitable instrument. Throughout Haitian history, few objected to the perpetuation of the status quo for the majority. Cosmopolites deplored the inflated gourde of the Leconte-Auguste-Oreste era, though it was not likely that the French market for Haitian coffee would be lost as a result. Fluctuations in quality, price, and supply did not deter French buyers until 1914, when shipping became unavailable. Those who found the inflated gourde most irksome included those whose salaries were paid in hard currencies: expatriates, politicians and other members of the urban bourgeoisie.

The European powers took their cue from local elites even as they helped shape the outlook of those groups. The least concerned metropole,

Britain, began to move away from its close identification with U.S. policies after 1912 but continued to believe that Haiti would eventually be drawn into the American orbit. As the Panama Canal neared completion British efforts in the Caribbean centered on asserting the right to equal shipping privileges in the isthmus. The Panama Canal Act of 1912 led the British to temporarily adopt a more vigorous stance in the region. The elevation of the British consulate in Port-au-Prince to a legation in 1912 indicated Britain's desire to strengthen its influence in the independent republics.[55]

The Foreign Office's renewed interest in Haiti developed slowly and did not mature until after the onset of the United States' protectorate over the island country, which circumscribed the limits of British commercial expansion. Britain failed to identify its interests soon enough in the game. As late as 1910, the Foreign Office did not know which Britons held Haitian bonds and had to acquire this information from the American legation in Port-au-Prince.[56]

The eve of the Great War found Britain trying to back out of the corner into which it had painted itself by its past acquiescence to American objectives in the Caribbean. The outbreak of war forced the Foreign Office to delay pursuing a more independent Caribbean policy. When the Wilson administration agreed to equalize British shipping rights in the isthmus, Britain resumed for the moment its customary passivity in the region.[57]

While insurgents accelerated their attacks on Théodore, World War I increased France's and Germany's concern with Haiti's status. When the news that the United States wanted a customs convention with Haiti reached the European ministries, both France and Germany indicated their desire to be included. The Americans, however, shied away from multilateralism. Removing Haiti as a pawn in the power struggle in Europe coincided with Wilson's neutrality program and with the administration's commitment to American supremacy in the hemisphere. When the German ambassador sent a note on this subject, Bryan indi-

55. Warren G. Kneer, *Great Britain and the Caribbean, 1901–1913: A Study in Anglo-American Relations* (East Lansing, 1975), 178; James Pyke, Annual Report on the Republic of Hayti, 1913, FO 371, Vol. 2000.

56. A. P. Murray to Secretary of State for Foreign Affairs, October 7, 1910, FO 371, Vol. 915.

57. On Anglo-American conflict in Haiti, 1917–1921, see FO 368, Vol. 1755, *passim*; Director of H.M.'s Petroleum Dept. to Ernest Weakley, October 19, 1921, and enclosed report, FO 371, Vol. 5577.

cated that the United States opposed all situations in which a European power could rise to preeminence in the Americas. He maintained that any arrangement that Washington made with the Haitians would be in everyone's interest and implied that the question of a customs convention still depended on the Haitians' will.[58]

The early twentieth century marked France's retreat from Haiti. Some French officials continued to stubbornly oppose any protectorate by a great power over the republic. The French minister of foreign relations suggested in 1913 that his government ban arms sales to Haiti, as the civil wars for which they were used would simply precipitate American intervention and thus further lessen French influence. The French legation in Port-au-Prince, however, argued that arms sales contributed to the stability the Haitians needed to resist such an occurrence. Some diplomats arrived at the conclusion that American control would mean little. "Haiti is a French corner of the world after all, and we must make all effort to see that it remains so," wrote Carteron from Port-au-Prince in 1908. "The Bank has all that is necessary to assure us this result."[59]

After 1910 the French believed that they could rely on the United States to ensure that Haiti met its obligations. War at home forced the French to marshal their military resources and abandon most of their Caribbean concerns. As long as France enjoyed the same privileges in Haiti as did any other power, it was willing to acquiesce to American control. Although it had to contend with the bad impression that its seeming capitulation made at home, France's endorsement of the Open Door in Haiti gave the State Department the green light it wanted there. The French acceptance of U.S. exclusionism was not dictated by wartime exigency alone. The disengagement from Haiti had been a gradual process, and the American preemption, accompanied by guarantees, gave the French the opportunity to make a graceful, and not wholly undesired, exit.[60]

58. Bryan to Count Bernstorff, September 16, 1914, in Arthur S. Link (ed.) *The Papers of Woodrow Wilson* (55 vols.; Princeton, 1978), III, 34–36.

59. Minister of Colonies to Minister of Foreign Affairs, August 11, 1914, QDO, Vol. 15; Minister of Foreign Affairs to Minister in Haiti, April 17, 1914, and D'Arlot de Saint-Saud to Ministry, April 25, 1914, QDO, Vol. 9; Pierre Carteron to Conty, April 29, 1908, QDO, Vol. 13.

60. Girard to Théophile Delcassé, April 17, 1915, and Minister of Foreign Affairs to Chargé d'affaires in Washington, July 29, 1914, QDO, Vol. 11; Minister of Foreign Affairs to J. Jusserand, June 16, 1915, QDO, Vol. 28; Bryan to Wilson, February 15, 1915, in U.S. Department of State, *Lansing Papers*, 465–66.

The French did, however, demand equity and a share in reorganizing Haitian finances. They also required special protection for the BNRH. Shortly after the U.S. Marines disembarked at Port-au-Prince, the secretary of the French embassy in Washington called on officials at the Division of Latin American Affairs. Professing to speak for his embassy, the official urged intervention. Making reference to the BNRH's importance to France, he encouraged American policy makers to proceed forthrightly in assuming control over Haitian affairs. [61]

The French embassy's action cannot be separated from a growing wartime anxiety, which exacerbated Allied hostility toward German residents in Haiti and led France to accept the view of the still neutral United States that Haiti's multilateralism was dangerous. The Germans indeed possessed considerable leverage in Haiti, but their critics enlarged their actual numbers and the scope of their power. German influence had never depended solely on official encouragement. Subjects of the Hanseatic cities had lived and traded in the Black Republic before the rise of Bismarck. Merchants from Hamburg and other commercial centers did not rely entirely on imperial power to make a place for them in Haiti. They diffused opposition to their position by "Haitianizing" their assets. When Americans grew alarmed at their financial prosperity, the German merchant-bankers began "Americanizing" themselves. Naturalized Americans, accorded dual citizenship by Germany, they established links to prominent New York financiers, finding shelter under the very flag that opposed them. Their experience parallels that of the import-export merchants and dramatically underscores the Haitian problem of ambiguous nationality. [62]

Once in place through its own efforts, the German colony found support from the Reich. Sometimes this was overzealous, and the gunboat diplomacy and terse notes to Haitian ministers from German officials often poisoned relations. Haitian fear of German aggression made it easier for German merchants to do business in the Black Republic, but these traders' interests were not always identical to those of the German state. The 1910 plan for a Franco-German national bank, for example, would have deprived the resident financiers of their traditional role had it been fully achieved. Only its failure ensured that Haitian finances would

---

61. Minister of Foreign Affairs to Chargé d'affaires in Washington, July 29, 1914, QDO, Vol. 14; Jusserand to Bryan, October 27, 1915, *FR*, 1916, p. 514; U.S. Department of State, Division of Latin American Affairs, Memorandum, July 29, 1915, DF, 838.00/1352.

62. E. Jore to Minister of Foreign Affairs, October 12 and November 12, 1909, QDO, Vol. 22.

be administered in the usual way, with predictable results. Tied as they were to the commerce of such mercantile cities as Hamburg, German traders lacked contact with German industry, which was already restlessly seeking to surmount mercantilist restraints. When the mercantile sector of the German economy collapsed during the interwar years, the German colony in Haiti, weakened by determined American opposition and unable to come to terms with Nazism, faltered. The new Germany of the fascist movement and the industrial tycoons was not its world. Those Germans who weathered both fascism and the American occupation could continue in Haiti only if identified as pro-American or as partners in U.S. firms.[63]

The Germans lost more ground when the military demand for ships compelled the Hamburg America Line to suspend its West Indian and Central American operations. The shortage accompanied a growing Francophile sentiment in Haiti. Late in 1914 the German legation ordered its consuls to expel fugitives who had sought asylum because of the prevailing hostility. The German consul in Cape Haitian disobeyed the order because he knew what the refugees could expect "of the tender mercies of the authorities here," Farnham told Bryan, "but he succeeded in scaring a little German sympathy into them for the time being."[64] Resort to such a stratagem was a sign of weakness and attested to Germany's relative unpopularity, a fact that facilitated the subsequent high-handed treatment accorded local Germans by the U.S. Marines.

The Reich greeted the American takeover with alarm. The kaiser had never acquiesced to Yankee pretensions in the Caribbean.[65] Within seven weeks of the marines' landing, it had become clear to the Germans that their interests did not rank very high on Washington's agenda. American plans for the disposition of Haitian customs receipts contained no reference to reimbursing Port-au-Prince's various German creditors. Germany did not seek a direct confrontation on this issue, but it did make

63. Edmund Schaumann, "The Bugbear of German Competition," *American Exporter,* LXXII (February, 1913), 5–7; Schaumann, "German Revolt Against Export Middlemen," *American Exporter,* LXIII (March, 1913), 95–97; Furniss to Secretary of State, August 12, 1911, DF, 838.00/668; Carl Kelsey, Statement, in SI, 1256; Eli Cole, Memorandum, January 24, 1918, File SD 268/11, Bureau of Insular Affairs, Record Group 350, NA; Ferdinand Mayer to Secretary of State, April 5, 1939, DF, 800.20210/263; John Russell, Daily Diary Report, August 21, 1917, DF, 838.6113.

64. New York *Times,* August 12, 1914, Sec. 2, p. 3; Enclosure in Roger Farnham to Bryan, December 28, 1914, DF, 838.00/1128.

65. Holger H. Herwig, *Politics of Frustration: The United States in German Naval Planning, 1889–1941* (Boston, 1976), 67–76.

strong representations to be included in any customs control agreement. The United States deflected the request, as it had done with France's, by promising just consideration for all foreign claims. [66]

The United States had always resisted the presence in the Caribbean of other strong powers, whatever their ideological orientation. In the nineteenth century it had opposed Britain, a supposedly liberal democracy, with the same dogged determination with which it combated Germany, an authoritarian, militarist state, in the early 1900s. Before the American declaration of war in 1917, Germany soft-pedaled its claims to unrestricted access to Latin American markets. The Germans did not want to precipitate American belligerency on the Allied side, but they never abandoned their ambition to eventually enjoy to the fullest the benefits of Western Hemisphere trade and investment. [67]

The Americans saw the gathering storm in Haiti through the lens of a remarkably consistent foreign policy. The United States had historically dominated Haitian commerce and protected its own trade representatives. In 1904 it sent a military attaché to the legation in Port-au-Prince, an extraordinary action in view of Haiti's modest size and power. The U.S. Navy constantly patrolled Haitian waters during the Roosevelt years.

President Taft's Dollar Diplomacy accompanied the National City Bank to Haiti in 1910. Despite Taft's and Knox's belief that financial stability for Latin American governments would lead to peace and civilization in the lands to the south, American participation in the bank contract of 1910 drew little on the rhetoric of progress. The State Department's response to European exclusionism was singularly nationalistic. It made no attempt to demonstrate how Dollar Diplomacy could benefit Haiti, yet it insisted that such a policy be undertaken there.

Wilson's Haitian program did not substantially differ from Taft's, but he characteristically endowed American policy with a moralistic content. Wilson opposed revolutionary insurgency and extraconstitutional politics and demanded that Latin American leaders, including Haitians, demonstrate their political respectability in his terms, thus limiting the choices available to them.

---

66. Robert B. Davis to Secretary of State, September 15, 1915, and Lansing to American Legation in Port-au-Prince, September 15, 1915, DF, 838.00/1308.

67. E. Malcolm Carroll, *Germany and the Great Powers, 1866–1914* (Hamden, Conn., 1966), 474; Holger H. Herwig, *"Luxury Fleet": The Imperial German Navy, 1888–1918* (London, 1980), 100–101.

Wilson also continued Taft's policy regarding overseas banking. Like Taft, he acknowledged the need for reforms that would facilitate the competitive movement of American capital abroad. He also worked out an accommodation with banking interests. Wilson's link with financiers rested on his appreciation of the advantages of new capital and commercial markets. This concern overrode his solicitude for Latin Americans as expressed in the Mobile address of 1913. The anticolonial solidarity Wilson alluded to more properly belonged to relations among equals. By 1913 the United States had pulled far ahead of other states in the Western Hemisphere. Its relationship to them, one of metropole and satellites, was poorly concealed behind a veil of sentimentalism.

One aspect of the Mobile address survived in the policy formulations of Robert Lansing, who later succeeded Bryan as secretary of state. The Lansing Doctrine emphasized the need to prevent European hegemony from developing in troubled Latin American nations as a result of financial control. It dispensed entirely with professions of brotherhood, however, and saw neutralization of European ambitions chiefly as promoting the interests of the United States and its own vision of hemispheric security. It shared Wilson's concern with combating the interloper, but its goals were realist rather than Pan-American. The request for the Môle St. Nicolas and consultation rights, though it preceded the Lansing Doctrine, harmonized with the strategic concerns of the Wilson administration. The bid for the Môle, though feebly pursued, aimed to prevent the possible alienation of territory, control the presidency, and reprove the Haitians. That the State Department made these proposals in 1913 indicates that even before the turmoil of the 1914–1915 period, Washington had begun to assume preemptive rights in Haiti.[68] The dramatic debut of American capital continued a pattern of exploitation begun a century earlier. Like its commercial analogue, American financial penetration was based on the United States' perceived national interest. It did not mark a new departure in the character of Haitian-American relations.

As for the import-export sector, the advent of banking improved its position and ensured its permanence. American traders and manufacturers sought intervention because they believed it would improve business conditions. Their impact on policy makers, however, was not as direct as that exerted by the business community in 1898 regarding the war with

68. Arthur S. Link, *Wilson: The Struggle for Neutrality*, (Princeton, 1960), 534–35, 535*n*138.

Spain. The State Department responded to merchants' and manufacturers' calls primarily because rivalry for concessions added to the turbulence of Haitian politics and retarded the development of nonspeculative businesses. The terms of trade and international relations had exacerbated a deplorable condition. Haitians and foreigners alike called for a complete overhaul of Haitian society. The consensus broke down, however, over the question of who would administer and benefit from needed reforms.

Epilogue

Tête caille cap' trompé soleil, main li pas capab' trompé lapluit.
The roof fools the sun, but it can't fool the rain.

—Haitian proverb

IN 1915 the United States began a military occupation of Haiti that lasted twenty years. Citing widespread violence, anarchy, and imminent danger to foreigners' life and property, the U.S. government ordered marines landed at Port-au-Prince. The Haitian occupation was unprecedented in both its duration and the overt racism that characterized the American presence. Racist violence peaked during the "bandit-suppression" campaigns in the countryside. Peasants rose in arms against the marines in 1918–1919. The Americans responded by launching counterinsurgency strikes against villages and guerrilla encampments. They officially acknowledged the deaths of more than three thousand persons in these conflicts.[1]

The subsequent congressional investigation of the warfare, the suspension of the Haitian constitution and legislature, and the use of forced labor resulted in a reorganized but still firmly repressive administrative structure. By virtue of a treaty that the United States insisted upon, it enjoyed sweeping powers, including control over customs receipts and the national budget. It also imposed on the island republic two successive presidencies, that of Philippe Sudre Dartiguenave and Louis Borno, both generally recognized as American clients with little popular following.

The occupation effectively neutralized northern military opposition but did little to bring the promised prosperity and improved living standard. Some rural people emigrated permanently, going to the Dominican

---

1. Hans Schmidt, *The United States Occupation of Haiti, 1915–1934* (New Brunswick, N.J., 1971); David F. Healy, *Gunboat Diplomacy in the Wilson Era: The U.S. Navy in Haiti, 1915–1916* (Madison, Wis., 1976).

Republic to cut cane or take up residence along the still disputed frontier. The road-building program had consumed a considerable amount of state revenue in a country where few owned cars. Occupation officials and technical "experts" meanwhile drew lavish salaries.[2]

Complaints about these matters were not made only by Haitians. C. C. Woolard, a businessman and the U.S. vice-consul at Cape Haitian, conveyed his disgust with American policy in a newspaper interview. "In eight years of occupation the country has made no progress whatever," he asserted. "What the Americans have done is to create an antagonism of races that did not exist before. The officials of the Occupation in Haiti, sent from Washington, are all politicians with no conception of Americanism." Woolard did not believe that the imported technical specialists had accomplished anything, and as for the marines, many had come to Haiti only "to get a gook."[3]

Woolard's superior, Damon Woods, endorsed his views. Woods served as consul in Cape Haitian for nineteen months. Upon resigning in October, 1923, he let his opinions be known to the State Department. His strongest criticism concerned the incompetence and offensiveness of marine and gendarmerie officers. Woods saw the work of improving Haiti hampered by the attitudes of the American military, whose numbers, he felt, should be reduced as soon as the native gendarmerie established its effectiveness. Woods also pointed to infringement of dissidents' rights and the gross disparity between American and Haitian pay scales. The official agricultural engineer's salary, paid from Haitian state funds, equaled that of 150 rural teachers. Armed forces personnel also drew salaries paid from the Haitian treasury but at American levels.[4]

In economic matters, the occupation followed an intensely restrictive fiscal and monetary policy, as Hans Schmidt has demonstrated.[5] Commercial policies were also characterized by an innate suspicion of innovative ideas. This official rigidity stultified business initiative and led to considerable friction between American authorities and foreign traders. American conflict with Europeans in Haiti was moreover a product of the

2. Winthrop Scott to Secretary of State, December 4, 1924, DF, 838.00/2060.

3. Dantès Bellegarde, *L'Occupation américaine d'Haïti: ses conséquences morales et économiques* (Port-au-Prince, 1929), 24n2; John Russell to Secretary of State, August 13, 1923, DF, 838.00/1963; C. C. Woolard to Secretary of State, September 26, 1923, DF, 838.00/1968.

4. Damon C. Woods, "Some Observations and Suggestions Relative to the Work of the American Occupation in Haiti," October 31, 1923, DF, 838.00/1985.

5. Schmidt, *The U.S. Occupation of Haiti*, 108–34.

United States' jealously preserved imperialist prerogatives in the Caribbean, a concern often cloaked with moralism. During this epoch, American moralism was embodied in a set of political and social ideas espoused by the middle class and loosely referred to as Progressivism. Deeply concerned with reform, rationality in government, and the missionary role that the United States was to play abroad, Progressives readily embraced the Haitian occupation as a field for the realization of cherished ideals.

Just before the Wall Street crash, an Indiana sociologist worked out a rationale for the occupation of Haiti that treated intervention as a pragmatic response to that nation's problems: "Before the people can be really free there must be an elaborate process of building; there must be constructed the material equipment through which society may function, and there must be developed the intelligence and the civic spirit which are absolutely essential in a democracy. The impossibilists argue that it is better that a nation be allowed to work out these results for itself, even at the expense of waste, muddling and violence. The pragmatists insist that intelligent guidance from without may sometimes accelerate the process of national growth and save much of the waste."[6]

Despite this paternal zeal, widely shared during the 1920s, the United States failed to fit the Black Republic into a ready-made framework built from the reform ideas of the period and wasted phenomenal sums of money in attempts to do so. By the end of the decade, policy makers were less certain that developing countries could absorb much "intelligent guidance," and they clearly lacked the resources to provide it. Before disillusionment set in, however, the positivist thought of the epoch, filtered through the ideology of Progressivism, helped create a moral rationale for foreign domination of Haiti. On a highly stratified society American authorities overlaid an elitist technocracy that ignored the traditions of the country and thus ensured its own failure. The occupation regime was much more effective militarily. The United States Marines and their creation, the Gendarmerie d'Haïti, permanently destroyed the old *caco* insurgency pattern.

American policy makers placed peculiar limitations on real change in Haiti. Streets were cleaned, roads were paved (especially those leading to areas of guerilla insurgency), customhouses were protected from fraud and embezzlement, and obligations to selected creditors were paid on

---

6. Ulysses B. Weatherly, "Haiti: An Experiment in Pragmatism," *American Journal of Sociology*, XXXII (1926), 363.

time. These improvements had little impact on the underlying societal structure. The sterile moralism of the treaty regime differentiated it from the formal colonialism of Europe but also prevented officials from asserting vigorous policies that would change the economic and social structure to the benefit of the majority of Haitians. The occupation remained literally a holding action. Like all bureaucracies, it generated its own momentum and exercised a repressive control over free political expression.

The authoritarian state, well advanced under Nord Alexis's aegis, continued to guarantee a system of privileges for the wealthy. During the course of the twentieth century, many such persons remained unscathed despite the supposedly random terror visited on society by one or another apoplectically enraged governor. Only through the perpetuation of privilege could such a large number of people be kept so destitute. Survival necessitated the collusion and collaboration of the poor with the patronage-distributing and law enforcement agencies of government, a process expertly documented for the contemporary period by Michel S. Laguerre.[7] The *cacos* were the early twentieth-century counterpart. Prompted by need as well as by adherence to traditional personalist values, ordinary Haitians were foot soldiers for those who regarded them as ultimately expendable.

The conquest of Haitian caudillismo by the U.S. Marines is not therefore synonymous with the defeat of the Haitian peasant as a potential insurgent. Rural unrest had been skillfully channeled into mercenary pursuits by the proprietor class. The occupation broke the back of this personalist peasant mercenarism, which resulted in tragic loss of life as rural people took up arms in unsuccessful attempts to repel the invaders. The generals nevertheless remained powers in their areas, and, just as such presidents as Michel Oreste and Davilmar Théodore had provided emoluments for threatening rivals, the occupation government bought off the troublemakers of 1915.[8] Forced to accept a transformed pattern of power distribution, the former militarists shifted their focus but not their intentions.

The limitations of real change can also be observed with respect to race, class, and color. Most scholars agree that the occupation neither tran-

7. Michel S. Laguerre, *Urban Life in the Caribbean* (Cambridge, Mass., 1982).

8. Winthrop Scott, "Political and Economic Conditions in Northern Haiti During Feb. and Mar. 1924," April 1, 1924, DF, 838.00/2019; Russell to Secretary of State, January 12, 1925, DF, 838.00/2067.

scended American race prejudice nor altered the Haitian class structure. No Haitian middle class was promoted, nor was the existing bourgeoisie wooed with guarantees. Americans widely criticized the failings of this class of Haitians, but similar faults had not deterred American cooperation with bourgeoisies in other Latin countries. Why was Haiti the exception?

Hostility to mulattoes played a part in maintaining the distance. The belief that mulattoes subverted the established order in a rigidly bipolar world of race underlay antagonism toward them. White Americans, whose own cultural grounding remained fragile at best, resented the claims of people of color to membership in a global Francophone society and culture. The mulattoes' European connection, moreover, raised political questions. Could cosmopolitanism be separated from the ambitions of France and Germany? Persons of mixed blood thus constituted a multiple challenge, which could be met in part by denial of their personal worth. Genuine deficiencies of the Haitian bourgeoisie helped Americans to justify this denial, but their terms of rejection had as much to do with race as with politics. The bourgeoisie included blacks of ostensibly unmixed ancestry who were functional mulattoes in that they had assimilated European cultural values. Americans equally resented them as Negroes who did not conform to accustomed behaviors. Evoking the conservative philosophy of the black American educator Booker T. Washington, treaty officials sought a world where blacks knew their place, did not wear frock coats, and did not flaunt law degrees from the Sorbonne. Ironically, Washington himself did not agree: he openly opposed the role that the United States was playing in Haiti.[9]

The American attitude cannot be separated from the question of political legacy. Which class would inherit the state after the occupation was over? In a letter to a State Department official, U.S. Consul Winthrop Scott described a "class of young Haitians who have served with Americans, since the occupation began, as interpreters, supervisors, clerks, etc." This group, the core of a nascent middle class, came to depend on the American presence. Treaty officials worked closely with these intermediaries but showed little interest in grooming them for future respon-

9. For American perceptions of mulattoes, George M. Fredrickson, *The Black Image in the White Mind: The Debate on Afro-American Character and Destiny, 1817–1914* (New York, 1971), 76, 80, 117–18, 120–24, 161–62, 163n, 234–35, 277–78, 321; Carl Degler, *Neither Black Nor White: Slavery and Race Relations in Brazil and the United States* (New York, 1971), 102, 107; Booker T. Washington, "Haiti and the United States," *Outlook*, CXI (1915), 681.

sibilities. This new class remained parasitic. As for the peasantry, occupation policy makers consistently denied the competence of the Haitian majority.[10]

The customs receivership was the linchpin of the occupation structure. Local merchants, regardless of nationality, deplored the way it operated. Although the receivership owed its existence to funds paid in by the import-export sector it entangled members of this business group in an almost impenetrable web of bureaucratic regulation and petty vindictiveness. A major commercial grievance concerned the 291 different circulars that explained the tariff regulations. All had the force of law, but no one could manage to acquire a full set or keep up with the constant and unannounced changes. For many firms, "it is found cheaper to pay up than to fight."[11]

Of sixteen import-export firms in Cape Haitian, fourteen were owned and directed by foreigners; and 95 percent of the local yearly revenues from customs duties were paid by aliens. The functioning of the receivership thus impinged directly on foreign concerns. Official complaints issued from France and Germany, which pressed for customs reorganization. In drafts addressed to the French minister and the German chargé in Washington, the State Department pointedly declared that if it ever undertook to change Haitian customs regulations, it would not invite the participation of other nations. The message for the French ambassador was not as curtly worded as was the note addressed to the German chargé, Haniel von Haimhauser, but the intent remained clear. Washington developed a standard reply to queries about tariff reform: revenues for each tariff category were pledged to repay the debt; tampering with the duties would harm Haiti's credit standing.[12]

The Americans never made the tariff structure consonant with Haiti's

10. Roger Gaillard, *La République authoritaire* (Port-au-Prince, 1981), 17, 167; Scott to Francis White, February 18, 1929, DF, 838.00/2500a; Josephus Daniels to Woodrow Wilson, August 2, 1915, in Josephus Daniels Papers, LC; H.M. to William Phillips, October 31, 1918, DF, 838.00/1547; Sumner Welles to Secretary of State, April 1, 1924, DF, 738.3915/265; Scott to White, February 18, 1929, DF, 838.00/2500a; White to Secretary of State, October 30, 1929, DF, 838.00/2600; "Reminiscences of William W. Cumberland," Oral History Collection, Columbia University; Schmidt, *The U.S. Occupation of Haiti*, 180–81.

11. Richard U. Stines to High Commissioner, June 8, 1923, in Russell to Secretary of State, June 14, 1923, DF, 838.51/1562.

12. Damon C. Woods, Memorandum, June 29, 1922, DF, 838.51/1316; State Department to Baron von Haimhauser, July 21, 1924, DF, 838.51/–.

development requirements. The receivership often taxed primary materials imported by artisans at a higher rate than imported finished goods, with attendant bad effects on local production. Authorities tried for a time to protect such commodities as tobacco, which could be grown in Haiti, and increased the tax on certain other luxury imports, but Haitian production was not substantially improved by these gestures. Some officials suggested new bond issues, as well as internal taxes that would allow reduction of export duties on agricultural commodities, but export duties were not as heavy a burden for the merchant as for the peasant producer.[13]

The occupation regime endorsed a Haitian law of July, 1925, that enabled any foreigner who paid the appropriate license fee to engage in any business in Haiti. Trade would henceforth be unrestricted and nondiscriminatory. The prohibition against aliens undertaking retail commerce had been dropped. Nationalist elements in the Chambers later managed to amend this legislation to require foreign traders to pay an occupational tax as consignees before they could engage in retail trade. As most Americans and Europeans were doing business on a scale large enough to weather the fee, and some Syrians had acquired Haitian citizenship, the amendment did little to curtail the inroads aliens had made in commerce.[14]

Treaty officials saw the opening of retail trade to foreigners as a healthy phenomenon, but they remained insensitive to the needs of native Haitian entrepreneurship. When American retrenchment brought a nationalist transition government to power in the early 1930s, Haitians once more tried to limit the scope of foreign business activity. In 1931, as the impact of the world depression was being felt in the less developed countries, the Chamber of Deputies considered barring aliens from retailing goods of "prime necessity." The proposal reflected the impact of the global market's high tariffs and low agricultural commodity prices, a circumstance that cut deeply into the value of the exports from which Haiti financed its import-dependent economy. In New York City, the Merchants Association of New York responded to the proposal by asking the State Department to intercede on behalf of those, mostly Syrians, who would be adversely affected. The arguments were by this time conventional: such commercial restriction meant losses for American firms.

13. *Crisis*, XXV (December, 1922), 55; Bellegarde, *L'Occupation américaine d'Haiti*, 22–25, 33; Woods, Memorandum, June 29, 1922, DF, 838.51/1316.
14. Arthur F. Tower, Memorandum, July 22, 1925, DF, 838.111/121; *Le Moniteur*, May 10, 1926; Maurice Dunlap to High Commissioner, October 5, 1925, DF, 838.512/23.

Other American trade groups pressed the federal government to make the Haitians abandon the bill. These included the largest textile manufacturers in the United States, whose appeal to the State Department spurred that agency to unequivocally support the traders. The United States acted consistently to eliminate Haitian discrimination against foreign commerce in order to forward American interests and keep European governments from assisting their nationals. In 1929, with the concurrence of the State Department, the high commissioner, the highest-ranking official of the occupation, was still engaged in preventing the return to Haiti of Germans he viewed as undesirable.[15]

The tensions that had long existed between foreign businessmen and the state persisted. Representing as they did the urban bourgeoisie, Haitian legislatures and administrations were bound to oppose a structure that left few employment opportunities for the white-collar class. As late as 1947, Senator Max Hudicourt fulminated against expatriates in commerce. "Possessors of all the foreign capital, they hide behind the puppet politicians, both mulatto and black, whom they control and through whom they maintain and increase their own economic power."[16]

Industrial entrepreneurship, by contrast, lacked both sustained interest and genuine development in Haiti. The corporate presence in the Black Republic flickered like a candle under the conditions the United States insisted on. Haiti could be profitable only if the maximum exploitation of its labor resources was permitted. The State Department, made sensitive to the faults of the occupation by American liberals as well as by local dissidents, limited American corporate leverage in Haiti. After an exploratory mission, the Sinclair Oil Company failed to reach an understanding with officials in Port-au-Prince about Haiti's share of possible findings and left the country. In the words of one of the American financial advisors, Texaco and Standard Oil, having also examined Haiti's modest resources, " 'prowled around' but [gave] it up as a bad job."[17] The

15. New York *Times,* June 10, 1931, p. 45, and July 5, 1931, Sec. 2, p. 4; Downtown Textile Credit Group to Secretary of Commerce, May 22, 1931, in Records of the Bureau of Foreign and Domestic Commerce, Record Group 151, NA; Russell to Secretary of State, January 21, 1929, DF, 838.52/Germans/2.

16. C. F. Wood, Political report, June 1, 1931, DF, 838.504/18; Max Hudicourt, quoted in Bernard Seeman, "Haiti's Economic Bondage," *American Mercury,* January 1947, in Clipping File, Haiti, Schomburg Research Center, NYPL.

17. William Dunn to Secretary of State, September 1, 1923, DF, 838.00/1964; W. W. Cumberland, in New York *Herald Tribune,* December 22, 1929, clipping in the Papers of the National Association for the Advancement of Colored People, LC; Arthur C. Millspaugh, *Haiti Under American Control* (Boston, 1931), 144.

Firestone and Goodrich corporations expressed interest in cultivating rubber in Haiti in the 1920s. Goodrich believed the peasants would make satisfactory estate workers and regarded the country's proximity to the United States as a decided advantage. The Haitian government would have to "assume a very strong moral and legal responsibility for the company" if the results of its pioneering efforts were to be kept out of German hands, but the onslaught of the depression and the success of Liberia as a rubber colony prevented the full-scale development of rubber cultivation in Haiti at the time.[18] The American regime invited the United Fruit Company to consider initiating Haitian operations. United Fruit could not be persuaded to locate in Haiti, however, and contented itself with recruiting workers for its installations elsewhere in the Caribbean.[19]

In the course of the 1920s, schemes to grow cotton, pineapples, and other crops were instituted. Most of these did not succeed. Consul Winthrop Scott reported that failures "appear to have been due not so much to local economic and political conditions as to weaknesses inherent in the management of the companies themselves. In certain cases the organizations have been little better than stock jobbing operations, in others the reckless expenditure of money in huge salaries, orders for unnecessary and experimental machinery and other unjustifiable purposes doomed them to failure at their inception."[20] The work of the agricultural companies was also hampered by uncertainties related to land and water use. The United States belatedly recognized the problems that unregulated exploitation could cause. In its haste to make the country hospitable for investors by setting aside Haitian prohibitions against foreign real estate ownership, it exceeded the limits imposed by both social custom and geography.[21]

Haiti was no El Dorado. The Cul de Sac plain was as highly developed as the current water supply permitted. Irrigation could reclaim some land, especially in the Artibonite Valley, which had been a focus of pipe dreams about internal improvement since the nineteenth century. A concession-

18. Russell to Secretary of State, April 6, 1925, Office of the Financial Advisor and General Receiver to William Castle, July 14, 1929, Dana Munro, Memorandum, August 29, 1929, all in DF, 838.6176/23.

19. Russell to Secretary of State, January 21, 1929, DF, 838.52/Germans, and October 28, 1927, DF, 838.504/5.

20. Scott to Secretary of State, March 25, 1924, DF, 838.159/21.

21. Clarence K. Streit, "Haiti: Intervention in Operation," *Foreign Affairs*, VI (1928), 622.

ary bid from a former U.S. congressman for the irrigation of the Artibonite obtained State Department approval in 1927, but the after-thoughts of policy makers delayed and finally aborted the undercapital-ized project.[22]

Ambitious entrepreneurs contemplating Haitian development con-fronted the complex Haitian land tenure system. Attempts to tamper with this structure were politically quite dangerous. The land issue constituted a critical obstacle to the growth of a plantation sector,[23] and the United States became embroiled in a three-way struggle over land with small-holders and the Haitian government. One American businessman noted that "the ownership of large areas of land by the political class, practically all of which was secured from complacent governments by graft, is one of the deterrent factors in the economic development of Haiti. Such owners have neither the money, energy nor experience to inaugurate or admin-ister agricultural or industrial enterprises and it is equally true that the Haitian employer seldom, if ever, pays even the prevailing low wages for labor but procures the services of the peasants by resorting to the old feudalistic system which for generations has held the great mass of the people in virtual bondage."[24] The Americans backed away from too close an association with the landed gentry. President Calvin Coolidge, in one of his rare statements on Haiti, disapproved of any latifundial develop-ment there and indicated his preference for small holding. He ascribed Haitian economic backwardness to retention by the state of land that should have been owned freely by peasants. Although nostalgic for plan-tations, the southern-born high commissioner endorsed giving public lands to the peasants by prescription to ensure political tranquillity.[25]

In 1928 the United States began a cadastral survey to establish clear titles. Land in the Artibonite and other parts of the country was aerially photographed, and the negatives stored in a warehouse. Haitians feared that the survey would lead to widespread evictions and the conversion of the rural people into a landless proletariat. Title registration could revive old feuds and political conflicts. These trepidations were temporarily laid

22. Frank Kellogg to Senator Shipstead, August 24, 1927, DF, 838.00/2313; "The Artibonite Irrigation Project," DF, 838.6113/52; Dana G. Munro, *The United States and the Caribbean Republics, 1921–1933* (Princeton, 1974), 101–102.

23. Millspaugh, *Haiti Under American Control*, 152; J. B. Romain, *Quelques Moeurs et Coutumes des Paysans haïtiens* (Port-au-Prince, 1969), 32; Louis Janvier, *Les Affaires d'Haïti (1883–1884)* (Paris, 1885); Paul Moral, *Le Paysan haïtien* (Paris, 1961).

24. H. P. Davis, "The Economic Problems of the American Intervention," July 16, 1923, DF, 838.00/1952.

25. Russell to Secretary of State, May 5, 1928, DF, 838.52/55.

to rest when an arsonist broke into the warehouse and set fire to the films.[26]

The possibility of creating such a proletariat was real and had been experienced across the border as a result of expanding Dominican sugar and lumber operations. Several American plantation firms acquired Haitian state lands for leasing during the 1920s. The Haytian American Development Corporation had 14,000 acres in sisal by 1929, and some of this land had been obtained through evictions. The Haitian Agricultural Corporation held 2,200 acres. The Haytian American Sugar Company leased 630 acres from the state and owned 24,000 as a pre-1915 concessionaire.[27] In 1930 the National Union, a pro-independence organization, attacked the sisal project. In a pamphlet written for the union, Perceval Thoby claimed that the Haytian American Development Corporation had razed and burned houses and reduced the food supply in various localities when sisal competed with subsistence crops for acreage. Its company store, staffed by petty government functionaries, kept peasants in debt peonage. While locally owned shops lost trade, laborers' money went to the United States in payment for imported food. The corporation, he charged, had diverted a stream for its exclusive use in the Fort Liberté commune and had even taken its workers to the polls under military supervision so that each could vote more than once for laws favorable to foreign interests.[28]

Plantation companies did not stand alone in influencing the direction of the Haitian economy during the occupation years. The history of Haitian finance during the 1920s cannot be separated from that of the large lending institutions. In 1921 a general retrenchment of Caribbean branch banking followed the war era expansion that the financier Frank Vanderlip had so enthusiastically promoted. Vanderlip had resigned as president of the National City Bank because of a policy dispute with its directors regarding unsecured loans to Europe. He now belonged to the Foreign Policy Association, a body that had criticized the Haitian occupation.[29]

26. New York *Times*, April 8, 1928, Sec. 3, pp. 1, 7; Russell to Secretary of State, January 18, 1928, DF, 838.00/2437.

27. Millspaugh, *Haiti Under American Control*, 152, 153.

28. Perceval Thoby, *Dépossessions* (Port-au-Prince, 1930), 21–23.

29. Carl Parrini, *Heir to Empire: United States Economic Diplomacy, 1916–1923* (Pittsburgh, 1969), 125; John K. Winkler, *The First Billion: The Stillmans and the National City Bank* (New York, 1934), 260; James McDonald to Frank A. Vanderlip, February 13, 1924, in Frank A. Vanderlip Papers, Columbia University.

Ironically, though Vanderlip firmly believed that only liberal credit flows to Europe could reconstruct those nations and thus restore health to the global economy, he did not prescribe a similar remedy for under-developed states such as Haiti. Vanderlip endorsed a generous policy of aid to Europe but simultaneously favored an aggressive campaign of competition against Europeans in Latin America. In notes for an inter-view on the one hundredth anniversary of the Monroe Doctrine, Van-derlip praised that policy for maintaining territorial integrity in the West-ern Hemisphere but criticized it for ignoring European penetration through investment there. Trade does not follow the flag, Vanderlip asserted. "Business follows the bond." The financier described a forty-million-pound British tied loan to Argentina, by which the Argentines had to purchase only British railroad equipment delivered in British ves-sels. The United States should not simply witness such deals passively, Vanderlip insisted. He advocated closer relations with Latin American states.[30]

Tied loans were hardly necessary in Haiti, where the character of the American intervention ensured continuity for U.S. business interests. Here it was not a question of precedence; the flag had followed trade in the Black Republic for generations. Despite the animosities between the treaty officials and the business community, and the tactical differences among administrative, commercial, and financial interests, all agreed on the task of exploiting Haiti's limited resources. As a former State Depart-ment official, Huntington Wilson, put it: "Those of our worthy publicists to whom Wall Street is *anathema* have, in the debauchery of their muck raking, been silly enough to insinuate that the Department of State was run by Wall Street. Any student of modern diplomacy knows that, in these days of competition, capital, trade, agriculture, labor and state craft all go hand in hand if a country is to profit."[31]

By 1930 the public sector in the United States could no longer so gleefully work with Wall Street. Economic depression made lengthy mili-tary interventions impractical and also increased general acceptance of Herbert Hoover's policy of stressing intrahemispheric cooperation rather than coercion. The question of normalizing relations with Haiti touched on the new realization by Progressives that Latin American problems

---

30. Frank A. Vanderlip, Notes for an interview with Latin-American News Service, 1923, in Frank A. Vanderlip Papers.

31. F. M. Huntington Wilson, "Secretary Knox Harnesses Wall Street to Serve Ameri-can Diplomacy" (Draft of an article in the Francis Mairs Huntington Wilson Papers, Ursinus College, Collegeville, Pa.), 8.

were clearly structural. As an exporter of raw materials affected by the global slump in commodity prices and the failure of Europe to regain its economic health, Latin America could not be changed through military intervention, nor could that expedient prevent the widespread defaults on government loans characteristic of the time. As Robert N. Seidel wrote, "the depression proved to internationalist Progressives that their schemes for progress and development stood and fell, ultimately, according to the actions of economic laws which, unlike civil or corporate law, could not be easily amended." Latin American governments were no less stable than in the past, nor were hemispheric politics less tempestuous. American priorities had simply changed.[32]

During the Hoover administration, the State Department raised the Port-au-Prince legation to an embassy, and sent Dana G. Munro to head it in 1930. His office did not exercise the blatant dictatorship characteristic of the old high commission, but Munro's role exceeded that of an ordinary ambassador. Late in 1931, because he disapproved of certain political appointments, Munro ordered all Haitian functionaries' salaries frozen, starting with President Sténio Joseph Vincent's. The occupation, though it was being withdrawn, was clearly not over.[33]

The retrenchment did not lay Haitian problems to rest. The revised treaty of 1932 abrogated all functions of the occupation structure except those relating to financial administration, the nonalienation of land, the conclusion of foreign alliances, and questions of civil order. By December 31, 1934, the gendarmerie, now called the Garde d'Haïti, would be completely Haitian and the marines withdrawn. President Vincent, elected in 1930 as a nationalist pledged to seek an end to the occupation, failed to support Haitianization, fearing his critics would accuse him of trying to prolong the American presence.[34]

Vincent also disturbed American liberals by his use of postal censorship and the persecution of dissidents. He began to see the national resistance movement as a greater enemy to his power than was the American government. Any extra-electoral challenges to his authority would

32. Robert Neal Seidel, "Progressive Pan Americanism: Development and United States Policy Toward South America, 1906–1931" (Ph.D. dissertation, Cornell University, 1973); Bryce Wood, *The Making of the Good Neighbor Policy* (New York, 1961), 123–35.

33. Dantès Bellegarde to White, June 28, 1931, and White to Ernest Gruening, October 28, 1931, in NAACP Papers.

34. Munro, *The U.S. and the Caribbean Republics*, 337–39; Smith to L. M. Little, September 26, 1932, in Louis McCarty Little Papers, U.S. Marine Corps Historical Museum, Washington, D.C.

meet sharp disapproval from Washington and possibly delay ultimate American withdrawal. After the honeymoon period of his presidency was over, Vincent ironically came to rely more on American support than on his own increasingly fragile coalition.[35]

Haiti emerged from the occupation only to slide into the middle of a world depression. It was left with expensive plant to maintain but few resources with which to do it. The United States, fearing a new cycle of foreign intrigue, objected to Haitian borrowing abroad. At the same time, it hesitated to make American assistance available in 1934–1935.[36]

Financial aid in the interwar period might have come from France, but officials in Port-au-Prince found it impossible to secure French credit. In the closed trading climate of the 1930s, the French equatorial colonies increasingly rivaled Haiti in the production of tropical commodities. Relations between France and Haiti had cooled during the course of the occupation, and France presented the Haitians with a list of imports for which it demanded special treatment. Haiti, bound by most-favored-nation agreements with other states and unwilling to forgo needed revenues, would not comply. The French refused to finance credits unless they could secure the same terms the Americans then enjoyed: control of customs and internal revenues. The Haitians were "angry and incredulous" at France's position. The Franco-Haitian treaty finally collapsed in May, 1935, when the French suddenly demanded payment in gold of the balance of the 1910 loan.[37]

Haiti had come full circle from the turn-of-the-century visits to foreign capitals by emissaries in search of desperately needed funds. The National City Bank rejected a loan proposal made by Abel Léger, whose father, J. N. Léger, had made similar approaches to American bankers

35. Ernest Clorissaint to Gruening, October 29, 1934, in White to James Weldon Johnson, November 30, 1934, in James Weldon Johnson Collection, Yale University; Committee for the Release of Jacques Roumain to Arthur Schomburg, n.d. [*ca.* Winter, 1934], in Arthur Schomburg Papers, Schomburg Research Center, NYPL; Carolyn Fowler, *A Knot in the Thread: The Life and Work of Jacques Roumain* (Washington, D.C., 1980), 54–57, 144–50; Streit, "Haiti: Intervention in Operation," 623; White to Johnson, May 8 and November 30, 1934, in James Weldon Johnson Collection; "Memorandum re Haiti," March 17, 1934, White to Charles Vincent, March 22, 1934, Bellegarde to White, April 14, 1934, White to Sténio Vincent, October 9, 1933, all in NAACP Papers.

36. Georges Séjourné, *Les Etats-Unis d'Amérique et la Banqueroute d'Haïti* (Port-au-Prince, 1932), 2–4, 8–9, 10, 16; Selden Chapin, Monograph on Haiti, 1935 (MS in Collection of the U.S. Embassy, Port-au-Prince), Pt. IV, Chap. II, p. 3.

37. Chapin, Monograph, Pt. 4, Chap. III, pp. 6–7, and Pt. III, Chap. II, p. 2; White, Memorandum, November 3, 1931, in Francis White Papers, NA.

decades earlier. Chase National Bank, the Morgan interests, and smaller banks also refused. The devaluation of the dollar, to which the gourde was pegged, made long-term dollar loans unacceptable to financiers.[38]

The collapse of Haiti after fourteen years of spiraling defeat from 1902 through 1915 was followed by a twenty-year period in which the country remained desperately poor and manipulable. The United States succeeded in imposing a formal structure of political domination on the country but never achieved the total suppression of extrahemispheric competition. European demands, concessionaires, political intrigues, and business ambitions continued to surface periodically like mushrooms. French, Syrians, and Italians especially dominated the import-export sector.[39]

The ongoing presence of an energetic resident alien business group continued to feed rivalries among the great powers. Metropoles continued their efforts to safeguard the interests of their nationals and to express dissatisfaction with any policies they deemed discriminatory, whether implemented by the Haitian government or by the treaty administration. Europeans were predictably unhappy with repressive political methods that adversely affected their interests. Although military occupation did not allow an opening for the direct expression of dissent, they could nevertheless vent their disaffection in oblique ways.[40]

The causes of Haitian impoverishment were only partially attributable to the exploits of alien traders. The reason for the near-total absence of industrialization and modern commercial farming also lay in traditional attitudes toward work, landownership, and national security. The American occupation failed to alter the status quo and left the island republic with the same slim resource base it had possessed when the marines arrived. The necessary corollary to the absence of capital in Haiti was the

38. Chapin, Monograph, Pt. 4, Chap. I, pp. 2, 4, 5, 7; Schmidt, *The U.S. Occupation of Haiti*, 234.

39. Munro to Secretary of State, July 21, 1931, DF, 838.512/53; J. Fanfant to Cabinet particulier, November 25, 1932, and Fanfant to Communal Magistrate of Jacmel, April 15, 1933, AN; George Gordon to Secretary of State, October 19, 1934, DF, 838.0443/28; Seeman, "Haiti's Economic Bondage"; John M. Street, *Historical and Economic Geography of the Southwest Peninsula of Haiti* (Berkeley, 1960), 408–409.

40. Oscar Huttlinger to Joseph Tumulty, February 7, 1920, DF, 838.00/1620; Dossier on the French, File 179, in Records of the Gendarmerie d'Haïti (Garde d'Haïti), 1915–1934, U.S. Marine Corps Records, Record Group 127, NA; Director of H.M.'s Petroleum Dept. to Ernest Weakley, October 19, 1921, FO 371, Vol. 5577; White, Memorandum, September 14, 1927, DF, 838.51A/59; Russell, Memorandum, March 26, 1930, DF, 838.00/2765; John MacGowan to the Marquess of Reading, November 3, 1931, FO 371, Vol. 15092.

exploitation of human capital, the labor force. Migration of labor to the canefields of Cuba and the Dominican Republic began in the early 1900s and has continued into the present, now supplemented by immigration to the metropoles. At home, affluent Haitians and foreigners refused to pay a decent wage and cemented the edifice of material deprivation with immiserization and political repression.

The great powers' attitude toward tyranny in Haiti remained highly pragmatic and cynical. The Europeans continued to regard the country as an emporium, whose modest size was compensated for only by the often extralegal goods and services its generally dire straits could make possible. They went on courting various regimes in an effort to neutralize competitors and continued to exploit whatever opportunities arose. The Americans, however, made claims to a moral stewardship in Haiti and insisted that all Haitian regimes remain unquestionably stable. That stability, as we have seen, was rarely distinguished from repression, and support for dictatorial presidencies has been a consistent feature of Haitian-American relations.

Continuity in the Haitian experience, which linked the 1902–1915 era with the years that followed, does not disaffirm the reality of change, which also strongly manifested itself in the course of the century. The temptation to see Haiti as a "living colonial museum" can obscure the subtle differences that time and circumstances wrought.

The development of a more highly organized, centralized state was a product of the occupation era, for its success depended on the suppression of rival power formations. Nord Alexis had hoped to destroy regionalism, a political threat to incumbency, through vigilant repression. Simon and Leconte wanted to accomplish the same objective by establishing an efficient northern railroad line. The growth of the state increasingly divorced it from the civil society with which it had come into being. The political culture of the society remained a thing apart. Nord Alexis had been the last president to attempt to nourish core values pertaining to that political culture. His successors, all either cosmopolitan or highly transient, were unable to follow suit.

The expanding state sacrificed the regional centers to its own economic imperatives, producing a skewed development that concentrated capital and infrastructure in Port-au-Prince and left the hinterland increasingly impoverished. A much less diversified and more dependent economy emerged as a consequence. The suppression of local industries to the profit of those based in the imperialist centers was reflected in the reduction of the foreign business community after 1915. Aliens continued to be a significant presence, but the ones who stayed on represented a smaller number of metropoles, were based in fewer Haitian towns, and were engaged in less varied activity. Between 1919 and 1933 the number of those who directly represented specific metropolitan manufacturers increased substantially.[41]

The capital that was not reserved for Port-au-Prince trickled into northern Haiti for military expenditures. Most of the treaty roads, for example, connected the seat of government to areas of insurgency. In contrast, the comparatively tranquil southwestern peninsula remained isolated. In 1927 a letter mailed from Jérémie took more than a week to arrive in Port-au-Prince. Neglect of such areas accelerated emigration. Minor ports such as Anse-à-Veau were victims of a discriminatory policy that localized foreign trade at Port-au-Prince. Most of Anse-à-Veau's ablest citizens left town to seek their fortunes in the teeming capital. An exception to this trend, the lively southern city of Aux Cayes, became prosperous in the 1920s as a result of the demand for labor in Cuba. Its population of twelve thousand increased, and so did the revenues and customs receipts associated with the contract labor trade. Characteristically, its success was associated with an extractive export enterprise, and the growing permanence of the exodus, which came to include entire families, was a cause for official concern.[42]

The desperate search for reform that had precipitated the Firminist civil wars no longer had strong local leaders to lend it impetus or, in many cases, dilute its strength. Instead, the state was called on to neutralize the social ferment produced in a country whose high birth rate assured it of a constant supply of restless youth. The militant nationalist voice that emerged during the occupation era and threatened several times to bring that experiment to an abrupt close was by 1930 allowed more open expression in urban areas. The Duvalier dictatorship could later list as one of its achievements the co-optation of that epoch's underground black consciousness movement.[43]

In their pursuit of political orthodoxy during the first sixty years of the

41. A comparison of trade directories before and after the American occupation reveals fewer nationalities represented in the alien community, an increase in the number of traders employed by or representing large American firms, and a decrease in the variety of occupations.

42. Dunlap to Secretary of State, January 14, 1927, DF, 125.72383/7; B. Danache, *Le Président Dartiguenave et les Américains* (Port-au-Prince, 1950), 154; Dunlap to Secretary of State, September 10, 1925, DF, 838.5612.

43. David Nicholls, *From Dessalines to Duvalier: Race, Colour and National Independence in Haiti* (Cambridge, England, 1979), 165–72, 212–38.

century, Haitian rulers had only to consider the domestic implications of their acts and their relations with the great powers represented in their country. The development of Caribbean policies by such states as Cuba and the Dominican Republic in the 1930s changed this. The presidents of these nations attempted to control Haitian government behavior through the leverage the presence of Haitian migrant workers offered them. Cuban politicians backed particular Haitian factions during the 1930s and 1940s, and the Dominican dictator Rafael Trujillo succeeded notably in thoroughly intimidating those Haitian administrations that had the misfortune to coincide with his long regime.[44]

The changes that occurred in Haiti foreshadowed to some degree Caribbean developments in general. Most societies in the region had lagged far behind Haiti and Cuba in articulating firm national identities, and even after many former colonies had gained their independence, nationalist sentiments remained weak. By the 1970s, however, more Caribbean peoples had begun to think of their homelands in terms that transcended mere nostalgic attachment to a particular outpost of empire. The new Caribbean nationalism precipitated strong tensions between conservative and radical elements within local intelligentsias. Here too, the Haitian experience of the early 1900s, with its armed conflict and barbed literature, antedated the experience of other Caribbean peoples. The Haitian battles were carried out in an age when the great powers watched Caribbean insurgencies impassively. Present-day civil conflict does not have the liberty to use so full an arsenal of political and military weapons in a world where every geographic location is perceived as strategic. Just as alleged fears of German ambitions gave other powers an excuse to conspire against each other, cold war rhetoric rather successfully disguises contemporary rivalries, which often have little to do with the Soviet Union.

Finally, the accelerated urbanization and migration experienced in Haiti, which resulted from the centralizing tendencies of the state, import-dependency, and the extreme exploitation of labor, came to characterize the rest of the Caribbean as trends in the global economy created the impetus for a massive population exodus after World War II.

44. Daniel Fignolé, Haïti et Cuba (Port-au-Prince, 1949); Haitian Minister in Santo Domingo to Abel Léger, January 30, 1931, in Kurt Fisher Collection, Schomburg Research Center, NYPL; Bernard Diederich and Al Burt, Papa Doc (New York, 1969), 57; Eric Williams, From Columbus to Castro: The History of the Caribbean, 1492–1969 (London, 1970), 438, 466.

Caribbean states continue to be burdened with underdevelopment and with neocolonial political and economic structures inherited from the past. These nations' needs, like Haiti's, are dismissed except when particular crises or new policy formulations in the metropoles dictate that they be showcased. Imperialist competition often provides the occasion and the rationale for such ministrations. For the most part, however, Caribbean imperatives remain neglected, and the most vigorous metropolitan assistance that the republics can expect lies in support for repressive government. Imprisoned in a universe of limited options, these peoples continue to struggle against the forces of deterioration. Many have joined a growing consensus that policies dedicated to preserving the status quo for humanity in one part of the globe can have only deleterious effects on all when the rest of the world is advancing.

Index